THE CONSUL

Map of Italy. Inset: Locale Pertinent to the Story

THE CONSUL

*To Pat O'Malley
With best regards
Carol Jose*

WALTER W. OREBAUGH
with CAROL JOSE

BLUE NOTE ⚐ BOOKS

BLUE NOTE PUBLICATIONS, INC.
FLORIDA

Library of Congress Catalog Card Number: 94-070993

ISBN: 1-878398-08-3

Second Edition
Retitled and Revised:
Blue Note Books
a division of Blue Note Publications, Inc.
110 Polk Avenue, Suite 3
Cape Canaveral, Florida 32920
1-800-624-0401

Cover Design by Scott Patrick

Printed in the United States of America

Chapter 1

From Consul to Captive

It was a sunny but chilly Friday in late November, 1942. I got up from my desk, where I'd been hard at work for several hours, and stretched. Suddenly, I heard a heavy, rhythmic, "thump!. . . thump!" out in the street. I stopped still to listen. Then I felt a cold chill as it hit me--it was the measured cadence of hundreds of booted, marching feet! I hurried to the windows and looked out. The Italians were invading Monaco in force.

Hitler's relentless rampage across Europe continued. At the order of the State Department, I had opened this U.S. Consulate in Monaco barely a week ago, in two offices on the ground floor of the Metropole Hotel in Monte Carlo. It was the first ever in that tiny principality, and was our fall-back position from Vichy-controlled France. The American Consulate in Nice, France--my most recent post--had been shut down immediately after "Operation TORCH"--the Allied landing in North Africa earlier in the month. We hoped that this new Consulate would afford us a safe listening post and would continue to show a strong American presence in this part of Europe.

Last week, elements of the Sixth Italian Army had raced across Monaco without slowing down, in desperate haste to reach Toulon, where the French fleet was anchored. They wanted to capture it while the French, not sure which way to jump, dithered around. A small contingent of Italian occupational forces was left behind in Monte Carlo.

The Consul

Prince Louis Grimaldi, Monaco's ruler, had objected strenuously to the Italians' flagrant violation of his country's neutrality, and had refused to comply with their demands that I be ejected from Monaco "Immediately!" The Italians retaliated by denying me the necessary passes to move about freely, so I was virtually under house arrest. The situation became more tense with each passing day. I had already briefed my current staff of four women about what to do in an emergency, but also tried to allay any fears. "This is just a precaution," I assured them. "Remember, we're on United States territory, under the protection of the U.S., the Allies and Prince Louis, so we have diplomatic immunity."

Now, I dashed for the door between the two offices and yanked it open. "This is it!" I exclaimed. "The Italians are invading Monaco. Use the emergency procedures."

The women froze for a moment. Then Nancy Charrier, the youngest of the four clerks, hurried over to the doors that opened into the hotel corridor, and quickly locked them. I turned to Amy Houlden, the senior clerk. "Go into my office, lock the door behind you, and do the bag with the seals and documents now. I'll stay here and try to keep them out." I turned to the others. "Quick, burn any papers we don't want them to see." I had been keeping a good fire going constantly in the fireplace, just in case something like this happened. I'd also packed a hammer and chisel in a valise with the seals, passport blanks, fee stamps and other sensitive documents, and kept it with me at all times.

"Remember, no one speaks Italian. Let me do the talking. Don't be afraid." I don't know why I said that. Of course they were afraid! I was nervous and apprehensive myself. Amy and Madame Eme, one of the two French clerks on my staff, had just locked themselves in my office with the valise when there was a heavy rapping at the locked door to the corridor. I needed to stall them, until we'd burned the papers and destroyed the seals. "Who is it?" I called. The voice of Mr.Sheck, the Swiss-born manager of the Metropole, came through the closed door. "You have visitors, M'sieu le Consul."

I turned to Nancy and Madame Goff-Lowenstein, the other French clerk, forced a reassuring smile to my lips, and whispered, "Be calm, now. Let's not provoke them. They won't hurt us."

The street was filled with hundreds of Italian troops, their weapons held at the ready, so my reassurances sounded a bit hollow, even to my own ears. I stepped to the door, but I didn't open it. "Tell them the Consulate is closed," I called to Scheck. "We will open again tomorrow at nine." I could hear voices outside. Sheck's voice came again through the closed door. "Er, Monsieur Orebaugh, I think they must speak with you now. They say they will break down the door if you don't open it."

I surveyed the room one last time. Then I shouted, loudly and indignantly, "They'd better not! That would be highly illegal! This is the Consulate of the United States of America! It is in a neutral country, protected under international law! This is damned illegal!" I could hear a trace of wry humor in Sheck's voice when he replied, "Monsieur Orebaugh, I don't think these men are lawyers. I think you had better let them in." I heard a command shouted in Italian: "Break the door open!"

I unlocked the door and swung it open. Two Italian officers shouldered roughly past me. Nancy and Mme. Goff-Lowenstein had seated themselves on the Louis XVI couch on one side of the room. I pulled the big, gilt antique armchair around and sat down in it, in a deliberately relaxed attitude. I gave the women a reassuring glance. To my surprise, Nancy began nervously fussing with her hair--flipping her mane of shoulder-length chestnut hair out, then patting it into place again. Then she began tugging at her skirt, crossing and uncrossing her long, slender legs. I was surprised at her. Nancy was a very attractive young woman in her early twenties, and usually very reserved. Then I realized that she was deliberately distracting the young officers, to give the women in the other room some extra time to do their destruction work. It was working, too. The Italians were all staring at her. Good girl!

Within minutes, at least twenty soldiers were milling around the outer office. The senior officer demanded, in Italian, "Where is the rest of your staff?" I pretended not to understand. "My staff at the Consulate in Nice, or my staff here in Monte Carlo?" More discussion erupted. I was ready to continue the verbal relay match, buying all the time I could, but I knew their patience would soon run out. A couple of them had already jiggled the locked door to my office.

Suddenly, one raised his rifle butt to smash the door open, but before he could do that, the lock turned and the door opened. Amy stood framed in the doorway, a triumphant look on her face. For a few seconds everyone stood transfixed, staring at her as if a mirage had suddenly appeared in the desert. Then they rushed past her into the inner office. I got up and followed. I saw immediately that the women had done their job well. Nothing of any value remained for the enemy's hands.

The Italians in the outer office continued to gaze in wonder at Amy. At the peak of womanhood, in her late thirties, she stood six feet tall without shoes. She had the rosy-cheeked milkmaid complexion typical of British women, and her hair, above a narrow face was a short cap of tightly curled light brown ringlets. Her slim body was more angular than rounded, and when she wished, she could draw herself up into a forbidding presence. I heard one of the Italian soldiers remark, "Eh! Quella non finisce mai!"——"Wow, there's no end to her!" Amy shot him a scathing look.

They finished their inspection and debated where to take us. Finally, as the discussion became more animated, I decided the time had come for me to speak up. "We absolutely will not leave this hotel!" I announced, in perfect Italian. At that, they were shocked into silence. My cool, assured manner, coupled with an unexpected command of Italian, threw them temporarily off guard. "My staff and I are going to the dining room for lunch," I continued, with as much hauteur as I could muster. "We're hungry." The senior of the two officers recovered quickly. "No one leaves here!" He looked at me belligerently.

"All right then, we'll dine right here," I countered, with calm finality. "Mr. Scheck?" I turned to look at Sheck, who had been standing quietly with the women, watching. He took the cue, and began bustling around. First, he pushed a small table over in front of the windows on the street side. Then he began ordering the enlisted men around. "Bring those chairs over here. You! Bring me the flowers. No! Those over there. Voilà!" The table arranged to his satisfaction, Sheck left to order our meal, having adroitly set up our table for five where the troops on the street would see us dining, unperturbed, with flowers and silver, while their officers stood around in confusion. I could see that he was getting as big a kick out of jerking them around as I was.

Soon, our dinner arrived. Sheck, ever the perfect majordomo, produced a five course meal, with appropriate wines for each course, deferentially served to us by the hotel's white-jacketed waiters. We ate and chatted amiably among ourselves, completely ignoring the intruders. I felt I was still in control of the situation, and was determined not to back down.

Suddenly, the door burst open, and an Italian colonel strode into the room. He was clearly not in the mood for the farce that was being played out right under his jurisdictional nose. He stamped around and barked orders at everyone. Then he whirled on me and shouted, "You! You are coming with me! Now! Immediately!" I sat, fork and knife poised, and fixed him with a cold stare. "By forcing your way in here, you and your troops and your country have already committed international crimes, and have forcibly invaded United States territory. Are you prepared to add kidnapping of a U.S. Consul to your list of crimes? My staff and I will not leave here and go anywhere with you." I resumed my meal with more outward calm than I felt.

"You come with me! Now!" he reiterated.

"We are on United States territory," I said. "You will have

to carry us out bodily, which I assure you will create an international scandal of the highest order."

The colonel hesitated. Then his face flushed with rage, and as he opened his mouth to vent his spleen on me, Sheck stepped in. "Monsieur le Colonel, I think perhaps you could allow Monsieur le Consul and his staff to be housed here in the hotel for the moment, but in an area where you can keep them under surveillance. That would avoid the kind of international incident Monsieur le Consul mentioned." He drew the Colonel aside for a whispered conference. The Colonel grudgingly acceded. "Come!" he said, turning to me. "Enough of this! Your meal is finished! You will come with me, please!"

It was not a request. We weren't armed, and there was no point in further resistance. "Let's go, ladies," I said, "stay close to me, and don't be frightened." They had been admirable, remaining calm although I knew they must be terrified. But now...I didn't know what might lay ahead for us. Four civilian women--two French, one British, one American, and I--an American diplomat---had just been formally taken prisoner by the Axis powers.

We followed in the wake of the booted colonel, who strode haughtily ahead. The two officers and several troops, guns at the ready at our backs, followed us. We entered an ingenious underground passage, hastily lined with Italian troops at attention, and followed along it until we came up on the opposite side at the hotel annex, where we'd be housed temporarily until the Italians decided what to do with us. I looked around my room. Our accommodations were comfortable enough, even a bit luxurious. Well, at least Sheck managed to get us imprisoned in decent quarters, I thought.

The next day, our personal belongings were brought to us, and I was glad to see that the canned goods, coffee, and soap I had brought with me from the States when I returned to Nice from home leave were still with me. Most of all, I was glad to see my two sealed canvas diplomatic pouches, which contained my hoard of dollars and francs, arrive untouched.

At about that same time, a cablegram went out from Washington, from Secretary of State Cordell Hull, to the American Legation in Bern, Switzerland, inquiring about my whereabouts and safety. State wanted to know if I could still send and receive messages. The answer from Bern, which had been unsuccessful in its attempts to contact me, was a terse, "NO."

Six days later, we all gathered in my room for a very different kind of Thanksgiving dinner. We tried to feel thankful for what we had, even though we were confined to our rooms, unable to communicate with the outside world, and uncertain of what would happen next.

The following day, Mmes. Eme and Goff-Lowenstein, as French citizens, were returned to Nice. We bid them a tearful farewell.

Ten days had passed, and confinement gnawed at my nerves. Physically active by nature, I loved the outdoors, and in that hotel room I was little more than a big, caged tiger, pacing up and down, with nothing productive to do except worry. "What do you think will happen to us, Walter?" Nancy asked anxiously, a quiver in her voice. "I don't know," I responded gloomily. "I have no idea what they intend to do with us. I imagine they'll use us for some kind of exchange." I worried constantly. Two attractive young women as prisoners of these troops--I slept lightly at night, one ear cocked to any call for help from them. "Well, whatever it is, you can bet it won't be pleasant," said Amy cryptically. She was probably right, but I longed for a change, any change, to relieve the monotony of our days.

That evening when our dinner arrived, there was a note from Sheck, hidden under Amy's bread. "Lester Maynard arrested," the note said, "being held incommunicado elsewhere in the hotel." Lester was the American Red Cross representative in Monaco. I knew him, though not well. I wondered what would happen to him, to them, and to all of us. I didn't have long to wait to find out—or for my foolish wish for a change to be reality.

The Consul

Monday, December 2nd, dawned unusually cold. I built a fire in the fireplace in my room and was sitting close to it to stay warm, when my door suddenly opened to admit two Italian officers. "You will be leaving for Italy today at one o'clock," announced the senior of the two. "Have your things packed and ready. You can take two bags with you. The rest of your things will follow later." I decided to try for one last concession. "I will not leave Monaco until I have met with the Swiss Consul," I said adamantly.

To my utter amazement, they returned shortly with the Swiss Consul, and the Vice-Consul. Then, in an even more surprising move, they stepped into the hall, leaving us alone. I gave two sealed diplomatic pouches, which contained hundreds of thousands of French francs--all the personal funds I'd brought with me--to Vice-Consul Alex Manz. "Please forward these through diplomatic channels to the Swiss Legation in Rome, and ask them to hold them there for me," I said, "and if you will, notify the American Legation in Bern, and ask them to notify my wife, and the families of the women, of these latest developments."

Manz looked sad, but tried to be cheerful. "Of course. Happy to do whatever we can. Have they said where in Italy they're taking you?" "No, nothing yet, what's the latest war news? How are things going for the Allies?"

"As well as can be expected. The Allies have met little resistance in North Africa so far." That raised my hopes. Maybe we'd be released soon. The explosions we'd heard a few nights before, he said, were from the scuttling of the French fleet at Toulon. That was a devastating blow to the Germans and Italians, who had hoped to get their hands on it. What good news! It must have been quite a show, I thought, if we heard it--Toulon was at least 100 kilometers away. Manz also gave me the disquieting news of the arrest of my Consular staff in Nice. I knew from what I'd seen happening to the Jews in Nice that Mme. Goff-Lowenstein was in the gravest danger of all. I quickly scribbled a couple of brief messages to the State Department, and one to my wife

Marguerite, who was back home in Virginia with our two-year-old son Howard. The two Swiss diplomats shook my hand, and gravely wished us well. "We will do everything we can to help you." Picking up the two canvas bags of francs, they left.

I sat by the fire in my room, thinking back to my experience with the Portugese money changer in Lisbon. I had brought about $2200 U.S. of our personal funds with me in a letter of credit, as an emergency nest egg. I had set out to change that, half into French francs, for use in Nice, the other half into American dollars. I didn't know that Lisbon had become a dump for all the French currency held by fleeing refugees, and that I was one of the few buyers for that currency. The $1200 I decided to change into francs had filled two big canvas bags with high denomination French bills, hundreds of thousands of francs--all worthless now, the clerk had assured me. Those were the bags I had just given Alex Manz to forward to Rome. I'd decided to keep the $1000 I had in American dollars, which were now hidden beneath the innersoles of my shoes, because I'd had experiences in the Foreign Service in the past where U.S. dollars could accomplish things that no other currency could.

Before I knew it, it was ten after one, and the Italians had returned. "Let's go," they said, hustling me out. There was nothing gentle or friendly in their manner. I found the girls and Lester already outside, waiting. For the next two days, we traveled interminably by car and by train. Our four OVRA guards (Mussolini's Secret Police) ignored our pleas for rest, warm clothes, or basic comfort. Exhausted and freezing, we were ordered off our fourth, and blessedly final train, high in the convoluted hills and mountains of central Italy. "Gubbio" said the small sign at the station.

As the train pulled away, Amy, Nancy, Lester and I were left standing on the open platform in our lightweight clothing, suitable for the temperate climate of the Riviera, not winter in the mountains. We shivered uncontrollably as the fierce, biting December wind swept down from snow-covered

Mount Ubaldo. A far cry from my arrival in Nice in chauffeured comfort just nine months ago, I thought grimly. No amount of grumbling on my part brought any response from our armed guards. Nancy and Amy stamped up and down, waving their arms to try to warm themselves. Tears trembled at the corners of Nancy's eyes. It had been a brutal trip. Two hours later, the chief guard returned. "You have been transferred to the jurisdiction of the Fascist party secretary here in Gubbio.

Just get us out of this damned cold!" I demanded. "We're freezing, we've been standing here for hours, and we need a toilet!" He wasn't interested. "You will follow me now," he said crisply. At his signal, we picked up our bags and trudged wearily after him, into the ancient town of Gubbio.

Chapter Two

Internment in Gubbio

The town limits were about a quarter of a mile from the train station, and we finally arrived at a large central piazza, or town square. There was a church at one end of the square, and some official looking buildings flying the Italian flag at the other end. On one corner stood a small, dun-colored stone and stucco building, in obvious need of paint and repair. Above it hung a weathered sign, "Albergo San Marco". Signaling grandly for us to enter, the guard announced, with a trace of sarcasm, "Eccoci. Siete a casa, Signori." ("Make yourselves at home, folks.")

We were met in the tiny lobby by the local Fascist Secretary. He, he informed us officiously, was charged with our "safekeeping". We would not be kept totally confined, he went on, but there were certain rules and constraints we'd have to live with. I translated for the others:

One, we were NOT, under any circumstances, to leave the city limits of Gubbio;

Two, we were NOT to attempt to use the telephone or postal service;

Three, we were NOT to speak to, or attempt to fraternize with, any of the local people;

Four, we were NOT to attempt to engage in any political or military discussion or activity.

"It is imperative", the Secretary concluded, "that each of you, without fail, report to me daily at the town hall." I stepped forward. "I have diplomatic status, and it is both improper and contrary to international law for me to do this. I also inform you that we are entitled by law to access to the protecting power, Switzerland, through communication and contact with the Swiss Legation in Rome." It was a long shot, but worth a try.

My comments clearly upset the Secretary, but he didn't challenge them. Like most Italians, he was conscious of rank and position, and nowhere in Italy did the word "Consul" carry more weight and meaning than in the ancient Roman towns of Umbria, particularly Gubbio. After all, their own most important and historic building was called the Palazzo dei Consoli, the Palace of Consuls. And now a Consul stood before him, in the flesh. He was aware that I had come to Gubbio escorted by no less than four of Mussolini's OVRA agents, that his government considered my detainment of great importance, and I spoke Italian fluently, a mark of education and high status. He slowly turned all this over in his mind. Abruptly he announced, "Signor Console need not report personally. The rest of you will report for him."

I let out my breath, then decided to press my luck a little. "I must let the Swiss Legation know where we are. Where is the telephone? I'll call them now."

"No,—no telephone!" he exclaimed.

I adopted a slightly more aggressive tone. "I am asking nothing more than my right to communicate with the protecting power. Why do you deny my request? "

"Signor Console, please understand. We don't have a telephone," he said, embarrassed.

Signorina Vera, proprietress of the hotel, stepped in. She showed none of the class consciousness of the Secretary. "Signore", she said acidly, "we are in a war, you know. Our telephones are not working. You cannot telephone. It is against the rules."

The Secretary beat a hasty retreat, leaving us to Signorina Vera's ministrations.

She led us up the staircase to our rooms. Throwing open the door to a tiny, cell-like room, she indicated Nancy and

Amy were to share it. "Gawd!" said Amy, as they stepped inside. "Walter, ask where the toilets are, for God's sake!" I asked. Signorina Vera pointed down the hallway, and the girls quickly headed that way. She showed Lester into a slightly larger room. The last, and largest of the three rooms, was reserved for me alone.

As soon as Signorina Vera left us, I went back down the hall to Lester's room. "Lester, before you unpack, let's talk about this. I've got a huge room with two beds in it, and you saw that tiny cell where she put the two women. Why don't you bunk in with me, and we'll let Amy have your room? That way, each of them will at least have some room. My room is plenty big enough for the two of us." He hesitated, so I added, "They're very young, like your wife, and this is awfully hard on them, you know." Mention of his young French wife touched him. "All right, Walter."

We began unpacking, with great sighs from Lester. He'd be a gloomy roommate. He had whined continuously since leaving Monaco. I looked around me. It was pretty dreary, and God only knew how long we'd be here. But it was good to be out of that damned freezing wind, even though the rooms were damp and unheated, and the chill in them penetrated to the bone. I wandered around the room, repeatedly stopping to lay my hand on the cold radiator, as if my touch might conjure heat from its frigid surface.

Aside from the armadio—the elaborately carved wardrobe standing against one wall—the room was sparsely furnished. Two narrow iron beds, a dresser, a square lamp table between the beds, a washstand with a porcelain pitcher and basin. A small table with a straight-backed wooden chair. The brown tiled floor was devoid of even a scrap of carpet to cushion the shock to bare feet on a cold morning. A tall, narrow window looked out on a small, unkempt garden below. All in all, it was a depressing, uninviting haven.

There was no such thing as a private bathroom. The hotel's only bath was down the hall and around the corner from our rooms. I went to check it out. Its ancient cast iron tub, housed in an unheated room, was plumbed for cold water only. The toilet was in keeping with the medieval character of Gubbio. When the flush chain on the commode was pulled, the rush and roar of water, out of all proportion to its effectiveness at flushing, echoed throughout the hotel.

Our clothing situation was pitiful. Lester didn't own a single garment suitable for this rough winter climate, not even a pair of woolen socks. The girls and I had little better. We'd need to buy or acquire warm clothing, and quickly. Winter in these mountains, as I knew from my Colorado days, would be fierce. Soon, it was dinnertime, and Signorina Vera's order that we be on time for meals was superfluous— we were famished. Amy's eyes were red-rimmed, and I knew she had been crying, but she said nothing, and no one mentioned it to her. We filed quietly into the dining room. Signorina Vera shooed us to a table in a far corner, then quickly pulled a wooden screen around us, concealing us from the view of the other hotel patrons. We were served a cup of thin, bland, minestrone soup, then a plate of grayish looking pasta, accompanied by broiled onions and chunks of coarse, hard bread. Ersatz coffee followed, and we were able to soften the bread somewhat, to make it edible, by dunking it in the murky brown liquid. As unappetizing as the meal was, we forced down as much food as we could to fill our stomachs. There was little conversation, and we wasted no time in returning directly to our rooms following "dinner". Sleep came quickly and heavily to all of us that first night.

The next morning, while Amy, Nancy, and Lester went out to make their first "report-in" to the Secretary, I drafted a letter to the Swiss Legation in Rome. "This location is unacceptable as a place of internment for civilians of diplomatic rank," I wrote. "Also, we are all sick with colds and in need of medical attention and warm clothing. We are not getting any of these things from the Italian authorities. Most of all, we need Italian lire to buy clothes and medicine." I had just finished the letter when the others returned. "What's the town like?" I asked.

"Grubbio, but interesting. You won't get lost," was Nancy's succinct reply.

I set out across the piazza to deliver my letter to the Secretary for forwarding to the Swiss, welcoming an opportunity to get out and stretch my legs. "How can I exchange some dollars or francs for lire, so that we can purchase necessities like medicine and warm clothing?"

The Secretary shook his head dubiously. "I do not think that will be possible, Signor Console."

"Well, why don't you make every effort to make it possible!" I snapped. "We're all sick and cold, and we don't have any warm clothes! You wouldn't want us to die while in your care, would you?"

"No, No, Signor Console! I will contact my superiors and see what can be done in this regard."

I walked out and went to explore the town. An ancient, walled city, Gubbio was a cloistered mass of gray stone buildings with orange clay tile roofs. It appeared to have stood still in time. During my walk, I saw fifteenth century bronze tablets that placed activity at the site of Gubbio as far back as the second century B.C. As I wandered around, and ascended the hill upon which the town sat, I came upon the street called "Via dei Consoli" (Street of the Consuls). Meandering along it, I noticed that some of the older houses had the "porta del morto", one of the curiosities of ancient Italian culture. A secondary door above the main door, used for the removal of dead bodies. It was an ancient belief that it was a bad omen to take a dead body out through the main front door of a home.

At the northwest corner of the Piazza della Signoria stood the battlemented Palazzo dei Consoli (Palace of the Consuls). I stared up at it, wondering about the role of those powerful Roman Consuls of old. Well, this Consul is nothing but a captive in Gubbio now, I reminded myself--diplomatic immunity or no.

Retracing my steps, I noticed that shops lined both sides of the square. I went "window-shopping," though I had no

Italian lire with which to buy anything. I was pleased to find a Farmacia, though it looked like it would offer little in the way of modern medicines. When I got back to the hotel, Isa was there cleaning my room. She was old, but how old was a matter of conjecture. She began chattering the minute I entered the room, and continued nonstop as she mopped, cleaned, and made the beds.

I learned her family history,---that she was a widow, with two sons sent to war in Greece. They were reported missing, and feared dead. Every day, I listened to Isa's tale sympathetically. By the third day, I felt she just might be the local ally I needed. I made it a point to be in my room every morning when she arrived, and every day I found some little thing to give her. She was always happy and grateful. After ten days, I dared ask, "Isa, could you possibly do me one small favor?"

"Certainly, Signor Console," she replied, "if I can, I will." "I need two stamped postcards. Can you get them for me? I want to write to an old friend, and I don't feel like sending it through that nosy Fascist Secretary." I didn't add that I wasn't allowed to use the postal system. "Not for Fascist bastards to read," she declared, with a fierce expression, turning her head and making a spitting sound. "Don't worry, I fix for you, Signor Console."

With that, I got my first glimmer of how the peasantry hated and mistrusted the Fascists, and the government in general. Playing a trick on them was a pleasure for old Isa, and she smiled conspiratorially as she waddled away.

The next morning, Isa slyly pulled two stamped postcards out from under her voluminous black apron. I thanked her, and while she nattered on with her daily litany about her dead husband and missing sons, I quickly wrote a message in Italian on one of the cards and addressed it to my old friend Manfred Metzger in Trieste. "Here we are in Gubbio. We don't get out as much as before. The war is hard on our pocketbooks, and we must bundle up against the cold. Hope you are enjoying the ping-pong table. Regards, Felice."

I gave the card to Isa and she assured me she'd get it mailed. A few days later, I gave her the second card, my backup in case the first one was confiscated, on which I'd written a similar message, again mentioning the ping-pong table.

If anyone in Europe could help us it would be Manfred Metzger. He and I had been good friends since 1938, and before leaving Trieste in 1941, I had given him an Abercrombie and Fitch table tennis set, which I was sure he'd remember.

Scion of a wealthy family of Austrian merchants, he had been born in Trieste, which was then a part of Austria. Manfred already had everything anyone could want from life when I first met him. We were close in age, and quickly became friends. He was nearly six feet tall--just a few inches shorter than I--and had a stocky build, with a broad chest and powerful legs. He wore his straight, sandy hair parted on the left and combed neatly over. It always looked well groomed, in contrast to my thick and unruly dark brown locks, which continuously fought any discipline. Where my face was craggy and square-jawed, Manfred's was softer and rounded, punctuated by pale blue Nordic eyes, and an aristocratic, aquiline nose. He had an air about him that demanded a second look. Wherever he was, and in whatever he did, Manfred Metzger never took a back seat to anyone. We were both young, physically fit, and adventurous by nature. Once, when we were out hiking, he bet me that he could jump a deep, rocky chasm. I half-heartedly took the bet, and without hesitation he jumped, landing on his feet on the other side. "All right, Walt," he called, laughing, "now it's your turn-- double or nothing!"

I looked down at the yawning chasm, which seemed a mile wide. "Are you nuts?" I said. "I'm not going to jump that thing."

"Come on, don't be such an old woman--you're always too cautious!" he challenged.

Stung, I took a deep breath and jumped, falling to my knees as I landed, barely clearing the edge of the precipice. Manfred laughed uproariously, reaching for his wallet to pay me off. I got to my feet and dusted myself off. "You bastard!" I said, laughing with relief. "I'll never bet you again, on anything! You're crazy as hell! It's a wonder you're still alive."

But Manfred, miraculously, managed to stay alive. He was an accomplished horseman, a skilled skier, a fearless bobsledder and an excellent yachtsman. He had been to visit me the previous spring. We'd had a fine time together, and when he left, he gave me a beautiful Vacheron-Constantin watch, which I treasured, and was still wearing. I knew I had no better or more faithful friend in all of Europe than Manfred Metzger.

Technically, with Austria now under German rule, he was on the other side, but I knew he would help me if he possibly could. I felt sure that in his heart he probably sided with the Allies. The family tank-car business, in which they transported wines, would permit him to travel widely, with few restrictions. He spoke French, German and Italian so impeccably, one could only speculate about which of the three was actually his native tongue.

We settled in and waited. We had no other choice. Without help from either Manfred or the Swiss Legation in Rome, we couldn't do anything. The weather was so cold we could rarely go outdoors. Amy summed up the daily menu in one word— "hideous". There was little or no news of the war, or for that matter, of the outside world. There were no newspapers. Once in a while, an outdated copy of the Vatican newspaper, "L'Osservatore Romano" would be left in the hotel lobby by someone, and I'd pounce on it, devouring every word. It was as if we were living in a dream, out of sight and touch with the real world.

Inevitably, boredom set in. Nancy decided to learn Italian, and studied with me every day. An Italian version of the life of Winston Churchill, which I had found in a dark corner of the lobby, served as our training manual. We also played cards, mostly Hearts.

Early one morning there came a gentle but insistent

rapping on my door. I looked at my watch. It was barely five a.m.! Even the Fascist Secretary wouldn't be out at this hour of the morning. It must be the girls, I thought. Shivering in the predawn cold, I pulled on my pants, scampered barefoot across the icy tile floor, and yanked the door open. "Yes? What?" A gaunt little man in a gray suit, carrying a valise, rushed past me into the room. Lester sat bolt upright in bed, his eyes wide with fright.

The man was struggling for breath, as though he had run a long distance. He hurried to the window and peered out, then scurried back to the door, looking up and down the corridor. Satisfied, he turned back into the room, and gasped out, "Mr. Metzger, he send me......he command me.......he tell Signora Orbaw where you are....Mr. Metzger he keep in touch..." The little man opened his suitcase, and scores of thousand lire and five hundred lire notes fluttered out of it. Without another word, he bolted out the door. So Manfred had gotten my message! I was thrilled that he'd somehow managed to get word of my whereabouts to Marguerite. At least she'd know I was alive and reasonably safe, so far.

Lester and I pounced on the money and began counting it. There was at least a thousand dollars in lire there. Lester ran up the hall to wake the girls, and we immediately began devising shopping lists. I couldn't help chuckling at their enthusiasm. They wore the first smiles I had seen in weeks, and were chattering together about what to buy first. "Put your biggest necessities at the top of the list, and we'll try to get those taken care of," I said. In my own mind, I was determined to do something special for all of them for Christmas, which was drawing near.

To cover our windfall of lire, I asked the Secretary to arrange a meeting for me with a local banker, to discuss a loan. I told him I was willing to put up American dollars as collateral. At the Monte dei Paschi Bank, I was ushered into the office of a short, swarthy Sicilian, Signor Meletti. "I need to negotiate a loan," I said. He waited politely. "We're ill, and we need medicines and winter clothes. We'll soon be receiving funds on a regular basis from the Swiss Legation, but in the meantime I am willing to put this money up as collateral for whatever funds you are willing to lend me." I placed a hundred dollar bill on the desk. Signor Meletti picked it up and fingered it for a moment, saying nothing. I waited nervously. Then he got up, went to the door and called for a clerk. "I will loan you twelve thousand lire against this hundred dollar note, Signor Console, at interest until you repay the loan." I agreed, and we processed the loan. My transaction in Lisbon was already paying dividends. I was glad I had insisted on some American dollars, and had managed to keep them with me.

As soon as we all left the bank and rounded a corner, safely out of sight, we hugged each other, laughing gleefully at our sudden stroke of good fortune. I gave everyone some money, and they went off to shop. Fortunately, it was also market day. I headed first for the "Farmacia" to get some medicine for our colds, then to find woolen sweaters and socks. We were all in high spirits. Even Lester was smiling, for a change.

"Ooh! Look!" cried Nancy suddenly. She stopped, and pointed at the window of the butcher shop, where a turkey was on display. We all moved closer and stared, pangs of homesickness knifing through us. It was holiday time. I made a mental note to try to buy it, and bribe the hotel cook into preparing it for us for our Christmas dinner. Bless Manfred! Without him, life would be bleak indeed.

Back at the hotel, I pulled a chair up to the window and sat looking out at the small walled garden. I lit one of the two cigars I had treated myself to at the tobacconist, and puffed contentedly. Beyond the garden, the last few orange- tiled roofs of Gubbio straggled down and away toward the lower plains. I smoked quietly, thinking of my family back in Virginia.

I was snapped back to the present as an old peasant woman suddenly appeared in the garden below. Without ceremony, she found a likely spot, hiked her skirts, and squatted. Apparently the hotel garden was the only facility available for the wives of the farmers come to market in the piazza. The scene reminded me of a Brueghel painting. There was a peace and permanence about it, and about this place. How many centuries, I wondered, had seen this same scene? If it weren't for the homesickness, the deprivations, and the restrictions placed on us, one could almost forget we were prisoners, caught in the midst of a terrible war.

Before I knew it, it was Christmas Eve. The turkey had been sold to someone else, and there was nothing decent left in the shops. I made a feeble attempt to decorate our room with bits of colored paper. I was depressed and didn't want the company of the others. I wanted to be home with Marguerite and little Howard for Christmas. My spirits fell to an all-time low. Early in the afternoon, as I sat slumped in a chair, feeling sorry for myself, there was a brusque knock at the door. I opened it to find Signorina Vera and two workmen, trundling in our baggage from Monaco. I couldn't believe my eyes.

I raced off down the hall to round up Lester and the girls. Excitedly, we all began to unpack the goods that Margueirte had insisted I bring with me from the States. "Wow!" Nancy exclaimed, "look at this! Ham!" Triumphantly, she held up a canned ham that had not been purloined.

"That will be Christmas dinner," I said.

"And look! Here's some cheese!" cried Amy, "Coffee, too!" They were like children at a Christmas tree, and suddenly I found myself choking back tears. I gave each of them a bar of soap from my hoard, and told them to go pretty themselves up and come back that evening for a Christmas Eve celebration. What that would be I wasn't sure, but I knew I had to pull one together for all of us.

I walked quickly along the streets of Gubbio, feeling frustrated and angry. Why in hell hadn't we heard from the Swiss? Why in hell hadn't they, or someone, done anything about getting us out of here? As I turned blindly into a small piazza, still fuming, the smell of fresh-baked bread assailed my nostrils. I looked into the window of the bakeshop, and there sat a big, beautiful pannetone, the traditional Italian Christmas bread. My mouth watered at the sight of it. High and golden, studded with jewels of citron and plump, crisp nuts, and capped with a dusting of snowy sugar, it was the perfect treat for Christmas Eve. I splurged on two bottles of spumante in the wine shop. Then I searched out a hardware store, and grabbed up the one hot plate in stock and a couple of pots and pans. My shopping was finished.

Exiting the hardware store, I found myself at the end of the piazza where the church was. I stepped inside. In the dim light, I could see the flickering votive candles and the festively decorated altar. Several old peasant women, swathed in black from head to toe, knelt in prayer, silently fingering their rosaries. They seemed impervious to the bone-penetrating cold that emanated from the stone walls and floor of the unheated church. On a step near the altar was a manger scene made of beautifully detailed ceramic statues. I stood there, awkwardly holding my packages, looking down at the exquisite tableau of the little Family, and felt tears welling up in my eyes. I thought of Marguerite and Howard, safe and warm at home in Virginia. Suddenly, I felt ashamed of my frustration. "Thank you, Lord," I whispered. Saying a silent prayer that we'd all survive and return to our loved ones soon, I turned and tiptoed out past the kneeling women. I knew that their prayers, though voiced in a different tongue, probably reflected the same fervent hope for peace as mine. With a lighter heart, I headed back to the hotel, eager to surprise the others with a Christmas Eve treat.

I unpacked my purchases and began setting up my "kitchen." A shelf in the armadio would serve as a pantry. I opened the window and put the bottle of wine out to chill. Next, I dug into one of the trunks and found the little coffee mill I had bought years ago in Trieste.

Carefully, I spread a layer of precious green coffee beans across the bottom of a pan, and put the pan on the hot-plate. Soon the smell of roasting coffee beans was tantalizing. What a treat! I hoped I would know when the beans were roasted enough. I hummed a few bars of "Deck the Halls" as I draped a clean linen towel over the little table, and set four plates out on it. When the coffee beans started oozing oil, I judged them to be roasted enough and took them off the stove to cool. Then I poured them into the mill, ground them. Whistling now, pleased with myself, I filled my new pot with water and set the coffee in it to brew. That done, I wrapped the presents in some blue tissue I'd found at the market, and settled down to await the others.

Without a knock, the door burst open, and the girls hurried in. "Walter, we smell something cooking—what's going on?" cried Nancy. They both stopped, astonished. Pinned to the curtains was a crudely lettered sign, "Welcome to Trattoria Gualtiero". (Welcome to Walter's Cafe). On each plate at the table was a thick slice of pannetone, and a slab of butter, and each place had a cup for coffee and a glass for wine. "Oh, Walter, how wonderful!" exclaimed Amy. "How did you ever do all this?"

"Coffee!" squealed Nancy, hanging over the pot and inhaling deeply. "I can't believe it! Real coffee! What a Christmas present!" The room was cold as always, but the steam from the coffee, and the smell of it, gave us a feeling of warmth and coziness. When Lester arrived a few minutes later, he found us in a happy mood that even his usual depression could not dampen. I proudly poured a round of my freshly roasted and brewed coffee, and we all attacked the pannetone. Nothing ever tasted so good as that one small cup of hot, real coffee, and that first meltingly delicious mouthful of pannetone on that lonely Christmas Eve in Gubbio.

I retrieved the spumante from the window sill, uncorked it with a grand flourish, and we toasted one another and sipped it as we opened our gifts. We had all had the same thought—everyone gave something warm to wear. At midnight, the church bells rang out. We looked at each other silently, our thoughts inevitably turning to our loved ones far away, and our tenuous situation. Nancy was the first to speak and break the spell. Jumping to her feet, she proclaimed, "I'm stuffed like a toad! I'm going to bed. 'Night everyone! Thanks for a wonderful evening, and especially to you for a wonderful Christmas, Walter." She hugged me warmly, and I hugged her back. The other two rose and gathered up their things. "Pannetone for Christmas breakfast, and more coffee!" I promised them. It wasn't such a bad Christmas after all, I reflected, as I settled in to sleep. Lester was already snoring.

The new year, 1943, entered raging, spewing forth bitter cold and wind. Even our new clothes were hardly a match for it. Nancy and I tried to stay occupied with reading and studying indoors. They all looked forward to afternoon coffee and treats in the "Trattoria Gualtiero" corner of my room. Lester whined ceaselessly about our miserable conditions and the separation from his family. We were all glad to escape his company whenever we could.

Amy, though generally cheerful and helpful, seemed to have few hobbies or interests outside of making observations about the local men, primping, and sniping at Lester. What she did with her time, day in and day out, mystified me. She refused to accompany Nancy and me on our walks. I knew that every night, she painstakingly wound every strand of her hair into metal curlers, and every day appeared with the same immaculately coiffed head of light brown ringlets. She kept herself impeccably groomed and looked younger than her age. She was extremely worldly, in a social sense. I knew that she was a friend of Somerset Maugham and had often frequented his villa on the Riviera. She occasionally talked about her romances, even shocked us with references to sexual escapades with various men. However, she remained, for the most part, a cool, solitary person who rarely talked about family or home, and had no ties anywhere. The Riviera seemed to be the only home she counted. I often felt sorry for her. Our situation was for her a bore and a nuisance, nothing more.

One brisk morning in mid-January, when Nancy had

begged off from our walk, pleading a cold, I set out alone. I had only gone a short distance when I heard "Psst! Walter!" from somewhere nearby. My scalp prickled. There was no one within my range of vision. I turned carefully, quickly scanning the area around me, and almost jumped with shock. There, at the hotel entrance, casually leaning against the wall, stood Manfred Metzger!

Dapper as ever, he was dressed in a tan cashmere topcoat over his business suit. On his head was a fashionable brown fedora, and his tan Italian leather shoes were polished to a high gloss. He stood out among the poor natives of Gubbio like a sore thumb. "Go away!", I hissed. "Are you crazy?" Manfred just looked at me. "Walter, dear friend....." he began. With as much urgency as I could muster, I cut him off. "Go away! You're crazy to come here! It's too dangerous."

Shrugging, he stepped to my side. "Walk along with me," he said in a low voice. I fell into step with him and we continued down the street. "Tell me what I can do for you—Felice." His tone was slightly mocking, and although I didn't dare turn my head to look, I knew there was probably a grin on his face. I didn't speak. Furious, frightened at the risk he was taking, I turned abruptly and began walking rapidly away from him toward the upper gate of the town. He quickly caught up with me.

"Metzger, you're mad," I whispered tersely, "I'm watched constantly! You run the risk of being arrested!"

"Hey, mon cher ami, relax! Talk normally. I'm just a stranger here, looking for directions."

"How did you get here?" "Why, I'm here for perfectly legitimate reasons, Walter. I'm here to buy wine. My papers allow me to go almost anywhere I want."

"How did you find me? How did you know where to look?"

"Easy. You're quite a celebrity here. I just asked an old man where they keep the American prisoner. He told me all about you, and that you go for walks every morning in good weather."

"Were you able to contact Marguerite?"

"Yes, dear friend, she knows where you are and that I am in touch with you.

I felt a wave of relief. "How can I ever thank you, or repay you, Manfred? You don't know what the money you sent us has meant to us. We still haven't gotten any funds from the Swiss Legation."

"Don't worry about it. Look, I can't be seen with you for long, 'just asking directions,' but I promise you I'll do everything I can. At the moment, it's too sticky to attempt anything official, but I wanted to see you myself and see how you are. Here. This will keep the wolves at bay." Thrusting a small packet into my coat pocket, he turned down a narrow side street and disappeared.

In the packet was more than enough lire to tide us all over until the Swiss Legation started sending us funds. I knew I could never adequately repay Manfred for his generosity or his deep and abiding concern. How lucky I was to have him for a friend! Several days later, I decided I might as well go to the bank and pay off my loan--I wanted to redeem my hundred dollar bill.

I was once again ushered into Meletti's office. "Buongiorno, Signor Meletti," I said cordially, shaking hands with him. "I received some funds. I'm here to pay back my loan and redeem my hundred dollar bill." Meletti looked startled. Then he launched into a protracted monologue about Italian banking practices, complex accounting procedures, and terrible bureaucratic red tape that surrounded everything. I listened politely, then repeated why I had come. "So if you will get me my hundred dollar bill now, I'll be happy to have this note paid up."

"Signore," Meletti replied, as if speaking to a simpleton, "you do not seem to understand. This is now a new year."

"We have an agreement in writing here," I said, waving the agreement at him, "and you, Signore, are flagrantly violating it! I insist you adhere to the terms of our written agreement."

At that, Meletti flew into a rage. "You!" he screamed. "You are one to talk about violating agreements! You and your Jew-loving President Roosevelt! You Americans think you own the world! Hah! Now you are no longer masters of the world! It's high time you were humbled and shown a thing or two! Agreements! Hah! You deserve whatever you get, filthy American!" With that last, he ripped the agreement, and slammed his open palm down on the desk.

Furious, I wanted to reach across and strangle him. I knew my rage was out of all proportion to the situation, but everything was about to boil over. I checked myself in mid-move. Any move I made on him would be dangerous to all of us. With great effort, I turned on my heel and stomped out, slamming the door as I went. I stormed furiously across the square to the hotel.

My mood lightened somewhat the next day, when we finally received a message from the Swiss Legation in Rome. They were prepared to remit each of us up to 5,000 lire monthly (around $250) against signed receipts. We all breathed a sigh of relief at that. But the best news was "we are requesting permission from the Italian Ministry of Foreign Affairs to send a delegation to meet with you as soon as possible." We were certain now that the Swiss in Rome were involved, and knew our whereabouts; we would be released shortly. Amy started a betting pool on the date.

I wrote back immediately, suggesting that we be moved to Rome as quickly as possible. I felt I'd have a better base of operations for getting us released if I could just get us to Rome.

The days and weeks dragged by. Then, in the middle of February, we were visited by two members of the Swiss Legation. We were overjoyed. Just to talk to someone from the "real" world, the world outside this ancient, isolated hill town, was a treat beyond imagining, and we devoured every scrap of news they gave us.

"What about getting us exchanged or released?" I asked the senior representative, Mr. Antonini.

"That is a ticklish situation, at the moment, Mr. Orebaugh," he replied. "The Italians want the members of their Armistice Commission, who are prisoners of the Allies in North Africa, recognized as candidates for exchange. The Americans claim that as a diplomat serving in a neutral country, your seizure and arrest was illegal and a gross violation of international law. They want you released forthwith, with no terms, exchanges, or restrictions imposed. The Italian Armistice Commission numbers one hundred twenty. Many of them are high-ranking members of the Italian government. You can see what a complex situation we have to resolve here. I'm afraid your release is not imminent, since your government adamantly refuses to negotiate on the basis of an exchange."

My spirits fell on hearing that. We were in a far more precarious position than I had thought, now that we were of some bargaining value to the enemy.

"We shall certainly express our distress at the accommodations and treatment you are being accorded, and will seek to get you transferred immediately to a more acceptable location," said Antonini, as he shook hands to take his leave. "Please try to get us moved to Rome," I implored. "I think that would be best in the event that an exchange is ever considered. The young women, especially, should be moved to a safer place."

"You have my assurance I will do all in my power," he replied.

When March arrived, cold and blustery, with no further word, we were more discouraged and depressed than ever. March 19th was my thirty-third birthday. Out of the blue, the two Swiss reappeared, accompanied by two uniformed Italians. We greeted Antonini and his companion effusively. He looked pleased. "Please go and pack your things, Signore," said one of the Italians politely, "We will be moving you and the others today."

"Today?" I was jubilant. "Where? To Rome?"

"No. To Perugia," he replied. "I think you will find your accommodations there satisfactory."

Although I was disappointed that we weren't going to Rome, where I'd have better channels to work on our release, I was happy to be leaving Gubbio. None of us had ever been to Perugia, either, but we all agreed that whatever it had to offer had to be better than the cold rooms, the tasteless food, and the noisy, inadequate plumbing of the Albergo San Marco.

Chapter 3

Transfer to Perugia

Our transfer by train to Perugia, about fifty kilometers to the south and westward, went smoothly enough. After a brief orientation about our restrictions and about the town, during which I learned that there were over a thousand foreigners being detained in Perugia, the officer handed each of us a small brochure giving detailed descriptions of the major points of historical interest in the area. This polite and cordial treatment, such a marked contrast to what we had experienced before, made us feel more like tourists on holiday than war prisoners. The feeling was reinforced when we entered the Hotel Brufani, only a short walk from the police station.

Nancy gasped as she glanced around, taking in the gilded, red velvet chairs, the sparkling chandeliers, the beautiful tables. Everything spoke of timeless luxury. It was a complete contrast to what we had just left in Gubbio. The clerk apologized for the limitations the war had placed on the quality of service the hotel was accustomed to offering its guests. "I am so sorry to tell you, Signore, that hot water is available only from eight o'clock in the morning until eight o'clock in the evening. From time to time, we must make substitutions in the items on the menu, due to shortages. Also, we have had to curtail the hours when the bar is open. It is open only from five o'clock in the evening until nine. " Our registration completed, he rang for a porter to come and carry the luggage to our rooms. Nancy, Amy, Lester and I looked at each other. Porters? Hot water? Bar? Menu? "My

God, if Signorina Vera could only see this," I whispered to Nancy, "she'd keel over!"

"Pinch me so I'll know I'm not dreaming!" she whispered back.

We were shown to our rooms, which were all on the second floor. This time, each of us had our own room. Nancy's, Amy's and mine were all to the back of the hotel, overlooking the well-tended garden, and Lester's was around to the front, overlooking the square. Best of all, there was actually heat coming out of the radiators! Not as much as we would have liked, but at least enough to take the worst of the chill out of the atmosphere. We wouldn't have to wear coats in the room all day, as we had at the unheated Albergo San Marco. We were grateful to find that each of our rooms boasted its own reasonably modern bathroom. We decided that a hot bath was the one thing we all wanted first, even though it was already past lunchtime and we were pretty hungry.

My large, high-ceilinged quarters were partitioned into two rooms--a bedroom and small sitting room. I opened the doors and stepped onto the balcony for a look around. Like many of the ancient cities of Italy, Perugia was walled, built on the crest of a hill for protection from invaders. Its main thoroughfare, on which the hotel was located, bisected the very top of the hill, falling off into a maze of twisting, narrow, cobbled streets snaking around the upper slopes. From the very edges of these narrow streets, with barely a foot of walkway, sprung homes and shops, and at various levels of descent I could see smaller squares or piazzas showcasing large important buildings, or ornate fountains and statuary. From my vantage point on the balcony, I could see the monochromatic brown pattern of barren hills, dotted here and there with sparse patches of evergreen forest, stretching into the distance. It was a peaceful, pastoral scene that made it difficult to believe the circumstances which had transpired to land me there.

In the dining room, we were courteously and quickly

ushered to a table. "You may order anything you like from
the menu and, of course, if you wish something special, it is
possible to request it, for a consideration, of course." "Of
course," I echoed casually, trying not to laugh at the looks on
the faces of the others. "May I suggest a wine, Signore?" I
thought Amy's eyebrows would rise up into her hairline.

That evening, I invited the others to join me in the bar for
an aperitif before dinner. "But of course,—how kind of you
to ask us," responded Nancy, laughing gaily. Then we
adjourned to our table in the dining room, where we dined on
an excellent antipasto, rich chicken soup, and roast squab.
Cheese and fruit were offered for dessert, along with coffee.
If it hadn't been for signs pointing the way to the air raid
shelter, it would be hard to tell that a war was going on. Only
the coffee, which was thin and bitter, reflected any wartime
shortages. The mushy gray pasta, hard coarse bread, and
hostile atmosphere of the Hotel San Marco seemed worlds
distant, instead of a mere 59 miles away.

Life in Perugia settled into a comfortable routine. I ran
into Jack Kutsukian, an old acquaintance from Trieste. He
and his wife Florence were also interned in the Brufani. Jack,
an expatriate metals and machinery dealer, knew the black
market better than anyone, and could get us almost anything
but coffee. He kept the wardrobe in their room crammed
with fresh eggs, cheeses, butter, honey, olive oil, and even
fresh sausages and meat! There were things in his room that
we hadn't seen since leaving the States, and the Kutsukians
often invited us for breakfast or dinner to share some of their
bounty. Florence Kutsukian made us the world's best rice
pudding, cooked in an old coffeepot on a hot-plate.

We also relished the luxury of having more news, as well
as more contact with the outside world. Amy and Nancy
soon made friends with other young single people who had
been students at the Universita per Stranieri, the College for
Foreign Students in Perugia. We attended the movie theater
once, unsure of whether or not it was "allowed". The newsreel
was so propagandistic, I snorted out loud in disgust, earning

me a sharp jab in the ribs from Nancy. However, we could glean from what we saw that things were not going well for the Axis forces. The reference to "strategic withdrawal and regrouping" suggested that the Allies were at last gaining in North Africa.

I was also able to initiate more frequent contact with the Swiss Legation in Rome. When I managed to get through the quirky Italian phone system to them in April, I was assured that a Mr. Riva would be coming to Perugia shortly to discuss our situation. All in all, we agreed, this was the best way to sit out a war, if we couldn't be home.

Manfred learned of our new location, and sent one of his "clerks" with a large basket of food. Food, to someone of Manfred's tastes, included such things as pâté with truffles, pickled quail eggs, tiny cocktail sausages, and chocolates. We laughed as we unpacked these treasures, the most precious being a store of Swiss coffee.

A few weeks later, stepping out of the Brufani for my morning walk, I spotted Manfred's distinctive green Willys, with its 1938 New York license plate, parked in front of the bank, next to the hotel. Seated at the wheel, smiling and waving as though seeing me was the most ordinary of social occurrences, was Manfred himself! He beckoned me over. "Hello, old friend, good to see you've moved to something more civilized. Did you get my packages?" "Manfred, I got your most welcome food package. But don't you realize how dangerous it is for you to be seen here, talking to me? How do you manage to get around like this? With a license plate that is four years out of date, to boot?"

"You worry too much about petty details, Walt, as always. There's no law regulating foreign license plates in Italy. This plate is good for as long as it is on the car. Come on, we'll go to your hotel and have a drink together. I have to call some clients." Over a drink, Manfred told me how he had managed to acquire the code words for getting through on the long distance military networks. "It only backfired on me once, a few months ago," he said. "They changed the code, or I had the wrong words. Anyway, I thought I was being put through to my associate in France, and instead I was connected with Hitler's staff headquarters in Berlin. That was a surprise!" He laughed with delight at the memory. "So, Walt, would you like me to call the Fuhrer and tell him to send you home?" I couldn't help chuckling with him at that idea. His visit certainly perked me up, and restored my flagging spirits. Our conditions were a thousand times better than they had been in Gubbio, but being a prisoner, restricted to one place, not knowing what the next day or the next week would bring, was not easy. At times, the year since my arrival in Lisbon seemed more like ten.

A few days later the ear-splitting wail of air raid sirens shattered the silence. We froze. Nancy came bounding out of her room, wide-eyed with fright. She ran to me, and I put my arm around her reassuringly. We hurried to the stairs and looked down into the lobby. People were milling about, not knowing what to do. Some of the women started crying.

Men shouted orders: "Here! This way! Quickly!"

Everyone scrambled to the stairway that led down into a subterranean area. I was surprised and fascinated to find that it was an enormous cavern that dated back to Etruscan times. Here and there on the walls were remnants of ancient mosaics and murals. Huddled together, we heard the drone of aircraft passing overhead. We tensed for the sound of bombs falling, but there were none, and after about an hour, the all-clear signal sounded and we filed upstairs again, shaken but relieved.

During the next week, the air raid sirens sounded several times a day. It was nerve-wracking. It seemed like we were constantly on the run, dashing to shelter somewhere. One day, the sirens sounded while I was out on a walk.

"Over here!" someone shouted.

I was directed down an alleyway and through a gate, then downward, and I found myself in a hidden underground city. Remnants of streets, houses, and shops from late Etruscan times were there, and Perugia was just built on top of them. It gave me an eerie feeling, — a sense of the fleeting nature of time, and life. But although we were kept in a state of constant tension and nervousness, no bombs fell on us, or near us. The Allied planes seemed headed for targets farther north.

As the war came closer, rumors abounded. In June, Amy heard from the Swiss Legation that she'd be leaving with a group of British subjects. She all but jumped for joy, and we were elated and rushed to help her pack. Then word came that it was a mistake. Her spirits were crushed, and ours with her. The air raids resumed. We could see squadrons of Allied bombers passing overhead, flying north at high altitude. At night, from my balcony, we could make out the glow of enormous fires far off in the distance. By July, the bombings were coming closer every day.

Nancy had become acquainted with a group of young people her age from the International University in Perugia, and she spent most of her time with them. A couple of the young men were showing some romantic interest in her, and I found myself feeling a little jealous about that. Nancy had divorced her French husband Pierre Charrier, and had shown enormous courage for a woman her age in slipping through the German lines to Nice, where she had come to work at the Consulate, planning to eventually return to her home in the States. But the war, and then our capture, had intervened. Now, I found myself feeling overprotective about her.

"Look, Walter," she said to me in exasperation one day, "you've got to stop acting like you're my father or something." I was crushed. I wished she hadn't said "father". I wasn't all that much older than she was, after all. Besides being young and attractive, Nancy was a charming, plucky woman, and I enjoyed her company a lot, especially her considerable wit and intelligence. Yes, I was jealous of her attention to those young men of the International University. I also felt somewhat responsible for the fix she and Amy were in.

But I, too, had developed new friends. A technician at one of the chocolate companies in Perugia, Enrico, had even loaned me a key to his apartment so that I could go at will and listen to his prized Zenith Transoceanic radio. Despite some jamming, it was usually possible to bring in the BBC, or failing that, one of the Swiss stations, to get some reliable war news.

On July 10th, I picked up the news that the Allies had landed in Sicily. I raced back to the hotel to tell Nancy, Amy and the Kutsukians, and we discussed the possibilities that news engendered. We were hopeful that our liberation would come very soon. The tempo of bombing sorties rapidly increased. On July 19th, we heard the shocking and sobering news that Rome had been bombed, though we later learned it was the outskirts--the rail lines--and not that magnificent city itself. About a week later, Palmyra, a Greek woman who lived one floor below us in the hotel, and who had access to a radio through her boyfriend, knocked on my door. "Signore," she called out excitedly. "Such news! Such news!" In her agitated state, we could barely understand her English. She was jabbering in a combination of Greek, Italian and English. "Here, Palmyra, have some coffee and calm down," I said, handing her my coffee cup. "What news did you hear?" I tried not to show my anxiety.

"Mussolini!" She cried. " Il Duce, he go! Finish! Finito!" "What?" I exclaimed. "Where? Where did he go?"

"Is over, finished for him!" she continued. "He is quit!" We sat there, stunned. Did this mean what we thought it meant? That Mussolini was out of power? Throughout that night, tossing and turning on my bed, I could hear shouting and singing in the streets. I slept little. Jack Kutsukian and I were up bright and early, and as soon as we could safely go out on the streets, we rushed over to Enrico's to listen to the early BBC news broadcast. My hands shook as I twirled the dials. "Yesterday," came the voice of the announcer in clipped, British tones, "Benito Mussolini was expelled from power by the Grand Council of Italy. The King has asked Marshall Badoglio to form a new government." I was staggered. If the BBC was broadcasting it, it must be true.

Mussolini out of power, after so long! That was difficult to imagine.

We went back to the hotel and roused Amy and Nancy to give them the news. They dressed hurriedly and we all went out into the streets. Crowds were already gathering. I tried to buy a newspaper, but they had all been snapped up. It was several days before I managed to get my hands on one. When I did, I was startled to see a full exposé of Il Duce's longtime love affair with Clara Petacci. The Italians could hardly be classed as naive about such things, yet the people of Perugia seemed thunderstruck at this revelation of their leader's amorous indiscretions. Twenty years of strictly controlled press had built Mussolini into a demi-God to his people. Now, like Humpty-Dumpty, he had fallen, and with these revelations his image was completely shattered.

By that evening, Perugia was no longer a Fascist town. From our hotel balcony, we could see the bonfires dotting the hills and plains, as the peasants heralded the news in the traditional way they always greeted the occurrence of a "great event." In the town, Fascist posters were torn down, along with street signs named after Fascist heroes. Windows were broken in shops owned by known Fascists, or paint was thrown at them, but there was little or no looting or rowdyism. A group of students passed below us doing a snake dance to the tune of "Beer Barrel Polka", and we laughed and cheered them on. After dinner that evening, I produced a bottle of champagne, and we merrily toasted the fall of Mussolini and his Fascist government. We were positive that with that momentous event, our freedom was near, and we'd soon be back with our loved ones again. How wrong we were!

During the days that followed, demonstrations and reprisals were frequent, and air raids only increased in intensity. By August, the air raid sirens were screaming continuously, and our nerves were shattered. Bombing and strafing attacks on the rail lines, highways and marshaling yards could be clearly seen at night. Few people bothered running to the air raid shelters any more--they'd have to practically live in them. The American bombers flew high overhead during the day, headed for targets in the north. The British usually came over at night at low level, striking at nearby targets and striving mightily to put the local airfield, which served as a base for German and Italian pursuit fighters, out of business.

We felt the results of this stepped-up pace almost immediately. There were frequent power outages. Telephone communications became even more unreliable, and food shortages increased. The Brufani drastically cut its menu and services. Nancy and Amy, shocked at what they saw happening, looked to me for reassurance. "What do you think, Walter? " Nancy asked me almost daily. "We'll be okay, don't worry," I kept assuring her, though I knew the situation would probably worsen.

The political scene was chaotic. Already powerful and well-organized as an underground movement, the Italian Communists were openly flexing their muscles. Then the Germans started tightening the screws on the Italians. More and more young Italian men, both civilian and military, were rounded up and sent to Germany as prisoners, on involuntary labor details. The Italians were furious and confused. They had been allies of the Germans, after all. The general Italian populace found itself caught in the three-pronged trap of an oppressive ally, a destructive liberator, and an unstable government.

Then two delegates from the Swiss legation came to Perugia, probably in response to my continual correspondence requesting expedited action on getting us transferred to Rome. They did not bring good news. "Monsieur Orebaugh, the situation in Rome is not pleasant," said Monsieur Chauvet dolefully. "There are bombings almost daily, and food is in very short supply. The streets of Rome are full of German military. You would not be safe there."

When they left, they took what little optimism I had left with them. A few days later I was lying on my bed in a funk when Vittoria Vechiet, the floor maid, arrived to give my room its weekly cleaning. I watched her as she worked. She didn't look Italian any more than I did. "Where were you born?" I asked her. " In a small village near Gorizia, Signor Console, not far from Trieste." At my surprise at hearing her call me "Console", she smiled shyly. "I know who you are. A few years ago I worked in Trieste, and I heard your name mentioned." That interested me. "And what brought you to Perugia?" Women like Vittoria rarely traveled more than a few miles from their birthplace during their lifetime. "I came here to be with my sister Margherita, Signore. She married a Perugino, and he is in the Army, and has not been heard from for months. We are very worried."

For the next week, I continued to watch her carefully, turning options over in my mind. I remembered the good luck I'd had with old Isa in Gubbio. I knew we'd soon need some help from someone locally, and I hoped Vittoria might be that person.

By the end of the month, German troops were tearing around the countryside below Perugia. The sound of their mechanized units being redeployed could be heard up and down the plain from early morning on. Judging from the volume, it seemed as if every German division in Italy was being shifted. The Allies responded by stepping up their strafing and bombing runs. We kept to our rooms, for it was daily becoming more unsafe to be out and about. I knew we needed to make some plans. What they would be, I wasn't sure, but I knew we'd need escape plans or a place to hide out.

I called Nancy and Amy to my room. "I don't need to tell you that our situation is very precarious, and getting more so every day." Amy nodded. Nancy looked a little frightened, but said nothing. "Being held by the Italians is one thing. Falling into the hands of the Germans is quite another. As soon as they realize who we are, or more specifically, who I am, they'll grab us and ship us off to Germany as hostages, to exchange for some of their high-ranking prisoners. Conditions of imprisonment there would be much worse than we can imagine." I didn't add that with the Nazis there could be worse than just imprisonment. They had shown no mercy to any of their captives.

"Well, what do you think we should do?" asked Nancy.

"What can we do?" Amy spoke practically. She ticked off our status. "We haven't been able to get to Rome. We have no papers. The Swiss seem powerless to help us. I agree with you, Walter, there is far more danger from the Germans than from the Fascists. But what can we do? Do you have any brilliant ideas?"

"Well, I think we might need to go into hiding at some point, until the Allies or the Swiss can get to us, and we'll have to have a place to go to, if that need arises. Somewhere away from the Brufani. Somewhere unknown to anyone, including Lester and the Kutsukians. I think I can trust Vittoria, the woman who cleans our rooms, and I intend to ask her tomorrow if she knows of a place we can go to."

"Do you really trust her, Walter?" asked Nancy anxiously.

"Well," broke in Amy, "we have to trust someone. She seems as likely a prospect as anyone. God knows we can't entrust our safety to the Germans. And if we wait much longer, it may be too late. I think you should approach her immediately, Walter, and see what she says."

"Nancy?" I looked over at her. She was clearly shaken by this serious turn of events. "Do you agree?"

Nancy pulled on a strand of her hair, and looked out the window for a moment, lost in thought. Then she turned to me. "Well, Walter, I really don't know what we should do. I'll go along with whatever you decide."

The next day, we were all in my rooms when Vittoria arrived to clean. "Vittoria," I began, "we need to talk to someone about our situation here, and we agree that you are someone we feel we can trust." Vittoria waited silently. Nervously I plunged on. "The Germans are coming closer, and we feel that it won't be long before they take over completely. That will put us in great danger, Vittoria, as I'm sure you know. We need your help, if you can help us. Do you know of a place where we could hide out from the Germans, if we have to get away from here in a hurry?"

Vittoria had set her mop aside. Now, she turned my request over in her mind. We waited. Finally, she spoke. "Of course I will help you Signor Console," she said. "I will discuss this with my sister tonight. She will advise me what can be done. I will come tomorrow and let you know." There was a collective sigh of relief from the three of us. I felt we had been right to trust her.

"Buongiorno, Vittoria," I greeted her the next day, and waited.

"Buongiorno, Signor Console," she replied. Wasting no time in small talk, she continued, "I have discussed the matter we spoke of with my sister, and she says she herself will shelter you if need be. She is very discreet. No one would know you are there. I would help you get away from here and go to her place."

I was elated. "Are you sure that would be all right?" I asked. "Of course," she replied, simply. "However, I must tell you, Signore, my sister's apartment is small and poor-- nothing like the rooms you have here at the hotel. We hope you won't mind the plain and humble accommodations you would have there. But it will be safe, and you will not be betrayed."

"Thank you Vittoria, and thank your sister for me. We don't want to be a burden, but we need help."

"Don't worry about it, Signore," responded Vittoria, "what we have we will share. You and the two Signorine will be safe with my sister and her family. She lives not far from here. It will be easy to get there quickly when you need to. I will watch and warn you if I hear the Germans coming."

She picked up her mop and began swabbing the floor as though no more than the weather had been discussed. I went to give the girls the good news.

The next day I received a letter from the Swiss. More bad news. "Negotiations with respect to an exchange between America and Germany and vice-versa seem to have come to a dead stop. This has probably caused the slackening, if not altogether the cessation, of the Italy-America negotiations." Up to then, I had not been aware that the Germans were involved in the negotiations. To learn that they were was a disquieting revelation, to say the least. They must know about me, and the girls, then. It made our situation even more dangerous.

That evening, we heard that the Allies had managed to cross the Straits of Messina and land in Calabria, breaching the mainland of Italy. We were jubilant. Once again, rescue seemed imminent. "We mustn't be too optimistic, though," I cautioned the girls. "Before it was just planes and bombings at a distance. But now the war has come to Italy proper, and it's sure to reach Perugia soon. We'll have to be very careful from here on, ready to make our move on a minute's notice. We need to stay in close touch with one another, and no one should go anywhere without letting the others know first. "Gawd, I hope they get here soon," said Amy. "I'm ready to get out of the sticks and back to civilization!"

On Wednesday, September 8th, I was again at Enrico's listening to the news. I could hardly believe what I heard, but General Eisenhower himself made the stunning announcement. "Today," he said, "the Italians have agreed upon an Armistice. Italy and the United States are no longer at war." Without waiting for further details of this extraordinary turn of events, I rushed back to the hotel, grabbed Nancy and Amy, and danced around, hugging them both.

Then I went to find Lester. "What do you think this means for us, Lester?" "Well," he responded, "I would think it means we are no longer prisoners of the Italians."

The fear of German reaction and retaliation still gnawed at me. We decided to go immediately to the questura to try to establish some official recognition of our status. "We realize how very busy you are, but we feel it is imperative that we be transported immediately to the Allied lines, before the Germans organize and take counter-measures." I decided to go for broke. "Will you please see immediately about having us flown out of here, today if possible, to an airfield behind the Allied lines? We would appreciate your assistance." At that, the police chief looked startled. "Signor Console, I regret that I have no idea what might be arranged for you and your party. I do not have authority to make decisions such as you request. However, I will be happy to send a telegram to Rome today for instructions. I will get in touch with you as soon as I have a reply. In the meantime, why don't you just go and enjoy the celebration in the piazza?" Realizing we would get no further with him, we left.

A celebration was certainly in progress. Just working our way across the plaza back to the hotel was an experience. By the time we reached the front door of the Brufani, we had been kissed, hugged, danced with, and cried over by townspeople of every age and description. I handed the doorman the bottle of wine someone had pressed into my hands. Inside, there was more celebration. I saw Nancy and Amy, laughing and dancing with some of the foreign students. "Walter! Walter!" shouted Nancy, catching sight of me, "Isn't it wonderful? I'm so excited! It's going to be over soon! We'll be going home!" She came running over to hug and kiss me. I hugged her tightly and held on to her. My instincts told me we still had a long way to go. Perhaps it's just as well they don't know, I decided. The Italians may have signed an armistice, but the countryside is still full of armed Germans, and THEY haven't signed anything. The next afternoon, having heard nothing from the chief of police, Lester and I and Colonel Rocke, a retired English army officer, returned to the questura. The police chief wasn't there, but the senior officer on duty greeted us apologetically. "Everything is topsy-turvy in Rome right now, Signori, and we have had no answer yet to our telegram. Would you like us to send another one?"

"No, not yet," I replied. "I'll check back with you again later."

Just then, the chief of police arrived. "I do not understand why our communications with Rome are not working," he apologized, "but I would suggest, Signor Console, that you go directly to the Army with your request, since they have jurisdiction over all aircraft in this area at this time." I immediately called to make an appointment to see General Luigi Renzoni, Commander of the military zone of Perugia.

Meanwhile unbeknownst to us, the telegram the questura had sent requesting air transportation for me by name was intercepted by the Germans. They forwarded it to their intelligence unit, where it was compared against a list of names of "Enemies of the State". My name was among those on that list.

The next morning, General Renzoni returned my call. "Signor Console," he began, "I understand your concern, and your wish to get to Allied-held territory as quickly as possible. However, I have no capability to give you access to an airplane. Nor can I get you rail transport. All civilian transport has been curtailed."

"Tell me, General," I asked, "if the Germans decide to attack and occupy Perugia, can you defend it?"

"I will be honest with you, Signore. The answer is no. I do not have the troops, or the arms. Also, I am not clear on just what my position is now. We are no longer at war with the Allies, and I understand that. But we are not at war with the Germans, either. So I have no orders to defend against them. It is all very confusing, as I'm sure you understand. Good day."

By that evening, rumors of every sort were flying around town. Lester came to me. "I've heard that the Germans are in control in Rome, Walter," he said. "So I think we can forget about getting transferred there anytime soon." "Walter," said Nancy later, " I just heard that the Pope has been taken captive by the Germans and sent to Berlin!" "Oh, I'm sure that's just a rumor, Nancy," I reassured her.

But it made me uneasy, and I hurried to Enrico's to hear the BBC. It was the only reliable source we had. The broadcast confirmed what I had feared. The Allies were managing to keep their toehold on the mainland of Italy, but the Germans, already there in force, were on the move and actively taking control in the vacuum of political power that existed in Italy. Rome, as Lester had informed me, was under German control. The Italians, not having declared against the Germans, were caught in the middle. The Pope was not mentioned, so that must have just been a wild rumor. However, the truth was more chilling for our personal situation than any rumors about the Pope.

As I walked back to the hotel from Enrico's, a motorcycle squadron of Germans roared into the Piazza Italia, pulling up in front of the questura. As they dismounted, every inch the imposing height and strong physiques of the much-touted Aryans, one walked right past me, smiling coldly and disdainfully at the small clutch of civilians gathered in the street. Stopping briefly, he deliberately unholstered his Luger and lifted it, snapping the chamber open, then closed. The effect was electrifying. The faces of the people changed, as though a switch had been thrown, from a mood of happy excitement to expressions of fear and dread. I quickly melted into the crowd, and made my way quietly to the hotel. The time had come to make our move.

Chapter 4

Hideout at the Casa Bonucci

I paced my room in agitation. I couldn't find Nancy or Amy anywhere. It wasn't like them to be gone at this time of day, or to go anywhere without leaving me a note. Damn! I must not have gotten through to them exactly how dangerous our situation was! As I paced, I could hear the rumble of armored columns from the highway below the city, and stepped out onto the balcony for a look. The Germans were approaching Perugia in force. Life here would change, and fast.

A sudden loud rap at the door startled me, and I hastened to open it. A little Italian girl, about eleven years old, stood there. She stared up at me, wide-eyed. "What do you want?" I asked sharply, annoyed. She continued to stare up at me in awe. I realized I was probably the first foreigner she had ever seen, and my gruff tone must have frightened her. "What is it?" I said, more gently. "What do you want?

The little girl looked shyly down, nervously twisting one of her braids around her fingers. Then, screwing up her courage, she blurted, "Mi mandó la mamma." (My mother sent me.)

"Your mother?" I asked in surprise. "Who are you?"

"I am Lucia Bonucci. Mamma sent me to tell you that your daughters are safe at our house. Zia Vittoria told me how to find you." With that, she bobbed a small curtsy, turned, and bounded away down the hall.

Bonucci must be Vittoria's sister's name, and the girls must have had a scare that day which caused them to go ahead into hiding, without waiting for me. I worried about what had happened to them, but I didn't dare leave the hotel, it was too early in the evening, and still too light. I was relieved to know they were safe for the moment, at least. I began to get myself ready to go as soon as darkness fell.

Once again, I carefully weighed my alternatives, and my decision. By remaining right here in the hotel, exposing myself to certain capture by the Germans, I could still hope that my diplomatic status might afford us all some small margin of protection, and safety. But I didn't really believe that, and couldn't trust it. I also knew, better than the girls did, that the Germans would not treat us kindly if we escaped from them now, and were eventually recaptured. And we would be exposing Vittoria, and her sister and her family, to terrible consequences for their complicity in helping us.

On the other hand, if we could just stay out of German hands we might have a chance, however small, of reaching the Allied lines, or having the Allies rescue us, in the near future.

For now, I thought, the Germans will probably be more interested in getting the Italians under control than in rounding up foreign internees, and we might go unnoticed for awhile. Maybe we shouldn't move in with the Bonuccis just yet. Maybe we'd be safe here at the hotel awhile longer. No sense overreacting.

Nevertheless, something had occurred today that made Amy and Nancy flee to the Bonuccis by themselves. Sending Lucia to me here meant Vittoria and her sister agreed the time had come, and had accepted the risk associated with sheltering us.

I worried about Lester, and the Kutsukians, too. What would happen to them? A few weeks back, I had cautiously probed Lester and Jack about the idea of going into hiding, without giving them any hint of my own thoughts or arrangements. The less they knew, the less the Germans could pry out of them if the occasion arose. Lester was vehemently against the idea. Jack had been cool and noncommittal. No, I decided, Amy, Nancy and I would have to do it alone, just the three of us. That was risky enough. Having weighed everything carefully, I decided that going into hiding, now, was my only viable option. That decided, I sprang into action, and changed into my oldest suit. My valise was not so large that it would be conspicuous. I surveyed myself carefully in the mirror. I hoped I looked like any ordinary Italian businessman on his way home from work.

Shortly after darkness fell, I slipped quietly out the service entrance at the rear of the hotel. I had checked out Vittoria's sister's place several times already, approaching it from different directions, until I knew I could find it easily, even by myself in the dark. After about fifteen minutes of walking, I had reached the cross street above the one on which the house stood, and I glanced down the darkened street to make sure no one was around.

The houses in that area were joined together in a row, with common partitioning walls, so I didn't have to worry about anyone lurking between them. The buildings stood right at the edge of the street, with only a few inches of curbing between them and the street. The street was deserted. Just to be doubly safe, I circled the block again, approaching the house from the opposite direction, keeping to the shadows. Slipping into the entryway, I glanced up the dimly lit stairway. Empty. Slowly, I made my way, step by careful step, up the stairs. I passed apartments on the first, second and third floors without rousing anyone. The door to the apartment on the fourth floor stood slightly ajar. I drew a deep breath and pushed it open just enough to slip inside, swiftly closing it behind me.

As I turned into the room, which appeared to be a kitchen, Nancy threw herself into my arms, sobbing. "Oh, God, Walter, I'm so glad you're here!" she wailed. "You won't believe what happened! We were so scared!" Amy grabbed my arm and was tugging on it, talking excitedly at the same time.

"Sssh. Sssh. Quiet! It's okay. Now, calm down," I ordered in a whisper. "One at a time. Tell me what happened. You first, Amy," I said quietly. "Tell me what happened."

"Oh, Walter!" she burst out, her ringlets fairly dancing in outrage, "it was perfectly horrible! Those Fascist bastards tried to shoot us!"

"Shoot you!" I exclaimed, forgetting to be quiet. "Why would the Fascists try to shoot you? What is all this?" I patted her hand. "Look, just take it from the beginning, and tell me everything that happened. Exactly as it happened." I reached over and hugged the shaking Nancy again, keeping my arm across her shoulders. I was glad they were there within reach, safe and unharmed.

"Well," began Amy, "it was about two o'clock, and you weren't back, so we decided to go out and find a newspaper to see what was happening. We were about three blocks from the hotel, not far from that news stand you always go to, when we heard a gunshot just behind us." She paused to draw breath. Nancy chimed in, "It was really loud, Walter, and scared the hell out of us!" "Sssh, I know it did," I hushed her, stroking her hair, "let Amy finish."

"Right after we heard the first shot," Amy continued, "I grabbed Nancy and pulled her toward the buildings. Then there were a whole lot of shots from the other direction. We dropped to the ground and crawled along close to the building to a doorway, and slid in there. We heard bullets hitting right above our heads. It was terrifying! We crouched there, not daring to make a sound. I don't think we even breathed. It seems like it must have been a long time, but probably only half a minute, or a minute, when more shots hit right in front of us. We thought we had been hit too, but it was only flying splinters from the paving stones. I poked Nancy and said, 'I've had enough of this—let's get the hell out of here!'"

"You didn't go out into the street!" I exclaimed.

"No, the doorway led to an alleyway behind some shops. We slithered backward into that alleyway, then we scurried along at a half crouch, trying each door as we came to it. One of the doors, maybe the third or fourth one, opened, and we barged right in. It was the back room of a poultry shop, and the proprietor was sitting there finishing his lunch, drinking a glass of wine. I said 'scusi, scusi' and dodged the chickens and we ran to the front door of the shop. Poor man! He just sat there with his mouth open, thoroughly stunned. He never moved a muscle!" Amy smiled at the memory, and I was relieved that she was beginning to calm down. "Then what happened?" I prompted.

Nancy took up the tale. "We turned a corner, and suddenly there was a big roar and here came a whole column of German soldiers on motorcycles, right at us! God! We were scared out of our wits! We jumped into another doorway, and I said to Amy, 'We'll never make it back to the hotel, let's head for Vittoria's sister's place." And here we are," she concluded, smiling bravely through her tears.

"You both did very well," I praised them, "you really kept your heads in a crisis. I'm glad you came here."

"Margherita—that's Mrs. Bonucci—decided it was safer to send Lucia to let you know where we were than for us to go back there ourselves," said Amy. I sat back in my chair, mulling over what they had just told me. Amy poured me a glass of watered wine. Gratefully, I downed it.

It was doubtful that the Fascists had been shooting at the girls. More than likely, it was a skirmish between newly emboldened Italian factions, and the two girls just happened to be in the wrong place at the wrong time. Also, I doubted that the German motorcycle unit was there to begin a roundup of foreigners. There were not enough German soldiers in Perugia to do that...yet.

It was probably just an advance party, for show, to instill the proper degree of fear into the populace. I was still sure the Germans were more interested in demobilizing Italian military units and rounding up young men who might be partisans or Allied sympathizers than they were in taking custody of a few stray foreigners.

"We've got to consider our next move very carefully,

girls. Life in hiding here won't be pleasant, or easy. You also need to consider that there will be severe consequences if we're caught, not only for us, but for the Bonuccis and Vittoria too." Our hostess had not yet appeared. Apparently she was giving us privacy to exchange our stories and weigh the pros and cons of our situation. I appreciated her tact and understanding.

"What do you have with you?" I asked. "Only our handbags. That's all we had with us," replied Amy. "Everything else is still back at the hotel. What about you?"

"I just brought what I could fit into a small valise. I can't risk going back. I know the Germans want me, so I have definitely decided to go into hiding, and now. Whether or not you want to do that is up to you. If you decide to join me, I think it would still be okay for you to slip back to the hotel tonight and get some of your things." They thought it all over. We sat in silence for a few minutes. "I've decided," said Amy suddenly. I'm coming into hiding with you, now."

"What about you, Nancy?" I asked gently.

She nodded her assent. "Me, too. I'd rather be here with you than at the hotel."

Amy stood up. "Let's go and get our things, then," she said briskly, heading for the door. She turned. "We'll be back here tomorrow, bag and baggage." She forced a thin smile.

"Once in hiding, we won't be able to go back until Perugia is liberated by the Allies," I warned. "We know that, Walter," said Nancy quietly, "but we'd rather take our chances here with you and the Bonuccis, than sit and wait for the Germans at the hotel." With that, they slipped out the door and were gone.

Margherita Bonucci suddenly appeared, detaining me with one hand on my arm, the other to her lips to signal silence. "It is better for you to stay here, Signore," she said. "Do not worry. The Signorine will be watched, and guarded, until they are safely back here tomorrow."

I looked at my hostess. She was a little shorter, and a little darker than Vittoria. "You are most welcome in our home,

Signore" she informed me graciously, "we are honored to have such a distinguished guest as you to share our poor and humble home." She was a strong, vigorous woman. Her graying brown hair was tied back with a strip of ribbon, and she wore an old, shapeless, gray cardigan over her simple, dark brown, woolen dress. A gold wedding band and a string of inexpensive beads around her neck were her only adornments.

"It is I who am honored, Signora," I replied, also in Italian, "and I am grateful to have such friends as you to help me in this time of need." She smiled, showing large, slightly crooked teeth. "I am happy you speak our language so well. You have no worry, Signore," she assured me, "we will see to your safety and comfort, and that of the Signorine when they return." Putting her finger once again to her lips to signal that I must be careful not to wake the others, she led me to my room.

Being the only other bedroom in the apartment, I knew it would turn into "our" room when the girls returned. I wondered how we would handle that. Margherita must have moved her children into her own bedroom with her. It was going to be a horribly crowded situation, with little or no privacy for anyone. I hoped it would be of short duration, that we would be liberated before the month was out. I stretched out on the bed and was soon sound asleep.

I woke suddenly, completely disoriented. Dawn was breaking. For a moment I couldn't remember where I was. Then it all came back to me. As I looked around the room, my new home, I knew what Margherita meant. It was definitely a humble abode. The dim light that filtered in from the single shuttered window revealed my bed to be a huge, cast iron affair that stood nearly four feet above a bare, red tile floor. Two ancient, overstuffed armchairs crouched disconsolately on either side of a doorway which, upon investigation, led to the bathroom. The iciness of the tile against my bare feet brought memories of Gubbio flooding back. If it was already this cold in September, I didn't want to think of what January might be like! Hopefully, we'd be safely behind the Allied lines long before November.

In the bathroom, I found an old bidet, a toilet which looked to be of the same vintage and noise production capability as the one in the Albergo San Marco, and a small sink. I tried both spigots, but only one worked—the cold. Hot water would have to be heated on the kitchen stove and carried in. It was probably reserved for weekly bathing. Shivering, I washed and shaved in cold water, and got dressed. I hoped the girls had made out all right. I was hungry and worried, and suddenly not all that sure I had made the right decision. Already, I missed the amenities of the Hotel Brufani.

When I stepped into the kitchen, I found Margherita already there, preparing breakfast. The kitchen was large--about fifteen feet wide by twenty feet long--with a large, black cast iron cooking stove against one wall. The smell of burning wood, and a tiny amount of heat, drifted from it. Across the room was a sink. Against another wall was a plain wooden cupboard, and in it Margherita stored and displayed her meager store of kitchen utensils--one or two pots, a few dishes, some glasses and tableware.

Above the sink was a small window, and from it extended a line and pulley arrangement for hanging out laundry. A couple of sagging shelves served as a pantry, and there was a battered old icebox. Lucia and a young boy of about eight were seated at a well-scrubbed wooden table, finishing their morning meal. Above the table hung a framed and faded print depicting Christ on the cross.

Margherita motioned for me to sit. "Franco, this is Signor Orebaugh. Say hello," Margherita commanded her son. Franco gave me a cursory stare, mumbled "buongiorno" and darted out the door before his mother could demand anything further of him. Lucia set a large mug of coffee before me, then stood close by me, smiling shyly. I smiled back at her. "Lucia! Sit down and finish your breakfast. Don't stare at Signor Orebaugh, it's not polite," said her mother.

I winked at Lucia, then literally caught my breath as a stunningly beautiful girl appeared, like a vision, in the doorway from the bedrooms.

"Buongiorno, Signore, I am Valentina", she said in a soft, husky voice, advancing into the kitchen.

I rose to greet her. "Buongiorno, Valentina, I'm Walter Orebaugh," I replied. "I'm pleased to meet you, and to be here in your home. Your mother is most gracious to help us." She gave me a warm, open smile, revealing even white teeth. "It is nothing, Signore, as my mother has told you. We are happy to be of help."

She went over to the stove and poured herself coffee, giving me a chance to regain my senses and observe her. Valentina was tall, about 5'8", with a slim, full-breasted figure, and she radiated youth and energy. Thick chestnut color hair fell to her waist, curling softly at the ends. It was held back from her face by a simple, black ribbon headband. And what a face it was! In Valentina, the strong Vechiet features of her mother and aunt had been softened and refined. Her huge, dark brown eyes appeared even larger, set in a delicate oval face. It was hard to believe that the stolid Margherita and her as yet unseen husband, Gregorio, had produced this beauty!

Quickly finishing her coffee, Valentina departed to do the morning errands. Without her presence, the kitchen somehow seemed dingier. But her casual departure, like Franco's, alarmed me.

"Margherita, I am worried that the children might leak information about us being here. Can we trust them to keep our secret?" "Don't worry, Signore, they understand well," she assured me, refilling my cup. "I have given them orders. They will obey. And anyway, no one pays attention to children's prattle."

Just as I finished my coffee, Amy and Nancy arrived, breathless from the long climb up. "Here we are, for better or for worse, as they say," smiled Amy bravely, hugging me. They'd had to slip past two German guards who had already taken up stations at the entrance to the hotel, so had managed to bring only a few essentials in a shopping bag, in order to get out without attracting the guards' attention. "However, not to worry," said Amy. "We arranged with Vittoria for the rest of our stuff to be hidden, and it will be brought here after dark."

We sat at the kitchen table with Margherita as she outlined the new household rules and arrangements. As I had expected, the three of us would share the bedroom, and all seven of us would share the single bathroom in the apartment.

"The children have been ordered to respect your privacy," Margherita told us. "You will be served your meals first, then the family will eat." I demurred. "It is best that way, so that if anyone comes, there will not be too many places set at the table. Also, there are only four chairs," she concluded, on a practical note. "Valentina and I will do the shopping and the cooking." I handed her what ration coupons we had. They would provide little, but she was happy to get them. I also insisted on paying her a sum every month for our board. She protested, but I was adamant on that. "Signora, you can hardly be expected to feed and house us out of your own pocket," I said, pressing some lire into her hand.

Over the next couple of days, our baggage arrived, piece by piece, carried by Vittoria, Valentina and Margherita. They even managed to cover up the expensive, telltale leather of my luggage, to conceal it from curious eyes. I turned the foodstuffs, —flour, sugar, coffee and canned goods,—over to Margherita, with the exception of a few bars of soap, which I stored behind the armadio in our room. They were as good as money, and might help us in some unexpected way some day. Margherita was thrilled with everything. Much of it hadn't been seen on the markets in town for many months.

Our adjustment to our new life began. The first night, I tried to sleep on the floor and let the girls have the bed, but the tile floor was so icy, I barely lasted an hour down there. We had only one sheet and two blankets, and we'd need all of them on the bed to keep warm. After a few nights of sleeplessness and nervous adjustments—Amy's prickly metal curlers and her continual snoring kept Nancy and me awake; I was a restless sleeper and kicked both girls until they had bruises; Nancy was a light sleeper, who woke with a start at every noise and turn—we finally became accustomed to sleeping three to a bed. Although it seems hard to believe, sex was never a consideration. Our miserable living conditions, and our fears, discouraged any thoughts of intimacy—we were always too tired, too cold, too hungry, and too frightened. Moreover, we slept fully dressed, wearing several layers of clothes, in case we had to make a quick escape. As winter moved in, and the temperature dropped, we were grateful for our enforced physical closeness—it made for shared body heat. Warmth, like food, had suddenly become paramount in our lives.

We nearly cried for joy when Naples was liberated in mid-October. However, we knew also that the Germans were now firmly ensconced, and in full control, in Perugia. Vittoria reported that Jack Kutsukian had been arrested when he left the hotel to go to the pharmacy. All detainees were now confined totally to the hotel Brufani, and could only leave if they had a letter of authorization. "Also, Signore," she reported solemnly, "today there were German officers in black uniforms, not in gray ones like the others, and they asked about you at the registration desk." At that, fear snaked through me. Black uniforms meant the Gestapo, the most dreaded force of the German military. They would not abandon the search easily.

Then, Margherita received the first word of her husband. His army unit had been surrounded by Germans and they'd been packed in freight cars and shipped to Germany to labor there. As the train passed along Lake Trasimeno, Gregorio and others whose families lived in the area tossed notes out, hoping they'd be found by friendly people and the information relayed to their families. Which is exactly what happened. The usually stoic and cheerful Margherita burst into tears on hearing that terrible news. We were devastated to see her so distraught, but after a few minutes she resolutely dried her tears and began preparations for dinner. "Sit and rest, Margherita," I urged her. "You've had a bad shock. We can manage to get our own dinner for once."

But she would have none of it. "No, Signore, I am all right now," she assured me. "Life goes on, and the children will be home soon, and hungry." She was an amazing woman--physically strong, almost fearless, endlessly resourceful, and a well of emotional strength for the whole household.

Not everything in our lives was glum. The forced closeness, and the family atmosphere, kept our spirits up, even when we were hungry and without enough food. "At least I don't have to worry about losing weight now," remarked Amy one morning, showing us several inches of gap in her skirt waistband. She and Nancy tried to help Margherita as much as possible with the household chores. I had little to do, but kept Lucia and Franco mesmerized for hours with tales of imaginary exploits with the Indians in the American West.

Lucia became my shadow. She doted on me, and waited on me at every opportunity. In the mornings, when I came into the kitchen, she'd be there, dressed and waiting to pour my coffee. Then she would sit close and watch me solemnly as I drank it. One morning I overheard her admonishing Valentina, "Remember, I saw him first! You already have too many boyfriends."

One evening, Vittoria appeared and silently handed me an envelope. It was from Manfred, and contained more money. She repeated the message that the anonymous messenger had passed, "keep your chins up, we're working on getting you to Rome." The Allies would take Rome long before they took Perugia, and our chances of eluding capture by the Germans would be better in a big bustling city like Rome than here.

From the little news we got, we knew that the Germans were fighting bitterly before giving up an inch of Italian soil. Also, they had rescued Mussolini and reinstalled him in a puppet government in north Italy, dubbed the "Republic of Salo". And neo-Fascists, worse than any of the heyday of Mussolini, had arrived in Perugia and begun arresting people, requisitioning homes and whatever else suited their fancy. They were, for the most part, the dregs of Italian society, recruited from the bowels of Naples, Palermo, and other urban cesspools. They were a blend of scum, ruffian, and ruthless cutthroat—hoodlums to be feared far more than the Germans. They began conducting periodic searches of houses and neighborhoods in Perugia, arresting Jews and foreigners. We now had real fear to live with every day. I had tried to make light of our plight, but now I had to face the ominous danger we were in, and worse, make the women and children live with it too.

Margherita and I carefully rearranged the kitchen, putting the table directly under the trap door to the attic. We kept a large wooden crate beside it, to boost me or the girls up to reach the trap door. I made Nancy and Amy practice putting the crate on the table, getting on it, pushing open the trap, and boosting each other into the attic. Then I'd climb up into the attic as fast as I could, and pull them up after me. We spent most of two afternoons practicing getting up into the attic under every possible condition and combination. When those practice sessions ended we were all exhausted, and every bone and muscle in our bodies hurt, but we had cut the time to less than two minutes from first warning to being in the attic, with the trap door shut and the crate down off the table.

As we lay in bed that night, trying to get to sleep, there was a noise on the roof, and Nancy gasped aloud and jumped a foot off the bed. "Ssh," I soothed her, "it's nothing. Probably just a roof tile falling. Try to go to sleep. You're just jumpy after this afternoon."

"Oh, Walter," she cried, and though I couldn't see her in the dark, I could hear the fear in her voice, "do you think we'll ever get out of here alive?"

"Christ I hope so," Amy piped up out of the shadows.

"With all that bloody climbing about, I ruined my last good pair of stockings. I'll need to go shopping soon." We all managed a laugh at that, and the tension was relieved. We slept deeply.

The next morning, for no good reason except I hated shaving in cold water, I decided I wouldn't shave again until we were liberated. Although at that time I had no thoughts of disguising myself by growing a beard, later it turned out to be a fortunate happenstance. At first, no one commented on my budding beard. A few nights after I had stopped shaving, Margherita and I were sitting up late, quietly talking about the day's big news bulletin—Italy had declared war on Germany—when there was a light tap at the door. I dived for the bedroom, waking the girls, and we huddled together in there, not daring to breathe. We knew that this was it, that we had been betrayed.

After all our practicing, there hadn't even been time to try for the attic escape. I hugged the trembling girls close. Suddenly, the bedroom door banged open, and we jumped in terror. A man stood there, laughing.

"Come out here, all of you."

I couldn't see his face, with the light behind him, but I recognized that laugh. It was Manfred! I leaped at him, yelling and cursing, pounding him on the back. "You crazy bastard! You scared hell out of us! How did you find us? What are you doing here?" Amy and Nancy threw themselves into his arms, hugging him. Margherita stood by silently, a stunned look on her face. She was terrified, and hadn't figured out what was going on.

We all crowded back into the kitchen. "Please, Signori, quiet, or you will have the Fascists out on us," Margherita cautioned us. I explained to her who this stranger was. Valentina, awakened by the commotion, appeared. Framed in the doorway, in a tattered old robe, hair tousled, she was still breathtakingly lovely, and I could see that Manfred was having the same reaction I did on first seeing her. After the introductions, he reluctantly tore his eyes from her. Valentina disappeared, reappearing a few minutes later in more presentable garb. By that time, Margherita had made coffee for everyone. Manfred turned and peered at me again.

"God, you look funny Walter," he said, "what's the matter with your face? Here, I brought some oranges." He reached into the sack he had dropped on the floor and pulled out an orange for each of us. The three girls immediately began tearing the peels off theirs. Margherita just held hers, turning it around and around in her hands, gazing at it in delight. I wondered how long it had been since she, or any of her family, had seen an orange. Manfred turned to the women. "Doesn't he look funny, ladies?" he demanded. "Yes, as a matter of fact you do, Walter," whispered Amy, looking closely at me. "What on earth have you done to yourself?"

"Nothing. I'm growing a beard," I shot her a sullen look. "And I'm not shaving again until we're liberated!" I whispered emphatically. "Oho!" said Manfred gleefully, "at the rate the liberation is progressing, you'll look like Methuselah. You'll have time to grow a beard down to your toes!" With that, he and the girls went off in a gale of giggles. Even though it was a pleasure to see them all laughing for a change, Margherita shot me a look of pure alarm. "Ssh! Hey! Quiet down!" I commanded in as stern a whisper as I could. "You'll have the Germans and the Fascists down on our necks if you keep that up. Shush! Whispers only! How did you find us, Manfred?" He picked up the sack from which he had pulled the oranges, and placed it on the table. Then he beckoned to Margherita, who cautiously approached him, curiosity overcoming her normal reserve. "I have my ways," he replied, "but so far they haven't been good enough to get you to Rome. I'm still working on it, though. Just wanted to see for myself that you're all right." As he spoke, he was pulling foodstuffs out of the bag. Margherita exclaimed softly as each new item appeared. She couldn't believe they were all for us. There was some sugar, and a little real Swiss coffee, and more oranges,—enough that each of the children could have one in the morning. There were canned delicacies. We pulled our chairs close around the table and sat there, slowly and carefully eating our oranges, savoring every morsel, eagerly listening to Manfred's news of the outside world. Never had an orange tasted so good to me. Manfred could not help noticing our obvious hunger, and turned serious.

"Walter, I know it is difficult to find enough food to keep all of you from being hungry, but you must be very careful about making purchases on the black market from here on," he declared solemnly. "Everyone and everything is being watched, and if Margherita spends too much, or too freely, for the size of her family, it will arouse suspicion. He turned and looked directly at Margherita. "You must be very careful," he reiterated, in Italian. She nodded her understanding.

Then, turning back to me, he said, "The Allies are not making any headway. It looks like you will be here for awhile, so take every precaution." With that, he pressed a wad of folded lire into my hand. Opening the door, he peered cautiously down the stairway. Then, with a casual wave, he was gone.

Our excitement kept us awake and whispering for another quarter of an hour, then we reluctantly turned off the single kerosene lamp to save precious fuel, and filed quietly to bed, each of us lost in our own thoughts. Manfred's news about the Allies had put a big damper on our optimism. The longer we were forced to stay there at Margherita's, the greater our chances of being betrayed, or discovered by the enemy, would become.

More weeks passed, and just finding food to feed us became Margherita's main occupation. She had a battered bicycle, which she or Valentina used for their long forays into the countryside in search of food. As the winter progressed, and foodstuffs became more and more scarce, the trips became longer and longer, sometimes reaching thirty to forty kilometers—almost twenty miles—round trip each day. Most days, we were lucky if these grueling trips produced a few carrots, or a cabbage, or a few handfuls of Brussel sprouts. With those, Margherita would concoct a thin minestrone, or a broth, more warming than filling. On the rare occasions when she managed to find rabbit, or a chicken, there was elation and celebration.

Never before in my life had food occupied such a paramount place in my thoughts. Never before had I known real hunger, either. I gained a new respect for cooks, and for the overwhelming responsibility placed on women like Margherita. The can of sweetened condensed milk, from the few that remained in the supplies I had given her, was accorded a place of honor in the kitchen. We were each allotted one teaspoonful of the thick, sweet milk a day, and we all looked forward to that treat. I repeatedly tried to give my portion over to the children, as did Nancy and Amy, but Margherita would not hear of it. "We need this to keep our strength," she said with finality. "If we fall sick, who will take care of the children? No, everyone must take their share, adults as well as children, to keep well."

Oddly enough, it was real coffee I yearned for, more than anything else. Our morning "coffee" was a roasted barley concoction. The real coffee Manfred had brought was drunk only on Sunday, only one cup each, and the used grounds were saved, dried, and mixed in with roasted barley, a scant spoonful at a time, all through the next week. Breakfast was a mug of that pale barley "coffee" and a couple of chunks of coarse bread, which we called bread only from force of habit. I didn't want to know what it was made of. Lunch was always a bowl of soup, or broth, carefully crafted by Margherita out of whatever she had held back from the previous evening's dinner supplies. In it, we dunked the stale, hard bread to soften it enough to chew it. The bits of soaked bread helped quiet our growling stomachs for awhile. There was no such thing as a "leftover," or a snack. Ceci (chick peas) were the standard vegetable at every meal. Sometimes ceci were the entire meal. There was no salt or sugar to be had, and very few other seasonings were still available, so everything was bland and tasteless. We ate to stay alive.

The evening meal was usually pasta—now a uniformly gray mush that was almost inedible. "Sauce" consisted of a thin tomato paste, or a ladle of broth from the lunch soup, unless it was one of those rare days on which Margherita had found a bit of dried sausage somewhere in her travels, or some other meat or game.

Manfred's occasional bags were our lifeline. He brought us small tins of canned meats whenever he came, but his visits were weeks apart, and we were seven people who needed to eat to keep functioning. Margherita had to somehow produce at least fourteen, and usually twenty-one, servings of some kind of sustenance each and every day! It was a phenomenal task, and was her constant occupation and worry. She did better than most, but I could see the weight dropping off everyone in the household. My own face, in spite of the bushy beard I now sported, reflected back a gaunt image when I looked in the mirror.

Vittoria kept us informed of happenings in Perugia. Jack Kutsukian had been sent to a concentration camp somewhere. The Germans now occupied the Brufani. "Eh, it is terrible out there now," lamented Vittoria during one of her evening visits. "They take everyone, every man under sixty—Jews, foreigners, Italians, no matter, and send them off to Germany to labor camps. All our men are being taken. Who will save us?" Being a man, and well under sixty, I now felt all the more exposed, and vulnerable.

Although it was of little comfort to us, we knew there were thousands of Italians and other foreigners in hiding, just like we were. "Macchia" is the Italian word for bush, and the phrase "darsi alla macchia" (to go into the bush) was the expression that described hiding out—whether it was in the hills, in the woods, in a barn—anywhere other than in one's own home.

This wholesale arrest of Italian men by the Germans and the neo-Fascists, or the mens' only alternative--to go to the "macchia"-- was having its inevitable effect on families. For Italians, nothing is as important as the integrity of the family unit. What may be lacking in them in the way of patriotism, civic loyalty, or religious ardor is more than compensated for by the deep and abiding devotion they manifest toward the family as an institution. The degree to which the integrity of the family was destroyed by the acts of the Germans and the new puppet Italian regime generated a hatred in the general populace that knew no limits.

The tenant farmers' families in the area around Perugia (and in other areas of Italy as well, we later learned) united to feed and shelter refugees who were hiding out from the Germans and the Fascists. Valentina, like Vittoria, returned from their forays for food with tales of the hills full of refugees—youths evading internment, British ex-prisoners of war, civilians of all ages and all walks of life—including, it was rumored, many aristocrats and some members of the deposed royal family— even police and caribinieri who had deserted their duty posts. All were labeled "brigands" by the neo-Fascists. Valentina heard from her friends that they were organizing themselves into guerrilla bands (partigiani) up in the hills, to take resistance action against the enemy. That interested me. I was determined to learn more.

"Valentina," I said one Saturday, as we slowly consumed our scant cups of soup, "I need you to find out as much as you possibly can about these guerrilla bands."

She looked at me seriously for a few moments, her dark eyes now huge in her thin face. Then she nodded. "I will find out what I can for you, Signore," she replied. "I will talk with my friend Renzo. He knows the leader of one of the bands."

I leaned toward her and placed a hand on her shoulder for emphasis. "Thank you, Valentina," I said. "Please do it as soon as possible, but be careful, be VERY careful," I cautioned. "We don't want anyone to have a clue that you are harboring refugees."

"Do not worry, Gualtiero," she assured me, smiling, "I will be very discreet."

The slothlike advance of the Allied forces gnawed at us as much as hunger did. We were deeply worried about how long we could continue to impose on Margherita. Never by word or act did she indicate that she was tired of having us there, but we had come in September for "a few weeks," and now it was November, and we were no closer to being rescued, moved, or liberated. Manfred was working on getting us false identity papers, so we could try to escape, but so far he had come up empty-handed.

It was the ever-watchful Amy who spotted the Fascists conducting a house-to-house search on our street late one afternoon. "Oh, God, Walter," she cried frantically, "here they come!"

"Quick, everyone! To the attic! Hurry!" I commanded. We all dashed for the kitchen table. I threw the crate up on it, and Margherita steadied it as I jumped up and pushed open the trap door to our "hell hole," as we had dubbed it.

Before I was in and fully turned around, Nancy was up on the crate, reaching to be pulled up. "Here, grab me Walter, hurry!" she begged. Amy was already clambering onto the table behind her. We could hear the Fascisti pounding loudly on the door to the apartment on the first floor. Our hearts were pounding almost as loudly. I got Nancy in, and together we hauled Amy up into the attic with us. As I slammed the trap door shut, I saw that Margherita had already removed the crate, and Valentina was calmly and quietly seating the two children at the table, with cups of soup in front of them. They were the picture of a poor family at their meager supper. Valentina checked the kitchen over, and Margherita slipped quickly into our bedroom to conceal any evidence of our presence.

We crept to the farthest, darkest corner, and crouched there, barely breathing. We were sweating from fear, despite the attic's icy temperature. The urge to sneeze or cough was unbearable, but we didn't dare to even clear our throats. We strained to hear sounds from below. Nancy had hold of my hand, and clutched it in a grip so tight I thought for sure the bones would be crushed. There wasn't a sound from our corner, except for our shallow breathing. After what seemed like an eternity, we heard the welcome sound of a broom being banged against the ceiling—it was the "all clear" signal! We let our breath out in a whoosh, and scrambled for the trap door.

Back down in the kitchen, we broke into a spasm of coughing and sneezing. I couldn't help laughing when Amy's face reappeared in the light—she was as black and filthy as a chimney sweep! The attic had built up its thick layer of dirt and dust for over a century.

Amy, ever the coquette, did not find her condition the least bit amusing, and burst into a storm of tears when she saw herself in the mirror. After that, it was difficult to get her to go into the attic. "Oh, Walter, I can't stand another minute of this!" she wailed. "I'd rather take my chances with the Germans. God only knows what's up there crawling around in that filthy attic!"

We cleaned up every trace of dirt, then wolfed down our sparse supper and turned in. In our undernourished condition, and weakened further from months of forced inactivity, we were exhausted, and fell asleep almost instantly. For once, Amy's snoring didn't keep us awake.

The winter became one of the most severe that any of the natives could remember. Perhaps, with sufficient food, the cold would have been more endurable. I prayed daily for a return visit from Manfred. There was no fuel for heat, and our breath made frosty puffs of clouds in the frigid air when we spoke. Dressed in all the warm clothing we owned, we spent day and night huddled together in bed for warmth. We were miserable.

Several weeks had passed since Manfred's last visit, and our small hoard of food had completely vanished. Margherita gleaned little from her long bicycle trips. She was weakening to the point where soon she would no longer be able to pedal such distances in search of food for us. I knew she secretly stinted on her own rations to give more to us and the children, but she never complained.

One evening, Vittoria came, and out of the lining of her

coat, like a magician, she produced two hard-crusted rolls, a pat of real butter, and about a third of a bottle of brandy. We were overjoyed. "I stole these from those pigs of German officers," she declared proudly. "They had stuffed their bellies and weren't paying attention."

We froze in horror. "Vittoria!" I scolded. "You mustn't ever take a chance like that again! If you had been caught, the punishment would have been out of all proportion to what you did! They might have executed you!" She was impervious to my outburst. "Never mind," she said stolidly. "Here, Franco, eat your bread." She broke a good-sized chunk from one of the rolls, dabbed it with butter and handed it to the child, who immediately wolfed it down. She gave me a look that spoke volumes.

I wished for something more useful to do than sitting around, watching my beard grow, which it did with a slowness as agonizing as the stalled Allied advance. "That beard is the ugliest thing I've ever seen, Walter," remarked Amy. "It rivals Joseph's coat of many colors!" That was true enough. Sandy in some places, black in others, salt and pepper gray in others, the beard was hardly an enhancement to my looks. But I was glad I had given up the torment of daily shaves in cold water, and had no desire to go back to them, no matter how mottled and ugly the result was. Besides, I had vowed not to shave until we were liberated, and I wasn't about to break that vow.

One evening, I asked for a few minutes alone with Valentina. I wanted to discuss news of the "macchia" with her, and the others all left the room without question. Lucia, however, flew into a rage. "First Signor Metzger, and now Il Console!" she spat at her sister, like an enraged cat. "Do you have to have them all? Don't you have enough boyfriends already?" Valentina flushed slightly, but said nothing back to her little sister. I was shocked, not only because of Lucia's tantrum, but because of the mention of Manfred and Valentina. It was true that on his few visits to us, Manfred had shown Valentina extravagant attention, but it was the kind of extravagant attention Manfred lavished on any pretty woman. I knew also that he'd given her some gold coins as gifts, in gratitude for what she and her family had done for us. Or at least I hoped that was the reason. For her part, Valentina had accepted his attention calmly, and didn't seem to attach any seriousness to it. I turned my attention back to the matter at hand. "Have you been able to find anything out about the partigiani?" I asked.

"Yes, I think I know of someone you can contact," replied Valentina. "His name is Bonuccio Bonucci. He is no relation to us, or to our family. He is well known in these parts, and it is rumored that he is head of a band of partigiani in the hills. I'm working on arrangements for you to make contact with him."

"Wonderful!" I exclaimed. "When?" My eagerness startled her.

"You must be patient, Gualtiero," she said seriously, "it may take awhile."

"Valentina, as casually and discreetly as you can, check this Bonuccio Bonucci out with one or two of your other friends, no more than that, okay? And again, take no unnecessary risks."

I shared Valentina's good news with Margherita. "It is possible that I may need to go to the macchia soon, if things continue to get worse," I informed her gently, "and I have asked Valentina to search out a contact that I can use if that need arises. She has heard the name of one Bonuccio Bonucci, an agriculturist. During the next few days, as far from the city as possible, please make inquiry among the farmers about him and see what you can learn."

"I don't know, Signor Console," said Margherita, dubiously, "it will be difficult to get the paesani (country folk) to talk about him. We do not talk to anyone about our people, and especially not to strangers, ever. The farmers are even more close-mouthed than we are. But I will try for you, Signore."

"Thank you, Margherita, thank you both," I said, sincerely.

"Please, whatever you do, don't take any chances, any unnecessary risks." Reaching across the table, Valentina covered my hand with both of hers. Looking directly into my eyes, she said, with uncharacteristic intensity, "Better to be in danger and hope to live, than to be safe and pray to die." With that, she got up and left the room. Her statement, wise for her seventeen years, hung in the air. It gave me plenty of food for thought.

Three days later, we again met in the kitchen.

Settling ourselves at the kitchen table, we each sipped from the thimbleful of brandy Margherita had poured into a glass. It was amazing how, even with little or nothing in the cupboards, tradition, the sharing of food or drink, still prevailed at any meeting or occasion.

Valentina spoke first. "Gualtiero, I have found out more about Signor Bonuccio Bonucci," she began. I leaned forward, hardly daring to breathe. "At first, no one would talk of him at all. Then two of my friends took me aside to ask why I was interested in knowing about him. 'Valentina,' they said, 'why do you want to know about such an old man? Aren't we good enough for you?' It was Renzo who asked me, while Pietro watched to see what I would answer. They are very suspicious of everyone, and if I were a collaborator, I could denounce him, and them, so they did not trust me. 'I can't tell you why I want to know,' I said. 'Then if you can't tell us, we can't tell you' Renzo retorted. 'I don't know if I can trust you,' I said to them again. 'And we don't know if we can trust you,' Pietro said. 'Well,' I said, 'I've heard well of this Bonucci so far, but I want to make absolutely sure. I want to join with the partigiani myself.' You should have seen their faces, Gualtiero! They laughed at me. I pretended to be angry. 'Damn you both!' I said. 'I can do as much as you can! I can help. You're the ones who want to sit here like women, and look good.' That really got them. 'Well, you can forget it, little girl,' that was Pietro, sarcastic. 'He only wants men—real men!' And that was the end of it. Really, men are so simple, so easy to manipulate. " She smiled triumphantly at her success. Then she casually dropped her bombshell. "Oh, and I also learned he occasionally comes to town on Sundays, and will be at the north corner of the Piazza Italia this Sunday afternoon."

Bonanza! That set my mind buzzing.

Margherita's news was also positive. "I could not get anyone to admit they knew Bonuccio Bonucci," she began, "but I could tell from what was said, and from what was NOT said, Signor Console, that this Bonucci is widely known and respected, and is a person of importance." So far, so good. There was one major concern, however. "Did either of you find out anything about his political affiliations?" Valentina shook her head. Margherita spoke up. "I learned that he is definitely a liberal, so we know he is not in the Fascist camp," she said. "Beyond that, the paesani would say nothing, and I felt it wiser not to press them further and arouse their suspicions."

I was elated. This Bonucci sounded like the contact I was hoping for. I didn't want to risk the women further, but I needed someone else to contact him directly before I did. I took a deep breath, and, not looking at Margherita, I addressed Valentina. "Valentina, is it possible that you could find a way to encounter this Bonucci on Sunday afternoon?" Margherita's eyes widened slightly, but she said nothing, and waited for her daughter to speak. Valentina sat in thought for a minute. "I think I could try to do that, Signor Console," she said slowly, "but what should I say to him?"

"If you succeed in making the contact, you should let him know there is someone important, an American, who wants to make contact with him. Above all, you must not let him know who I am or where I am staying." She nodded assent. "I will talk to Renzo again tomorrow morning." I raised the glass, with its few drops of brandy. "Buona fortuna", I said, and sipped, passing the glass to Valentina. She took it and raised it without drinking. "Buona fortuna," she said softly, handing it to Margherita. "Mama, you drink the rest," she urged, "it will warm your bones a little." Margherita took the glass and ceremoniously tipped it toward me. "Buona fortuna," she echoed, and drained the glass.

I felt an excitement I hadn't felt since Monaco. Although I was concerned for Valentina's safety, and hated to have to ask her to take a risk for me, I could hardly wait for Sunday. On that afternoon, December 14th, Valentina skirted the piazza carefully. As planned, Vittoria followed her at a discreet distance to be sure she wasn't followed. Then Vittoria stood in the shadow of a doorway and watched to see that nothing happened to her niece. When Valentina spotted the man she felt was Bonucci, she walked toward him, and, as artfully as any practiced spy, contrived to let her purse fall to the ground in front of him, as though the strap had just broken. She had, in fact, undone the strap moments before. As they both bent to retrieve her purse, she acted appropriately flustered. "Oh, how clumsy of me, scusi," she murmured. "Bonucci," she said clearly, as she picked up the identity card that had fallen out of her purse. The man unconsciously patted his own coat pocket. Then he realized she was reading the name Bonucci from her own card. "Why, that is my name too," he said, surprised. "I know," Valentina smiled her radiant smile up at him, and in the same tone of voice, as though thanking him for his assistance said, "I know an important man who wants to meet you. He cannot come out on the street himself."

Bonucci gave a slight bow, and countered, "Perhaps you and I should meet again first. A lot of important men would like to meet me. Some of them are not my friends." "This one is American," said Valentina, turning away to leave. Bonucci quickly slid his hand under her elbow, gripping it tightly. "Walk along as though we're friends," he said continuing along with her. "Why would an important American want to meet me?" he asked, with just an edge of menace in his voice. "To talk to you about joining your partisan band," replied Valentina quietly. They were silent for several moments while Bonucci digested this information.

Then he named a street corner about three blocks from the apartment. "Eight o'clock Friday. I'll wear a red scarf. The

American should wear a white scarf." He gave her a slight push of dismissal, and let go of her elbow. As she walked away, Bonucci stood and stared at her back for a few moments before turning away down a side street. Vittoria stood guard until both were safely out of sight, then rushed back to her job at the Brufani.

When Valentina recounted the story, I nearly jumped for joy. Then came a moment of concern—the white scarf! I didn't have a white scarf. Without a word, Margherita disappeared into her bedroom, and came back with a white linen dresser scarf. "Washed and folded, no one will know the difference," she said matter-of-factly. I hugged her in gratitude, then demanded that Valentina recount her adventure again, leaving out no detail. I made her describe Bonucci to me three or four times, until I had him fixed in my mind.

Valentina glowed. She was the center of attention, reveling in it, and rightfully so, I thought. To be naturally devious, yet basically honest, were qualities to be valued in times like this. And, most importantly, she had succeeded admirably in her mission. "You did a wonderful job, Valentina," I praised her warmly, "I will always be in your debt for the risk you took for me today." She flashed me a warm conspiratorial look— so she had enjoyed the adventure too!—Then she dropped her eyes demurely. "I was pleased to be able to be of help, Signore," she said modestly, grinning.

The icing on the cake came that same night when, just after nine o'clock, Manfred appeared. We all gathered around hungrily as he unpacked the two large bags of food he had brought. Lucia hugged the tin of powdered chocolate to her thin little bosom in delight. "Mamma! Can we have some now?" she begged. "Later, after the Signori have talked," decreed Margherita.

"The news is not good for either side right now, I'm afraid," said Manfred. "The weather is keeping the Allies from mounting an offensive. Bombings are giving the Germans hell in the north of Italy. Rail lines are a mess, and the Germans are shipping tremendous amounts of material, so travel now is impossible for most, and is becoming difficult and a little dangerous even for me. I don't know when I'll be able to come back here again."

What would we do without Manfred, I wondered? How will we survive?

"Walter, your plan for heading south is totally impractical now," he said, dashing my hopes in that direction. "However, there might be a better chance of you getting out of here and hiding you somewhere nearer Rome."

I decided not to mention my upcoming meeting with Bonucci to him, or my thoughts about going into the hills to join the partisans. It was not because I didn't trust Manfred, but because I had always considered it a sound operating principle not to give anyone information that could be pried out of them on interrogation, or under torture. "I agree with you, Manfred, but we can do nothing, nothing at all, without Italian identity papers. We need those, and the sooner the better. Have you had any luck on that?" I asked. "You know, with identity cards, we'd stand a better chance if we had to leave here suddenly. We could pass normal checkpoints, if we weren't questioned too closely. Nancy and I could probably pass as Italians." Then I smiled. "Amy would have to play a deaf mute." At that, Amy looked insulted, and Manfred chuckled. He always called Amy "Spinster Mary" when we were alone. I could see he was once again snared by the idea of intrigue and adventure. "I'll do my best to get cards for all three of you as quickly as possible, my friend," he assured me.

"I'll be back again as soon as I can, Walt. I know this is hard on you, and you need more food, with all these mouths to be fed every day, and I'll work on the identity cards so you can get the hell out of this mess as soon as possible. "

On Wednesday, Vittoria brought two more bags of food from Manfred. There was also a bag with gifts I had asked him to purchase for Christmas. I was more deeply indebted to Manfred Metzger than ever, to a point that could never be repaid, I realized. He was taking serious risks to help us, and had certainly shown us the true meaning of friendship.

The week dragged. I mentally rehearsed, over and over, what I would say to Bonucci when we met on Friday. My nervous tension was transmitted to the others. I had told Nancy and Amy I felt I had to consider going into the hills and throwing my lot in with the partisans. "You'll give up any shred of diplomatic immunity you still have if you do it, you know," said Amy.

"Yes," said Nancy, accusingly, "and you'll be abandoning us, all of us. You're the only man we have to count on! I don't think you should go. What will we do without you?"

"I know, I know, and I don't want to leave all of you either," I protested. "But if we're caught, and I'm with you, it will go much harder on you, and on the Bonuccis, than it would without me. I'm one of their prime targets. Harboring and aiding an enemy agent is no joking matter to the Germans. I'm putting you all in danger of torture, imprisonment, even execution. And I'm another mouth to feed. Don't worry, Nancy, if I go, Manfred will look after you all. He has promised to stay in touch and to do everything possible to get you and Amy out of here and safely to the Allied lines. We have to trust him."

"Have you told him what you're up to?" demanded Amy.

"No, I really don't want him, or anyone, to know my plans. I don't like it that you and the Bonuccis and Vittoria know. That knowledge is dangerous. I don't want Manfred, or any of you, at risk any more than we are now. "

Nancy burst into harsh sobs, burying her face in her hands. I felt terrible. For months now, they had depended on me to give shape, form and reason to our crazy situation. And to afford them some protection, though what I could do to save them was a mystery, given my present state of weakness. To make matters worse, Margherita shared their feelings of despair and abandonment. "It is good to have a man in the house, even if he is too young and too Inglese." I was in an impossible position, and began to have second thoughts about my upcoming meeting with Bonucci.

All the next night and morning I turned it over in my mind, but always came up with the same inescapable conclusion—it was best for us all for me to go. I knew that Manfred would not abandon the women. I knew the Germans were looking for me. I knew that rescue, in the form of the Allies, would be a long time coming. I knew I would be giving up all diplomatic immunity and all United States protection if I joined the partisans.

I also knew, without any doubt, that I could not continue to sit the war out in hiding in the Bonucci bedroom and attic. The inactivity, and my enforced helplessness, were killing me. Above all, I could not continue to depend on Margherita to find enough food to feed me, and all the others as well.

I will keep my rendezvous with this Bonuccio Bonucci tonight, I decided on Friday. I'll see what the situation looks like. Maybe he won't want me. Maybe he won't take me. But if he does, I'm going. That evening, I dressed warmly, putting a heavy wool sweater on under the old business suit I had worn to the Bonuccis that first night. I was startled at how the suit, snug when I left the Hotel Brufani, now hung slack on my body, even with the thick sweater underneath the jacket! Well, I thought philosophically, at least I've lost the twenty or so pounds I've always promised myself I'd lose. I knotted the white dresser scarf loosely around my neck and pulled on one of Margherita's husband's dark, shapeless felt hats. I looked in the mirror.

In the semi-darkness of the room, the white dresser scarf stood out like a beacon. Bonuccio Bonucci will have no problem spotting me, I thought. I just hope no one else spots me. My heart was pounding already. In the kitchen, the women hugged me tightly, and Nancy and Amy clung to me in a kind of quiet desperation, which only served to heighten my already frazzled nerves. I hoped that Valentina's assurance that the curfew was never strictly enforced would apply to this evening. I slipped out the door and moved stealthily down the stairs. It felt strange to be out in the cold. I hadn't set foot outdoors in three months.

The rendezvous point was only a few blocks away, but I dreaded having to go even that short distance. Worse, I had to pass the barracks of the local Fascists, which was in the next block. I had absolutely no identification on me. I made up my mind to break and run at the first hint of being stopped or challenged for my papers.

The few townsfolk I passed seemed shrouded in a cloak of wariness and weariness. None of the usual cordial greetings were exchanged when people passed each other. I crossed to the opposite side of the street to pass the barracks—I wanted as much space as possible between me and the young thug who guarded the entrance. I forced myself to count, to maintain an even gait and not hurry. I was relieved to turn the corner, and in a few minutes reached the rendezvous point. As I slackened my pace slightly, a tall, slender man swung in beside me, matching my stride. I noted his red scarf. Bonuccio Bonucci.

"Keep walking," he murmured in greeting. "Just act like we are going someplace, Signor Console." At the words, "Signor Console" my stride faltered. He touched my elbow lightly to urge me onward. I was jarred inside. If he knew who I was, how many others did? I glanced sideways at him. There was a half-smile on his face. "You are surprised that I know who you are?" he said. "Don't be. When a pretty young girl tells me an important American wants to meet me— well—I, too, make inquiries. It was not difficult to find out which important American is missing and has not been seen for awhile. I was glad to get your message, Signore,—I have wanted to meet you almost as much as our German guests have." He flashed me an open, boyish smile.

For whatever reason, I felt an instant trust and liking for this man. He seemed self-assured without being cocky, and able to communicate without braggadocio. He quickly and quietly outlined his operation. He had the rare gift for revealing just enough, and yet concealing enough, that made for a valuable leader in a clandestine operation. His goal for the immediate future, given enough food and arms, he said, was to raise a force of 150-200 men, commanded by no more than 10 officers. From there a force of several thousand could easily be recruited—all depending on arms and food. His terse summary had been completed by the time we reached the next corner. He stopped and turned directly to face me. "Well," he said in fairly decent English, startling me, "that's it. Do you want in?" "Definitely," I replied, without a moment's hesitation. "If Italy had had more men as courageous as you to call upon, I probably wouldn't be in the fix I'm in right now." "Thank you, Signor Console," he said sincerely, "I am honored. But think it over a bit more. We'll meet again Christmas Eve. Two blocks north of here, northeast corner. Eight o'clock. There will be many people out that evening, and we will not be noticed. Carry a package, as though you are going to deliver a Christmas gift to a relative." He turned down the next street and vanished into the gloom.

I doubled back to the apartment, going a few blocks out of my way in order to avoid the Fascist barracks, and to reach the apartment from the opposite direction. That way, any nosy neighbors or street watchers would only have glimpsed me once. I had to restrain myself from bounding up the stairs two at a time. I felt a great sense of relief and exhilaration. I had gotten a taste of being outside and moving about again, and, most importantly, I was finally doing something. The exercise of walking those few blocks was sorely needed. It was not much of a walk, but even so, as I reached the third floor landing I was winded, gasping for breath. Poor diet, and the restriction to the confines of the tiny flat for so long had taken their toll on my physical strength and stamina.

As I stopped to catch my breath before taking the final flight of stairs, I thought about Nancy telling me I was their only protection. Hah! In my present condition, I'd be useless as a protector of anything, I reflected wryly, — even a kitten.

Everyone greeted me happily when I entered the apartment. Margherita pressed a mug of hot broth into my

hand, insisting I sit and drink it before telling my story. I recounted our meeting, omitting that I had agreed to join Bonucci's band of partisans. Nor did I tell them how close I had come to asking Bonucci for help with our desperate food situation. Margherita had come up empty on two successive days of searching for food, which had depleted our scant hoard. Nothing but empty cupboards stared back at us from the kitchen walls. For the first time, driven by hunger and frustration, Margherita lamented having so many mouths dependent on her. Tears slipped down her cheeks as she looked around at all of us. "I don't know what I am going to do! I don't know where I can find food! I'm so tired!" she cried despairingly. We rushed to hug and comfort her and assure her that somehow, some way, we'd find some food, we'd manage. I was determined to send Valentina to find Bonuccio Bonucci the next day, if need be, to ask his assistance.

However, miracle of miracles, the following morning Manfred the Magician appeared. He brought a large basket of canned goods and other delicacies. "Well, in the 'nick' of time comes Saint Nick, I see," he greeted us jovially, trying to cheer us up. "I wish I could have brought more, and I can't stay long this time, but I will be back soon, don't worry." After a cup of coffee and some socializing, he drew me aside. "I haven't been able to come up with identity cards for you yet, but I'm going to Trieste soon, and feel sure I'll be able to get them taken care of there." "Good, we must have them, and soon. Any thought of escape is hopeless without them, and you see what a burden we have become for Margherita to feed. We can't stay here much longer, Manfred. We'll have to leave. So do whatever you can as soon as you can." Nodding, he left.

As Christmas drew near, we tried to get into a holiday mood for the sake of the children, and for our own drooping morale as well. Lucia disappeared for hours into her bedroom, doing something secret. She would reappear with a satisfied, knowing smile on her lips. I was alarmed at how she looked, —she had become little more than a thinly padded skeleton.

On the Thursday before Christmas, Franco came bursting through the door after school, gasping for breath. "Mamma! Mamma!" he cried to a startled Margherita, "Hurry! They have birds in the poultry shop! Big ones!" I grabbed for my wallet and thrust a thick wad of banknotes into Margherita's hand. Without pausing for coat or shawl, she dashed down the stairs and out into the freezing twilight on a run, headed for the poultry shop. Less than ten minutes later she was back, triumphantly holding aloft her prize. "Look! A goose! I got a goose!" she cried proudly, eyes shining. We sat, staring at it in absolute wonder and awe. Then we all rushed at her at once, hugging her and the goose and Franco, praising them for being so quick-thinking.

"No, no, Signore," she protested, catching her breath, "it is you we must thank for this blessing. We could never have afforded this, no matter how hungry we were." She clasped my hand gratefully.

The price, of course, had been astronomical. The goose was one of perhaps only a dozen in all of Perugia. Paying such a price posed somewhat of a risk, but at that point, who cared? Risk be damned! We'd have a Christmas Eve feast with that goose, and a Christmas dinner, and more. There would be good, hearty broth for Lucia's cough. Margherita called us all to her side and insisted we kneel then and there to say a prayer of thanks for our good fortune, adding a prayer for the health and safety of her husband Gregorio in Germany. Only then did she rise and begin preparations for dinner, a soup in which she used the feet and a piece of the neck of the goose.

The next day was Christmas Eve, and it really took on a festive air as the slowly roasting goose warmed and scented the kitchen. We all waited hungrily for it to finish cooking. Margherita hummed as she moved about the kitchen, preparing small dishes from some of the canned goods Manfred had brought. From time to time she would open the oven, releasing a mouth-watering aroma into the room, and she'd carefully spoon grease from the roasting pan into a jar, an act which required her utmost concentration, so as not to spill or waste any of the precious drippings. In Margherita's thrifty hands, I knew that goose would be paying dividends for weeks.

The apartment door opened, and Valentina came in, rosy- cheeked from the cold. "Hello everyone! Look what I got!" She beamed as she held aloft her Christmas prize — a current issue of "L'Osservatore Romano"! I grabbed it up, and read the key articles aloud, adding my own editorial comments as I went along. The situation in Rome was bad. Food shortages were critical there. On hearing that, every eye swung gratefully toward our well-charged oven. Milan, however, was by far the worst off. The industrial belt around the city had endured repeated bombings. There were vague references to "citizen unrest" in that area, but no details on how the Germans were reacting to control the problem.

Once we had digested every scrap of news, I took Franco and Lucia aside and did my best to tell them Dickens' <u>A Christmas Carol</u>. At one point, Franco interrupted to inquire seriously, "Is Scrooge a Blackshirt, (Fascist) Signore?" That he wasn't didn't dim their enthusiasm for the story, and I could see that they identified with the joy of Tiny Tim's family over the Christmas goose. Flushed with success, I launched into a fractured version of "Twas the Night Before Christmas" Of course it didn't rhyme, and I took literary license here and there—I didn't know the Italian word for reindeer, so I had horses pull Santa's sleigh. Lucia giggled at the idea of someone coming down a chimney. By the time I reached the end of the tale, Valentina and Margherita had joined the audience, and were sitting there enthralled, dinner all but forgotten.

When Vittoria finally arrived, her chores at the hotel finished, we were ready to sit down to our Christmas Eve dinner. We decided we'd risk eating together, just this once. Nancy, with help from Valentina and Franco, had hauled the two old armchairs from our bedroom into the kitchen. I was ushered ceremoniously to the seat of honor at the head of the table. I felt a lump rise in my throat as I said the grace, asking a special blessing on Manfred, and on all our distant loved ones. It was indeed a feast. We savored every morsel of our allotted portions. After the dishes were cleared away, Valentina set Manfred's "torta" of dried, candied fruit on the table, and the adults lingered over a half cup of Swiss coffee, while the children had a rare hot chocolate. We wondered if we would ever enjoy such a meal again in our lives. Margherita brought out the last of the brandy and poured us each a sip. I raised my glass, the others followed suit, and we drank a misty-eyed toast to all our absent loved ones.

At last, it was time for presents. Although they had been cautioned not to expect much, the children were on tiptoe with excitement, and if the truth be told, so were the adults. I gave Franco the book on the life of Winston Churchill that I had found in the hotel in Gubbio. It was the one I had used to teach Nancy Italian. Some day, I thought, as he hugged me gratefully, then sat down to turn the pages of the book—his first—I'll be giving my own son Howard a book like this, so he can learn from the lives of great men like Churchill. For me there was a diary, which served as a sharp and painful reminder of just how long I had been away from my family— almost two full years!

I presented Margherita and Vittoria with new sweaters I had acquired through Manfred. Valentina tore the tissue from her gift, and gasped in delight. It was a soft, dark brown leather purse, to replace the one whose strap she had broken to help me meet Bonucci. "Oh, Signor Orebaugh," she exclaimed, "it is much too beautiful and too expensive! I will be the envy of all my friends! Thank you!" "Look inside," I urged her, smiling. Inside was a thin gold chain with a medallion of the Virgin—from Manfred. She sat back in her chair, a soft blush suffusing her cheeks. "Now for Lucia," I said, and her eyes fairly glowed with anticipation and delight. I produced a huge box. How I had managed to smuggle it past them had them baffled. Lucia squealed with delight, and threw Valentina a triumphant look before turning to tear off the wrapping. She drew forth a forest green wool coat with a bright plaid lining, and a woolen head scarf to match. She threw herself into my arms, hugging me, and tears streamed down Margherita's and Vittoria's cheeks at the sight of the coat. "Oh, Signore," said Margherita, as Lucia put it on and danced around the room, "there is no finer coat on anyone in Perugia this winter! How can we ever thank you?'" "It is I who can never thank you, and your family, Margherita," I replied, embarrassed by the display of emotion I had aroused. I hastily excused myself to get ready for my second rendezvous with Bonuccio Bonucci.

I donned my sweater and coat, but couldn't find the white scarf anywhere. Strange. There wasn't time to search for it. I couldn't leave Bonuccio waiting, thinking I had changed my mind. I returned to the kitchen, ready to leave. Vittoria was waiting. She'd be walking with me part way. A man and a woman taking a Christmas Eve stroll together were less likely to arouse suspicion. Lucia stood by the door, with her new coat on, a package in her hand. Wordlessly, she held it out to me. I unwrapped it quickly. There was the missing white scarf, only it had been transformed into a real scarf, the ends carefully fringed and knotted. Near the corner, on one end, was a painstakingly hand-embroidered representation of an American eagle. Tears filled my eyes. I handed the scarf to Lucia, and ceremoniously bent down so she could place it around my neck. As she did, she shyly gave me a kiss on the cheek. "Thank you, Lucia," I said, "I will treasure this. " I hugged her, and hurried out the door.

When Bonuccio fell into step with me, I said quickly, "I want in. How do we arrange it?" "We'll be glad to have you with us. I must make a trip back to the hills first, which will take me a couple of weeks, but I'll be back here Sunday, January 16th. We'll meet in the Piazza Italia, where I first met your young lady friend, at four o'clock sharp."

"Okay," I replied, "I'll be there— the 16th, Piazza Italia, four o'clock."

"Be sure you know what you're doing," he cautioned me

again. "If you change your mind, I'll understand. But once you come with us, there's no going back."

"Don't worry," I assured him, "I understand. I'll be there."

Now that there was a prospect of action, time passed more slowly than ever. I had not yet informed the others of my decision to leave. If action was what I needed, it came sooner than expected. Late in the afternoon of December 28th, Margherita spotted a search squad of Blackshirts working our street. "Hurry! To the attic!" she cried. "They're almost here!" The girls and I clambered frantically up into the attic. I had barely finished pushing the discarded furniture and old crates between us and the trap door when we heard them pounding on the door of the apartment. We huddled in our freezing corner, not daring to breathe. We heard loud male voices below. Nancy was shaking all over. The voices grew louder, and in one I detected a decidedly German accent. Clammy sweat broke out all over my body. None of us moved a muscle. Not that we could have—we were paralyzed with fear. Suddenly, the trap door popped open, and the peaked cap of a Fascist militiaman came into view. His eyes barely cleared the sill of the trap door. From our dark corner, we could see him clearly, silhouetted in the light from the kitchen below. Fortunately for us, his eyes were not adjusted to the darkness. They raked the heaped-up articles obstructing his view of us. After a brief glance around, his head disappeared, and the trap door was pulled shut. Amy jumped at the sound. I moved only enough to pry loose the fingers painfully digging into my arm. I never knew whose they were—Nancy's or Amy's, though I suspect they were Nancy's. We didn't dare even whisper. We could still hear loud voices, and some shouts, below us. I was terrified for Margherita and the children. Then we heard the apartment door slam, and the sound of boots clumping down the stairs. We waited in silence, growing more frightened with each passing second. After what seemed like an eternity, the welcome "thump! thump!" of the broom came, and Nancy immediately burst into sobs, followed quickly by Amy. "Shhh!" I hushed them. "We're okay. They've gone. Easy, now. We'll be out of here in a minute."

We climbed down on shaky legs and washed the filth and grime from ourselves, then collapsed into chairs around the table to hear details from Margherita and Valentina.

"There was one German, Signore, and three Blackshirts," she said.

"Were they looking for us?" I asked. She shook her head. "No, I don't think so."

"Did they mention me, or Americans?" I pressed. "No, Signore, they didn't seem to be looking for anyone in particular."

"What did they want?"

"I don't know," she said, " I think it was just a routine search."

"They took our radio," said Valentina. "They said they were going to block the frequencies so we can only get the local station." Suddenly she burst into laughter. I was startled, then realized it was laughter from nervous relief. "Can you imagine such a prize for all their effort? That worthless old radio that gives us nothing but static? Let them have it! We'll never see it again, you can be sure."

We laughed with them at the idea of the four men carrying that virtually worthless radio down the stairs, — the big prize from their raid, when the real prizes were right under their noses--or rather, right above their noses!

We might not be so lucky the next time they decided to do "a routine search." And I didn't like the idea that there were Germans along with them now. I was relieved when Manfred showed up again that very night. I swiftly filled him in on what had happened that afternoon.

"Good thing then, that I have this for you," he remarked casually. Reaching into a pocket, he produced an envelope containing a blank identity card, with an excise stamp to be affixed to the reverse side of it.

I grabbed it excitedly. "Whoopee, you did it!" This was

a ticket to freedom! It was indispensable for going anywhere.

"I didn't have a picture of you, so I couldn't fill it out," Manfred said, as I carefully turned the document over and over in my hands.

"God, how much did you have to pay in bribes to get this baby?"

"You know, it wasn't too much," Manfred replied. "I said to the guy, 'what the hell, the Germans are going to lose anyway. You better start getting on the right side now, while you still can. I'll get you a note you can show to the Allies, to protect you afterward.' So a few thousand lire, and he gave it to me."

Yeah, I thought, a "few thousand" lire. I could only imagine how many thousand. "Okay, I'll do a note for the guy who gave you the blank card. Who was it?"

"Criminal lawyer," replied Manfred. "Big shot Fascist. Has been pro-Nazi, all that crap. Wants to cover his ass now. You can fix me a note for him?"

My mind raced. "I will, but only if he gets papers for Nancy and Amy. If he produces those, he'll get his piece of paper from me. Either we all get out, or he gets nothing." Without giving specifics, I told Manfred of my new plan. "I may join a resistance band soon, going somewhere into the Umbrian hills, so you'll have to see to getting the girls out." "Hmmm. You sure?" I nodded. "Okay. If you go, how can I contact you?"

"Why, you old bastard, how else? You'll just have to join up with us in the hills!" Then, knowing he just might take me up on it, I hurried to add, "No, Valentina will keep you in touch with me if I go. You'll enjoy that, you dirty old goat, staying in contact with a beautiful woman! You can always get to her through Vittoria at the Brufani."

"Well, it's your neck! I'll try my lawyer friend again about the cards for the girls. You be careful. Whatever you decide, don't worry. I'll take care of things here. We'll get the girls out." Wordlessly, I embraced him, and he slipped quietly out into the night again. I knew it would be the last time I'd see him for a long, long time.

I turned to the women. "Margherita, bring me your card so I can see what has to be done to make this look absolutely official." She brought hers to me and I examined it—Ooops! The raised official seal, necessary to validate the card, was missing from mine. Damn! I'd have to think of a way to fake it.

1944 arrived bitterly cold. We spent New Year's Day huddled in bed. The temperature in the apartment never reached forty degrees. When Margherita cooked, we all crowded around the stove, absorbing whatever feeble heat seeped from the weak cooking fire. The news from outside was even more chilling. Vittoria reported that several more large German military units had been moved into and around Perugia. This would make Perugia a bombing target for the Allies. Our "few weeks" stay was going into its fifth month. The extreme cold made it impossible for Margherita to forage for enough food to feed all of us. Manfred's supplies, and even the careful stretching of the Christmas goose, were almost at an end.

Houses in the immediate area were searched two days in a row—once when Margherita had our newly washed, obviously foreign underwear strung across the kitchen to dry. Stripping it all down in a panic, we'd dragged the cold, wet laundry with us into the attic. Afterward, it all had to be washed again, along with us.

Two more weeks passed, and Manfred did not return. I had just about finished the seal on my identity card. I had found an old passport picture among my belongings, and doctored it up and put it on the card. I named myself Michele Franciosi, unmarried, son of one Luigi Franciosi and Anna Maria Spada. For occupation, I decided on "clerk". Then Valentina wrote "`SFOLLATO" across the card.

This marked me as a bombed-out refugee. She signed the card as an official in Rome. I made up an address—Piazza Villa Fiorelli 8. For hours, using the point of one of Margherita's fine knitting needles, I had worked at duplicating the raised seal on her card. The finished product was perfect, and gave me a strong surge of pride in my counterfeiting craftsmanship. My identity card looked, and felt, as authentic as Margherita's in every respect.

When January 16th finally arrived, I took the card to my meeting with Bonucci. He was impressed and congratulated me on my ability to come up with such a valuable document. "Well, Signor Bonucci," I said, as we strolled along the shady side of the Piazza, "I am definite about joining you and ready to leave whenever you say."

"If you are certain about this, Signor Console, and understand that I can offer you no assurance of protection because of who you are, then I am happy to have you join us."

"I understand," I assured him," and I'm ready to accept the risks I'm undertaking. "Then it is decided," said Bonucci. "Four days from now, on January 20th, be at the railway station at six-fifteen sharp. You will take the 6:30 train for Ponte San Giovanni. You'll get off there and transfer to the train to Monte Corona, then take the local train to Campo Reggiano. At the station at Campo Reggiano, you will cross the tracks after the train leaves and begin to walk northward. My man Giuseppe will approach you and give you instructions. You must be quick and catch his instructions the first time. He will take the same trains you do, and will be in the same cars, but away from you. Should anything go wrong, he will do whatever he can to create a diversion, so that you can escape, if possible." I tried to absorb it all.

"All right," I replied, and repeated his instructions aloud, to be sure I had them perfectly clear in my mind. Reaching the opposite side of the Piazza, we went our separate ways. I mentally rehearsed my instructions several times, to fix them firmly in my mind. There would not be any allowance for screw-ups. The plan was a tightly scheduled one, which had only one chance to work. Since it was my hide at risk, I was determined to see that nothing went wrong on my part. Back in the apartment, I gathered everyone together. "I'll be leaving you for good in several days," I announced. As I gazed around at their stunned faces, a pang of guilt lanced through me, and I tried once more to assure them, (and myself) that my decision was in everyone's best interest. No one said anything negative, but I sensed their deep hurt.

"And when is this all to happen, Walter?" inquired Amy, in a tone that was chilling, if not icy."

"Four days from today--January 20th," I replied.

Margherita said nothing, but from the noise she made with dishes and pans as she set about preparing supper, I could tell she was deeply affected. After throwing me a look of anguish, Nancy got up to help Margherita. The vacuum of silence that ensued was depressing. Lucia cried loudly in her room.

After dinner, I carefully reviewed with the girls everything Manfred and I had discussed about getting them identity cards and getting them to Allied lines. "I'm trusting you both to do whatever Manfred tells you to do, whenever. He is your ticket to freedom. Your lives depend on it, so I'm counting on you to do it," I said.

The next morning, over coffee, I reviewed things with Valentina, and told her Manfred would be in touch with her through Vittoria, and that he would continue to provide food for them whenever he could. I told her that she'd be Manfred's contact with me, through Bonuccio Bonucci, and it would be her responsibility to get messages to me through him, and to assist Manfred in getting Amy and Nancy to freedom. She nodded from time to time, saying little, but I could see she was pleased and proud to be given such important responsibilities. "Don't worry, Signore," she said, briefly touching my shoulder as she got up to leave, "we will look after the Signorine, and I will get messages to you somehow. I am proud that you are joining Bonucci, Gualtiero . I wish I could go with you." With a fiercely loyal, partisan Valentina in my corner, I felt immensely reassured. Despite her youth, I knew that she'd see to it that all went well here without me.

Vittoria joined us for supper on the 19th, my last evening. I had packed and repacked the battered old suitcase I had borrowed from Margherita. I made room for the white dresser scarf so carefully reworked by Lucia. The mealtime mood was somber. I tried to lighten things up with joking remarks, but sounded corny, even to myself. I felt like I was participating in my own wake. Everyone just sat there and stared at me, wide-eyed and wordless. I escaped to our room as soon after dinner as possible. I had so much on my mind, dawn broke without me once closing my eyes.

As soon as I heard Margherita stirring in the kitchen, I got up, dressed, and joined her. Lucia was already there, and for the last time brought me my cup of coffee. Soon everyone was gathered in the kitchen. "Don't worry about us, Walter, we'll be just fine," Nancy assured me seriously, then burst into tears. Lucia followed suit, and soon they were all crying. When it was Franco's turn to say good-bye, he manfully shook my hand, then turned and bolted for the bedroom, bawling out loud. Lucia waited alone by the door. I picked her up and hugged her long and hard. "Bye, little Lucia," I said, "keep safe and keep smiling, and take care of your mother." "Oh, Signore," she cried, "please come back! Please be safe. God be with you and protect you. I love you." Gently, I set her down and untangled her arms from around my neck. "I love you too, little Lucia," I said, "take care," and hurried out the door. I didn't want any of them to see that tears were coursing down my cheeks.

Chapter 5

Michele Franciosi, "Il Console"

As I walked the twenty minute distance from the apartment to the train station, my head cleared and my emotions calmed. The predawn cold was invigorating, and the few people who were out gave me no more than a passing glance. Over and over I rehearsed my new name. Michele Franciosi. Michele Franciosi. I knew I needed the sound of that name implanted in my brain so well that I reacted instantly to it. I certainly looked the part. Bearded, thin, dressed in a frayed coat and battered felt hat, carrying a scruffy cardboard suitcase, no one could possibly associate me with the dapper, clean-shaven American Consul who had strolled the streets of Perugia a few months back. Would my own mother recognize me now? Probably not. I chuckled to myself at the thought of what her reaction would be if she could see me.

The tension that always crawled just below the surface of my skin rose steadily as I neared the railroad station. Stepping into the station house, I was relieved to see quite a few people gathered there, waiting for the train to arrive. That would make it easy for me to blend in with the crowd. I purchased a third class ticket to Monte Corona—the agent barely looked up as he shoved my ticket and change across the counter to me. Then I joined the line of people waiting to have their documents checked by the questorino, (police agent). He was seated behind a small table, hunched down in his chair, bundled against the early morning cold. I prayed silently as the line ahead of me diminished. This would be the acid test of whether or not my homemade identity card would pass inspection. When my turn came, I proffered my card, open to the photograph, and kept shuffling slowly ahead, as I had seen the others before me do. The agent's eyes flicked up at me briefly, then back at my card. There was no cry of "Alt!" as I shuffled on. Then I was out on the platform. I had made it! So far, at least. Taking my handkerchief from my pocket, I faked blowing my nose in order to wipe the nervous sweat from my face.

The train came chugging in, and I slipped into the third class car among a group of working men. The run to the junction at Ponte San Giovanni, my transfer point, took less than fifteen minutes. We had to get out and walk the final half mile to the junction station, since the railroad bridge leading to the town had been bombed out. As I walked, I tried to spot Giuseppe, the man Bonucci had hand-picked to shadow me for the journey. If he was tailing me, as I assumed he was, he was extremely good at it, and was being careful not to show his hand. The wait for the connecting train was agonizing. Although there were no tickets or police checkpoints to worry about, I felt exposed and vulnerable, standing alone on the platform.

When the northbound train finally pulled in, I scrambled aboard with the others. Searching for an empty seat in the crowded car, I was shocked to see that twenty or so passengers were German military, both officers and enlisted men. I proceeded, outwardly calm, down the aisle. The only available seat was next to two German soldiers. Screwing up my courage, I sat down, bracing my suitcase between my knees. Neither of them took any notice of me. We rode along for a few minutes, and they talked together in German and pointed at things they saw from the window. Suddenly, one of them turned to me and said, "Scusi, a che serve?" pointing to a row of mulberry trees pruned down to stump length. Praying they would not detect any foreign flavor to my Italian, I briefly replied that I thought that this was how grape vines were secured to the trunks and strung from tree to tree. That seemed to satisfy them, and they continued asking polite questions from time to time, when passing scenes caught their attention. "Scusi, Signori," I apologized at one point, "I'm not a farmer, so I don't know much about these things." They accepted my explanation without question. As the train slowed to a stop in Monte Corona, I rose to leave. The one called Christian reached across and shook my hand, thanking me for the company and the conversation. I jumped off the train as soon as it stopped, and crossed over to the odd-looking, midget-sized train already waiting on the narrow gauge line. I jumped aboard, and almost immediately the little locomotive tooted its whistle, and chugged upgrade to Campo Reggiano. All seats in the only passenger car of the two-car train were full, and about a dozen of us were left standing in the aisle. I scanned the carriage, hoping to spot Bonuccio's elusive Giuseppe. No luck.

The Campo Reggiano station was a small, weather-beaten masonry building, whose unpainted concrete interior offered a couple of wooden benches that served as a waiting room. Following the instructions Bonucci had given me, I crossed the tracks, turned north, and paused at the beginning of a slope. From this height, I could see the cluster of buildings below that made up the village of Campo Reggiano. Just beyond me, on my side of the tracks, was a dirt footpath that led over the brow of the hill.

The sun was shining, and it felt good on my back. I watched the few poorly dressed farmers head off in various directions. Some went toward the town, others set off down the narrow, overgrown footpath. Coming up behind me, a nondescript, middle-aged man muttered "follow me", and added, "not too close." Turning onto the footpath, he took off at a fairly brisk pace. My heavy suitcase slowed me down, so there was no possibility I'd follow too close. In fact, I was afraid I would lose my escort. The path narrowed as it led uphill, and the footing was treacherous. After just a few minutes, I was panting. Months of inactivity were taking their toll on my endurance. I plodded determinedly on. It was a full twenty minutes of toiling uphill before we reached a level clearing. Giuseppe stopped there, motioning for me to catch up with him. There were fields all around us, and in the distance I saw a couple of dilapidated stone farmhouses. "Benvenuto Signore," he said respectfully. "From here we can go together. It is safe. It is probably safer for you to be seen walking with me now, because any stranger walking alone here might arouse suspicion. With me, you will be taken as one of us—Bonucci's band—and therefore to be trusted." With that, he took my suitcase and set off. I caught up to him and tried to match his stride. He said nothing, but I was aware of his intense scrutiny of me. I couldn't even think about it though, as the agony of trying to keep up with him commanded my full attention. Since he was at least ten years older than I, and carrying my suitcase to boot, I was determined that I would, by God, keep up. But it wasn't easy.

After about an hour, when I had reached the limits of my endurance and thought I would drop from the effort, we reached a small cluster of old, weathered stone houses, and there we paused briefly. In the midst stood an old stone church, its square bell tower topped with an almost flat roof of red-orange clay tiles. The simple utilitarian buildings, and the church, looked as though they had sprung out of the rocky soil that surrounded them. Giuseppe stopped in front of the church and made the sign of the cross. Then he turned to me. "This is San Faustino," he said. This gaggle of old stone buildings could hardly be classed as a town. About a quarter mile later, we came upon a villa, a rambling, sturdy edifice planted foursquare on the crest of the hill, commanding a view of the town below it.

Constructed around the turn of the century out of native rock and tile, the villa did not compare in size or elegance to other villas I had known, but it was impressive enough to suggest substance and importance, especially in relation to the other buildings in the area. It boasted a square bell tower like the one on the church in the village, and its window frames, painted a bright azure blue, injected a jaunty note of color into the drab winter landscape.

We turned into the entrance path, passed through the old iron gates, and as we stepped onto the terrace, the front door was thrown open, and Bonuccio Bonucci himself appeared, smiling broadly, his arms wide in greeting. "Benvenuto, Signor Console!" he exclaimed warmly. "I am happy you made it without incident. I see you have met my right arm, Giuseppe." He walked up to me and clasped my hand in both of his. "You are welcome to my home," he declared. Putting an arm around my shoulder and signaling for Giuseppe to follow, he walked me into the main living room of the villa.

Seated in a comfortable armchair, with a glass of wine in my hand, I was at last able to take the measure of this man who had so dominated my thoughts, and my life, in recent weeks. Tall for an Italian, slim yet powerfully built, he exuded a boyish charm that was infectious and disarming. He moved with the natural grace of a jungle cat, or a well-trained athlete. The effect of the strong, masculine features of his face was heightened by his ability to impale his listener, and hold him mesmerized, with a steady look from those deep, liquid brown eyes. "Occhi parlanti", the Sicilians call them,—"eyes that talk". They were the most notable feature of his fair-complexioned face, which was framed by a thick mass of dark curls that belied his age, which I judged to be around forty.

Now, he paced the room, speaking in a rapid-fire staccato, his voice sparked with fervor and enthusiasm. His naturally gregarious nature reached out and, like a strong ocean current, pulled those around him into, and along with, whatever activity he was pursuing. The dread I had felt over having to adjust to a new way of life, a new set of associates, dissolved into insignificance, as he spoke to me with pride about his guerrilla "Band of San Faustino". After just a few moments, I felt like I could hardly wait to meet the others and start taking action against the Germans! No wonder this man was so well-liked and respected! No wonder his name was a household word to the peasantry of the region. Bonuccio

Bonucci was a real charmer—a born charismatic leader of men.

He left me for a few moments while he said good night to "Gigi," (as he called Giuseppe), then escorted me upstairs to the bedroom he had set aside for me. After the tiny, crowded apartment in Perugia, the spacious, light and airy room he ushered me into was a sight for sore eyes. It was high-ceilinged, with tall double windows on two sides. Its antique furnishings were dark mahogany, heavy and solid, with a large, comfortable bed, a dresser, and a washstand. An overstuffed armchair, upholstered in a deep green and red floral print that matched the side curtains at the windows, sat in one corner, with a low, square wood table at its side. Dropping into the armchair, Bonuccio continued his briefing while I stowed my gear.

"You have come at a good time, my American friend," he said. "Your presence will give everyone a boost, and will lend a lot of credibility to our efforts. And, your assistance in getting word of our existence to the Allies will be invaluable. We are just getting started as an organization, and there are many problems to be confronted and resolved. We are fortunate to have you join us at this stage."

"How can I be the most help to you right away?" I asked.

"By getting word out to the Allies somehow that we are here, and ready to begin operations, that we are badly in need of arms and of some means to communicate with them, but will begin operations anyway, hoping they can get help to us soon," he replied.

"What is your manpower?" I inquired, retrieving my comb and soap from among the sweaters in my suitcase, "What kind of numbers are we talking about?"

Bonucci got up and went to the windows, looking out over the fields that stretched to woods at the back of the villa. "Signore," he answered quietly, as if speaking to himself, "numbers have little relevance in our situation. In this area there are hundreds, probably thousands, of people who have taken to the macchia for various reasons. With little effort, we could recruit a force of a thousand good and able men in a week, if we were so minded. But we are unable to feed a force of such size. And we must also require that each man we take on have a weapon, that he be physically strong and hardened, which most peasants of this area already are, that he have previous military experience or training, that he be able to face the danger and hardship of guerrilla life, and that he be motivated to support our cause against the Germans and the Fascists. That is not an easy order to fill, by any means." He turned and flashed me a sardonic smile. "As you yourself have learned, we recruit slowly and carefully, Signore, to be sure that every man among us is fully with us, and fully trustworthy. It is the only way.""

"D'accordo", I agreed. "That's the only way it could possibly work."

Bonucci went on to clarify his own role. "Please understand, Signore, I am not the military commander of this movement," he said, pacing back and forth at the foot of the bed. "That is in the hands of Colonel Mario Guerrizzi, a seasoned professional. You will meet him soon. I represent the CLN, the Committee for National Liberation, which is the organization responsible for planning and coordination of resistance at the national level. The Band of San Faustino, which you are joining, is a non-political, partisan group that is ready to undertake aggressive military operations in our range."

"And what is our range?" I asked.

"Roughly two hundred square kilometers," he responded proudly. Then he turned, and with his finger drew an imaginary map on the wall at the foot of the bed. "The zone of our operations lies between the Parish of Morena on the north," he said, punching a dot with his index finger to indicate Morena, "to Città di Castello on the west," a line and another finger jab, " and Gubbio on the southeast."

"I know Gubbio fairly well," I told him, giving him a brief rundown on the time I had spent in the Albergo San Marco.

Bonuccio explained how the military presidios of the

partisan movement were organized. "We have already recruited several seasoned Italian officers for our organization," he said. "Colonel Guerrizzi's second-in-command is Captain Stelio Pierangeli, who is also responsible for the presidio in the Città di Castello sector. Other sectors are under the command of other Italian officers. Lieutenant Mario Bonfigli is in command of our sector here in the Pietralunga area, and he is the one you will be working most closely with."

"Where are the partigiani billeted?" I wanted to know.

He hesitated only a fraction of a second before replying, but it was enough to give me an idea of the inherent caution in the man. "Well, we keep them scattered in local farmhouses, two to three to a farmhouse, in an irregular pattern that will prevent detection, but one that allows us to round everyone up on short notice, if need be. Each cadre has twenty to twenty-five men."

I told Bonucci I had heard through Valentina's contacts that there were some British and American officers who were in some way connected with the partisan movement in this area—"Is that true?"

"Your information is absolutely correct, Signore," he replied. "There are several British and American officers sheltered in this area who have, somewhat casually, offered us their services. We hope to avail ourselves of those services in due course. But there are problems. One, they don't speak Italian, and two, they don't know the terrain, so their usefulness to us at this time is limited."

"Well," I said with American practicality, "there must be SOME way we can use them to our advantage, even if they don't speak the language. Are any of them trained in explosives, or demolition, do you know? Or bridge engineering?"

He thought a moment. "There is one," he said, "a Britisher named Ramsay. I heard only two days ago that he has a good working knowledge of explosives. Now that you are here to ease the difficulty of communicating with them, we can

certainly make good use of their experience and abilities."
Suddenly he stopped, and smiled his engaging smile at me.
"But I am being a poor host, Signore—it has been a very long
and tiring day for you. I will not keep you longer if you wish
to rest."

"No, Signor Bonucci, I am not ready to sleep. I want to
continue our talk."

"Well, then, we'll go back down and share a glass of wine.
And we'll talk no more of business! I want to hear about
you— about your home and your family, and your
background." We adjourned back down to the parlor, and sat
in deep armchairs in front of the fireplace, where he kindled
a warming blaze. Over a glass of wine, we exchanged
information about our families, our backgrounds, and our
respective careers— mine in the Foreign Service, his as an
agriculturist. It was easy to talk to him, and with each passing
moment, I felt more relaxed about my decision to join him .

"You know, Bonuccio," I said, when we had exhausted
the topic of ourselves and our families and careers, "I'm
curious about the local peasants. I'm particularly interested
in them, in their way of life, and their attitude and role in this
war. From my limited experience with them to this point, I
find they are difficult to get to know, and even more difficult
to understand. Can you enlighten me any?"

Bonuccio sipped the dregs of his wine, stared at the fire
for a few seconds, then shrugged. "I wish I could, Signor
Console," he replied thoughtfully. "I have lived among them
all my life, and as an agriculturist, I have been as closely
associated with them as anyone can be. I believe I have their
trust and respect. I am engaged in business dealings with
them almost daily. I often eat with them, and occasionally,
sleep in their beds. I am invited to their baptisms, their
confirmations, their weddings, and their funerals, yet I cannot
say that I really understand them, either." He set his glass
down on the small table next to his chair, and leaned forward,
hands clasped between his knees, looking at me intently.
"The peasants are, and always have been, an enigma, a

mosaic of contradictions, of conflicting values and desires. Yet today, beyond a doubt, there is a solidarity among them that has never before been seen in this country. One could almost believe that a magic wand has been waved over the countryside, brushing aside and covering over all their previous conceptions of political ideology." "So what will happen now?" I asked softly.

"Ah, that is anyone's guess, Signore," he said leaning back and tapping the tips of his fingers together thoughtfully. "Relative to what they want, no one is sure. We know that the Communists are at work, spreading their dogma among them. The only thing we know for sure is that they want no more of Fascism or any of its trappings. And they hate the Germans."

"What do they think of the partisan movement hereabouts, and of you, personally, as a key organizer?" I asked.

He smiled at the directness of my question, but did not hesitate in replying. "Surprisingly, their attitude is very favorable to us," he said. "We have never been refused by any peasant family when we've requested billets and board for our men. Even when their houses are full to overflowing with their own family, they take in 'sfollati (bombed-out refugees), and invariably offer to put our men up as well, even if they only have stalls or outbuildings available. It is truly amazing. And now, Signore," he said, rising and stretching, "we must stop this and get some rest. We will talk more tomorrow."

I gave only a brief thought to Nancy, Amy, and the other Bonuccis before dropping into deep, dreamless sleep. When I awoke, the sun was already up and shining. Looking about me, at my unfamiliar yet friendly surroundings, I knew without a doubt I had turned a page in my life. All that had gone before now receded from concern or concentration. I was irrevocably committed to Bonuccio Bonucci and his partisan Band of San Faustino, for better or worse. And, this morning, I knew beyond a shadow of a doubt I was glad to be there, and ready to get going. I bounded out of bed. After hastily washing and dressing, I headed downstairs, toward the kitchen, and the enticing smell of something like coffee brewing.

Bonucci and Gigi had already breakfasted and were just coming in from a morning meeting somewhere. Gigi put on a fresh pot of the inevitable barley coffee, and there was a loaf of good bread and some real butter, no doubt from one of the neighboring farms, waiting on the table. "Good morning, Michele," Bonuccio greeted me heartily. I stopped for an instant, confused, then realized he was using my new identity. Michele. Michael. I'll have to get used to using it, and hearing it, and certainly to answering to it better than I just did, I thought, chagrined.

"Morning, Bonnucio, Giuseppe." I said, pouring myself a cup, and breaking off a chunk of bread. "Sorry, I slept so late—I guess I was more tired than I thought. I haven't had so much exercise in months."

"You'll get back in shape fast around here," laughed Bonucci. "Gigi will see to that." He poured himself some barley brew and motioned for me to join him on the terrace, which was in a sunny corner just outside the kitchen. What a pleasure to breathe fresh mountain air for a change, I thought gratefully, inhaling deeply.

"So, my friend, you are glad to be out and free again, eh?" commented Bonucci, with a knowing smile. "You don't know how glad," I agreed fervently. "I hate being confined and helpless, the way I've been for the past five months!"

"Well, you don't have to worry about that any more,—as long as you don't get captured again," he said. He then began bringing me up to date on activities of the Band of San Faustino. Shortly after the armistice in September, they had hit a German convoy, and managed to destroy several trucks. They salvaged one for themselves, which was now hidden under hay in a barn near the village of Pietralunga. The Germans had retaliated with ferocity, executing several dozen innocent villagers,—including old folks, women and children. Bonucci's eyes clouded with pain at the memory, and his face twisted in hatred. "Pigs! Animals! They have no soul, no conscience!" he spat out, in fury. Then he took a deep breath, and continued. "After that raid, and the reprisals, we went through a period of fear and were pretty disorganized. To keep everyone frightened and demoralized, the Germans and the Fascists stepped up the "rastrellamenti",— the roundup. They took the young people away, and confiscated all weapons. Then, feigning to enforce the "ammasso", the farm tax, they requisitioned the major part of our wheat crop! As you can imagine, all of this had a devastating effect on people's willingness to be active, let alone openly resist."

"So how did you get going again? " I asked. Gigi appeared in the doorway with two visitors, and another pot of coffee. The two men were from neighboring farms, and were also members of Bonucci's resistance group. Both were dressed in the drab work pants and shirts and the frayed woolen jackets and caps typical of the peasant farmers of the area.

As they approached the table to be seated, Bonucci spoke quickly and quietly in an aside to me. "Signore, forgive me, but I think that when you meet others who are in our Band, I need to tell them your real identity."

He introduced me to the two men, who had been regarding me curiously since stepping onto the terrace. Their eyebrows rose in surprise when Bonucci told them I was the American "Il Console." Both men immediately pulled off their caps in a gesture of respect. "Benvenuto, Signor Console," they welcomed me gravely, then, raising their cups and murmuring "Saluti," they sat back and silently sipped their coffee, waiting for Bonucci to proceed.

"As I was telling Il Console," continued Bonucci, including them into the story, "we were inactive for awhile after the raid on the convoy, and the reprisals." The two men made a low guttural sound, either of hatred or acknowledgment. "Oh, there were some individual and small group actions here and there," Bonucci went on, "like sabotaging of telephone and telegraph lines—we did that so often that they gave up trying to repair them—and we removed or redirected road signs, so they'd get confused, or lost. We've disarmed, and stolen arms from, a dozen or more of the Fascists—that helped us with our need for weapons. But that is child's play. We haven't done anything big. Certainly nothing on the order of our September raid on the convoy."

I could see the potential for destructive action, given an organized and directed group, that would force the German Wehrmacht to divert some of its attention to protecting itself from the dogs nipping at its flanks. Yes, it was definitely time to get word to the Allies, and as quickly as possible, that there were organized and professionally directed partisan groups in the area, anxious to help the Allied cause.

By the time the visitors left, it was lunchtime, and although Bonucci continued to fill me in on operations, I found the offering of fresh meat, fairly decent pasta, and good local red wine a strong distraction from the business at hand. Bonucci smiled as he watched me. "Mangia, mangia", — eat, eat," he urged, putting more meat on my plate. It was an expression I was to hear often from the Italians, no matter how scarce food was. "Some meat, and some good red wine in your belly will get your blood going and your strength up, and we need you to be strong, Signor Console. This is not an easy game. It is not for children, or weaklings."

After months of subsisting on starvation rations, I needed no urging to eat a hearty meal, but was careful not to overeat, which I knew would immediately make me sick. As soon as I was reasonably sated, I pushed my plate back, got up, and stretched. "If it's okay with you, I think I'll take a walk around," I remarked to Bonucci, smiling. "I need some more fresh air, and some exercise, after all that good food. I won't go far," I assured him, "I just want to wander around the villa property a bit." I knew that, undoubtedly, Gigi would be ordered to guard me from a distance.

"Fine, Signore, enjoy your stroll on such a beautiful day, then maybe you should have a little nap," replied Bonucci, rising and heading back into the house. "Oh, and Gualtiero," he said, startling me with his first use of my given name, "there will be a major organizational meeting after dinner tonight. Please be so good as to prepare a draft of a brief message to the Allies about our need for recognition and assistance." I nodded, and set off on my walk.

I was excited, and exhilarated too. I thought of Nancy, and Amy, of Margherita and Vittoria and the children, and hoped they were getting along. I was confident that Manfred would come through for them. I had to think positively on that. This new venture would require all my concentration, and all my attention, if I were to succeed, and stay alive. The rest would have to be pushed into the background, like it or not. I looked up. I was about the length of two football fields from the villa, and had already been walking around, at a fairly brisk pace, for about half an hour. I decided to test my strength by jogging back to the villa. The sharp, clear air hurt my lungs as I chugged along, and after only a couple of minutes I realized just how out of shape I was, but I stubbornly stuck it out, and, arriving back in my room, threw myself on the bed, gasping for breath. God, I felt good! I felt alive again, and ready to face whatever challenges lay ahead.

I looked at my watch. It was almost five o'clock already! Time for me to get going and draft that message. I saw that Bonucci had provided pen and paper—it was lying on the table next to the armchair.

I sat down, and picked up the pen. "I'm Orebaugh, American Consul," I wrote," arrested by Italian Sixth Army, Monaco, Nov. 1942, detained Perugia, evaded capture by Germans. Am now with Bonuccio Bonucci, CLN partisan leader, have joined organized resistance group Pietralunga area. Resistance force here estimated 100-150, led by Colonel Guerrizzi and Captain Pierangeli. Ready to assist Allies by ops to harass and distract enemy forces, provide G2, in area bounded by Morena, Città di Castello and Gubbio. Need funds, immediate air drop arms, ammunition, medical supplies, grenades, radio transmitter & receiver. Locations for air drops: Morena valley: field directly across from church; or further up the valley. Code words for signaling air drops:

"Puoi Gioire" (You can rejoice) and "Abbia Fede" (have faith). Six bonfires mark drop area. Suggest message via BBC signal at 2:37 a.m., repeat at 4:12 a.m. Await acknowledgment, further instructions. W. Orebaugh."

When I finished, it was dinnertime. For the first time since opening the consulate in Monaco, I felt useful again, doing something positive. It was a great feeling. I headed down the stairs, whistling tunelessly. Giuseppe intercepted me at the bottom.

"Scusi, Signor Console," he said deferentially, "Signor Bonucci would like you to join him for a glass of wine before dinner. He is in the library waiting for you." He pointed to direct me. Bonucci greeted me and poured me a glass, and we raised our glasses in a toast. "Saluti".

"Saluti," I replied. "To our successful joint enterprise." I handed him the draft of my message. He sat down and read it through. When he finished, he stood up and shook my hand. "You have been here less than a day, and already you have made a valuable contribution to our effort. I can see that you will be very important to us. I am grateful to you, and honored to have you with us, " he said, sincerely.

"I'm glad to be of some help. We're working for the same goal, Signor Bonucci," I replied simply, and turned the talk to another subject. I continued to be impressed by the man. His manner was straightforward, but warm and sincere. He was genuinely interested in me, and wanted to know more about my recent experiences. I was flattered by his open admiration of how I had handled things at the time of my arrest in Monaco—he especially enjoyed the story of our impromptu dinner party. Bonuccio Bonucci was also a realist. He entertained no exaggerated illusions about the Band and what it could accomplish. Nonetheless, he was determined to have a go at showing the Germans, and the world at large, that the Italians were tough and ready fighters, and not feckless cowards as the British and foreign press often portrayed them.

If Bonucci had a wife, or a girlfriend, he didn't mention

her, and she was nowhere in sight. Giuseppe's wife was in charge of the kitchen, and she served us a tasty minestrone, which had a few vegetables in it besides the bits of pasta and the inevitable ceci, and was reasonably tasty. After the soup came a bowl of pasta, dressed with garlic, olive oil, cheese, and a little red pepper. With it, we each had a slice of some kind of locally made dried sausage, rather like a salami, and some bread. There was a flask of the villa's red wine on the table. It was an excellent supper.

We had barely moved from the table to the living room, when the first person arrived for the meeting. I was elated to find he was an American. The tall, slender, young man who came forward to shake my hand introduced himself as Lieutenant Joseph Withers, of the Army Air Corps. He had been shot down in June of 1943, he told me, on a mission over northern Italy, and was detained for awhile in a Prisoner of War camp near Brescia. Like many other Allied POWs, he had been turned loose to fend for himself when the Armistice was signed in September of 1943. He and some British officers had slowly worked their way south, keeping to the hills and woods, aided by the Italian peasant farmers, taking circuitous routes to avoid populated or urban areas. "We finally arrived in this area, somewhat the worse for wear, but glad to be alive. Friendly peasants put us in touch with Bonucci, and here I am." He smiled in an open, friendly way, and I looked forward to getting to know him better.

Shortly before eight o'clock, several others arrived. One Italian in particular, Captain Bice Pucci, both amused and annoyed me. Somehow having gotten the notion that Americans and Scotch whiskey were inextricably intertwined, he repeatedly assured me of his liking for Scotch, and declared, with utmost seriousness, "I like my whiskey straight and my women crooked." I tried not to laugh, and managed eventually to sidle away and introduce myself to Captain R.D.G. Ramsay of the Royal Tank Regiment, who had just arrived. I was particularly anxious to meet him, since he was the one Bonucci had mentioned yesterday as a possible demolitions expert. I liked Ramsay, who was always called that--I never did learn his real first name--on sight. "I'm really happy to meet you", I said "Bonucci has spoken highly of you." He flushed with pleasure at hearing that. "I look forward to seeing a lot more of you," I added, shaking his hand. Then I saw another face, which was familiar, but escaped the edge of my memory. I pointed him out to Bonucci. "Who is that?" I asked.

"Eh, Gualtiero, you've been gone from America so long you don't recognize another American?" Bonucci teased me, smiling. "His name is Mills. Leonardo Mills."

That brought the flash of recall. Leonard Mills was a young American graduate student whom I had met briefly, almost a year before, at the Brufani. He was one of Nancy's group of friends from the University. So he had decided to "go to the macchia." Good. I walked over and greeted him warmly. Mills spoke excellent Italian, and would be very helpful. By this time over twenty people had arrived, and Bonucci decided to call the meeting to order.

He acknowledged my presence, saying, "Il Console is to be protected at all times against any exposure to risk. His well-being and safety are the only guarantee we have that we will be heard, and listened to, by the Allies." Heads turned toward me, and I felt the frank stares of the assembled men. "He has already taken steps to establish a communication channel, and to request arms, ammunition, and other material by air-drops," he continued. There were murmurs of approval. "His very presence here will bolster our credibility, and be of incalculable help in getting assistance from local farmers, other partisan groups, and the CLN. It is imperative therefore," he paused briefly for the effect of the word to wash over them, " that he be safeguarded, and delivered unharmed to the Allies when the great day of the liberation of Italy comes." All eyes swung toward me. I felt awkward and embarrassed.

On the one hand, I couldn't blame Bonucci for making the most of me as an asset. On the other, I wasn't about to accept the role of a canary in a cage. I was determined to play an active part in the Band, to be with them on their raids, to share their life. I needed to make that known to them immediately. However, I would have to do it discreetly. I couldn't in any way offend Bonucci, or nullify his protective posture toward me. At that point, Bonucci formally presented me. "I give you now Signor Console, Gualtiero Orebaugh, our esteemed friend, and the man who can convince the Allies of our extreme need."

I stepped forward and faced them. I drew a deep breath, and began, in Italian, "I am happy to be here among you, and to have joined the Band of San Faustino." Eyebrows went up in surprise at my command of Italian. I smiled at them. A few, like Ramsay, Withers, Mills, and Pucci, smiled back. The rest just watched warily, solemn-faced, waiting to hear what else I had to say. I held up the papers in my hand. "I have here a draft of a communique to the Allies, which I want to read to you. But first, I would like to say a few words." I knew I would have to walk a tightrope now, to avoid offending Bonucci. I genuinely admired him, but I did not want to be the "show wafer" on their altar of liberation. "I would like to start off with an English epithet, 'Bull!' The sharpness of my voice quickened their attention. "By that I mean, I don't want you to treat me like some sort of magician, or special hero. I am here to be with you, to be one of you, and to do what I can to hasten the victory of the Allies over the Germans. Whatever I can do because of my position, I will do. But I also intend to help in other ways, because I am a man,— a man who cannot endure watching the rape of a country that I have come to love. Senz'altro potete contare su di me!" I concluded firmly. (You can damn well count on me!) At that, the Italians broke into loud whoops and applauded wildly. The Americans and the British looked puzzled. Seizing the advantage, I immediately translated the message I had prepared, reading it aloud for them. When I finished, any concern I had for Bonucci's reaction to my insistence on being one of the Band was dispelled. He strode up and grabbed me in a bear hug.

Then he turned to his men. "Tonight we have added an important officer to our ranks," he declared. "I propose Signor Console as Communications Officer of the Band, with command responsibility." The Italians shouted their unanimous approval of that, and applauded again. Ramsay looked puzzled by it all. I sent him an "I'll explain later" look, and he nodded.

We decided a special messenger would go to Florence, where the CLN had a clandestine transmitter, to send our message to the Allies. Then Colonel Guerrizzi addressed us, briefing us on the activities of the Florence partisan group, adding, "I welcome Signor Console to our midst, and wish to commend and recognize Signor Bonucci. Because of his organizational efforts, his contributions to our liberation effort, and his connections to the CLN, he is hereby declared the overall leader of the Band of San Faustino, with Captain Pierangeli as his second-in-command." At that, there was more shouting and applause. Everyone crowded around Bonucci to shake his hand and congratulate him. Then the meeting was over. By one's and two's, the men slipped quietly out into the cold January night.

When everyone had gone, Bonuccio took me aside and poured out two brandies from the bottle sitting on the little desk. "To our success," he toasted, raising his glass to me, "not just yours and mine, but the success of our countries."

"And to our health and perseverance," I rejoined, raising my glass. "Not just yours and mine, but all our comrades in this endeavor." We drained our glasses, and said good night. I had time for only fleeting thoughts of the girls, Marguerite and Howard, and the outside world, before dropping off into a deep, dreamless chasm.

The next morning, entering the dining room, I was startled to find two decidedly rough-looking strangers sitting there, calmly drinking coffee. Then Bonucci entered, and both men immediately stood up, and exchanged hearty greetings with him. "Eh, Gualtiero, what did I tell you?" he exclaimed, turning to me with a broad smile on his face. "You bring us good fortune already! See? These men will carry your message to Florence for transmission!" Noting my raised eyebrows, he went on to explain, "These are Special Service officers attached to the 'A Force' in Bari. That's a special regiment of Italians trained for underground operations. After going to Florence, they will head back to Bari. I gave them a second copy of the message, to send when they get to Bari. That will double our chances of getting it through to the Allies!" He poured himself coffee, obviously pleased and happy. I knew where Bari was, of course--pretty far to the south, on the Adriatic, but I had heard nothing about the "A Force" before. However, I trusted Bonucci completely. He gave them the message, and they left almost immediately.

By the afternoon of my third day with Bonucci, I was getting nervous. Far too many people openly came and went at the villa. Surely all this must be a matter of common knowledge by now! Why he had been left free to continue his activities for this long puzzled and amazed me. Surely the Germans and the Fascists were aware of Bonucci and his activities--they missed little.

That afternoon, over lunch, I expressed my concerns to him. "I also hate being here unarmed," I told him. "I know you must be worried, Gualtiero," he said. "And I'm sure you're right, some of my activities must be known to the Fascist authorities. But you mustn't forget, there are always a few of the Band, and Gigi, around here to protect me. And the farmers in the area will warn us if anyone strange appears." "Well, I still don't like it," I insisted, stubbornly." We're very careful, Gualtiero, I assure you," he smiled at me, "but to make you feel better, I will see that you have a weapon soon, for your protection. But remember, I want your role to be more passive than active, for the time being." He twirled some pasta around his fork and ate it, chewing thoughtfully. "You know, you're right, Gualtiero my friend, there <u>are</u> a lot of people around here. Maybe too many. It is probably not safe to keep you here. You are much too important for us to risk." He sat thinking for a moment, idly crumbling a bit of bread between his thumb and forefinger. Then he said, "For your security and safety, Gigi will take you tonight to a farmhouse where you will stay for awhile. The conditions will be primitive, but the family is completely trustworthy, and will look after you. You'll be safe there. I will stay in touch with you through Gigi." Abruptly, he got up. "Gigi will show you maps of the area. I'll be back at four o'clock."

I finished my lunch, and spent the rest of the afternoon poring over the maps Gigi brought me of the countryside. He pointed to a spot where the farmhouse was supposed to be. Painstakingly, I committed to memory the routes from the farmhouse where I was to stay to each of the partisan presidios in the district, as well as possible ambush areas. I paid particular attention to the escape routes that Gigi pointed out to me. By the time Bonucci arrived, I felt well-versed in the terrain of the area. "The farmhouse is only a stone's throw from here," I told him, pleased. "Ah, my friend," Bonuccio replied, "it looks only a little way on the map,—but to reach it you will have to travel eight kilometers, in very rough country." He pointed at the map, and I looked. "See here— the farmhouse looks to be located on the main route to Pietralunga, but it is actually well off to one side. Anyone seen heading that way has to have a reason for doing so. There, you will have plenty of warning if anyone comes looking for you." He got up, clasped my hand in both of his, then embraced me warmly. "Godspeed, my friend," he said. "Gigi will see you safely to your new home, and we'll be in touch. We will meet again soon."

"Keep safe, Bonuccio," I responded, giving him a firm handshake, "Thank you for all you've done, and for making me one of you. I have found a new friend in a strange land. Watch your back. See you soon." With a quick wave, he was out the door again.

That evening, I took an early supper in the kitchen with Gigi. We packed our stomachs with heaping bowls of rich rabbit stew, and, shortly after seven, we set out. It was freezing cold, and I was shivering before we'd gone fifty feet.

We retraced our steps along the muddy footpath through San Faustino. Then we turned onto another footpath not even wide enough for the two of us. Gigi spoke for the first time. "There is a regular road, Signore, but if we take it, it will add several kilometers to our walk." I tried to imagine what a "regular road" might be. "Then let's stay on the shorter route," I said. I wanted to get to somewhere warm, as fast as possible. It was slow and tedious going. There was no moon, and where the path wasn't mired in mud, it was blocked with snow, which we plowed with our "walking sticks"—two gnarled, thick branches trimmed from an olive tree. The cold gnawed at us. Even the stalwart Gigi grumbled and cursed as he stumbled and slithered from time to time.

It was close to midnight, and I was nearly frozen, by the time we reached the lonely farmhouse. The moon had finally appeared, bathing the area in its cold, gray light. Bonucci was right. This was certainly off any beaten path. An ancient, battered-looking building in sad disrepair, it was obviously not the abode of a prosperous family. Margherita's poor flat was a villa by comparison, and Bonuccio's a palace. As with most peasant farmhouses, the ground floor housed the livestock, farm equipment, hay and feed. The family lived on the floor above. I had seen many farmhouses just like this scattered on the plains around Gubbio—they all looked alike. The one we were standing before was just more dilapidated than most. Gigi shouted, but got no response. Now that we were standing still, the cold attacked us with knives. Gigi went from shout to bellow. "Eh! Ruggero! Si faccia vivo!" (Come alive!) " A shadow appeared in the upstairs front window, but nothing happened. Exasperated, Gigi yelled again. "Ruggero! Aprite!" (Ruggero! Open up!) With that, the window opened a tiny crack, and a face appeared. "I have here a good friend of Signor Bonuccio Bonucci, who needs shelter," shouted Gigi. The window slammed shut, and within seconds the upstairs door was thrown open. We scrambled up the stairs and into the house.

"Scusi, Signori," apologized Ruggero Bruschi profusely,

as he lit a candle in the cold room, and prodded the banked fire in the fireplace to life. "Sit, sit!" he urged us, pulling out two chairs. Despite his prior fear, his sleepiness, and the lateness of the hour, the rites of tradition were scrupulously observed. Our excited host scampered to the far side of the dimly lit room muttering, and groped among the flasks arrayed on a shelf. Returning to the table with one, he took down three glasses from another shelf and filled our glasses so full, some of the liquid slopped over the side.

The idea of drinking wine at this late hour did not appeal to me. I was nearly frozen, and so tired I wanted to crawl right into the fireplace and go to sleep. But Gigi had thought only of a warming glass of wine for the past hour. As soon as the glass was in his hand, he tilted his head back and quaffed it down in a single gulp. Then, with a roar that resounded throughout the house he spewed out whatever he hadn't swallowed. Ear-splitting curses followed. Our poor host was at first dumbfounded, then his face registered embarrassment. He grabbed for my glass. "Oh, scusi, scusi, Signori, what a fool I am! Please forgive me!" Salt, hard to come by, was hoarded in old wine bottles as saltwater. In the semi-darkness, Ruggero had poured our glasses from the wrong flask. Gigi had gotten a mouthful of strong saltwater instead of wine. Getting new glasses, and a fresh flask, Ruggero poured anew. "Scusi," he said again. Then he joined us at the huge, rough-hewn wood table that dominated the enormous room.

While we drank, and warmed ourselves before the feebly flickering fire, Gigi explained me to our host. He spoke some sort of local dialect, which I had difficulty following, but which I realized I would have to learn, and quickly. "Signor Bonucci sends you his regards," Gigi began. Ruggero nodded, and sipped his wine, waiting. "He has chosen you," said Gigi, with a trace of pompousness, "from among all the others, because he knows you can be counted on to handle the very heavy responsibility of being host and protector to his American friend, here." Ruggero raised his eyebrows on hearing that, but said nothing. "He is hiding out from the

Fascists and the Germans. No one is to know he is here. He goes by the name of Michele Franciosi,—a 'sfollato from Roma, capisce?" Ruggero nodded. "You and your family are to take care of him, and protect him, for Signor Bonucci, and for the cause of liberation."

At that, our host beamed. He was immensely flattered to be entrusted with such a big responsibility. In those parts, Signor Bonuccio Bonucci was a man to be respected and accommodated, if at all possible. He, Ruggero Bruschi, had been personally selected by Signor Bonucci to shelter this mysterious American, out of the scores of countrymen with whom Signor Bonucci had dealings. What an honor for the Bruschis!

Finally, Gigi made his farewells, and took his leave. He would not remain the night, despite Ruggero's urging. Suddenly, I found myself alone with another Italian stranger who was to be my host, in yet another Italian home, which was to be my home. We looked one another over warily.

Ruggero Bruschi was a short, sturdily built man in his early thirties, with dark, straight hair parted on the left and combed neatly back. His round face was ruddy-complexioned, and although clean shaven, it bore the shadow of a dark, heavy beard. It was saved from being a formidable face by his natural readiness to smile and laugh. Light, bushy eyebrows shaded clear hazel eyes. His smile revealed only a few remaining teeth, from a poor peasant's lack of any dental care.

"Make yourself comfortable, Signore, while I make sleeping arrangements," said Ruggero, and disappeared into the adjoining room.

I looked around me. The heavy wood table at which I sat filled the center of the large rectangular room, which was about thirty feet long by twenty feet wide. Ranged around the table were six rush-bottomed, straight-backed chairs. A large open fireplace dominated one end of the room. A heavily encrusted black iron kettle, which apparently was used for cooking, was set to one side on the stone hearth.

Beside it lay some wrought iron cooking implements, reminiscent of paintings of rural colonial America in the 1700's. There was no stove, nor any sink, but it was obvious that the room was kitchen, as well as dining room and living room for the Bruschi family. A wooden storage counter against one wall, with a few rickety wooden shelves above it, completed the meager furnishings. The walls were of the same dull gray stone as the floor. A small crucifix hung on the wall above the fireplace. It was the room's only adornment. There were two windows,— one at the end opposite the fireplace, and a larger one in the long wall overlooking the farmyard. Neither boasted any curtains. I looked around for a nail, or hook, on which to hang my hat, but there were no pegs in the wall where you could hang anything. The floor sagged rather precipitously toward the middle, like a giant saucer. The oaken beams upon which the heavy squares of stone flooring had been laid when the house was built had bowed over time under the weight of the stone, creating the bowl-like curvature. It took me awhile to get used to the strange sensation of walking down, then up again, to cross the room.

Before I'd fully taken in my surroundings, Ruggero reappeared, followed by his entire family. He presented his wife, Adalgisa, who shyly shook my hand. She was a short, plain woman, apparently older than Ruggero, but probably by only a few years, judging from the ages of the children. However, she looked to be at least ten years older. Her wispy, graying hair was drawn back into a plain bun at the nape of her neck, and her face, neck and hands were wrinkled and leathery, from years of hard work in severe weather. Cosmetics were as unknown to this woman as indoor plumbing. Her slight figure was already bent from years of hard physical work, but her brown eyes were warm and compassionate. Concetta, the daughter, was about fourteen. She was dark, short and stocky like Ruggero, plain like her mother, but not unattractive. The son Giuseppe, called Pepe, was a skinny, curly-headed youth of about ten who reminded me of Franco Bonucci. His eyes reflected wide-eyed amazement at this middle-of-the-night apparition. I solemnly shook hands with both youngsters.

Then I was ceremoniously escorted into the family bedroom, which was the only other room in the house. It was big, about sixteen by nearly thirty feet, and it contained two beds—a very large wood-framed bed, and a smaller iron cot ranged right next to it. The small bed was Concetta's. Ruggero gestured to it. "You will sleep here, please, Signore," he said politely. He waved aside my protests. "My daughter will sleep in the other bed, with us. You do our family honor to be our guest, Signore," he hastened to assure me. " I am sorry our accommodations cannot be better for a friend of Signor Bonucci," he added apologetically. Adalgisa showed me a small screen in one corner of the room. Behind it was the "bathroom", which consisted only of a chipped ceramic chamber pot, and a small wooden washstand holding a pitcher of ice cold water.

I gazed around me, dazed with shock. Never in my life had I seen or imagined anything this poor. I was suddenly struck by what luxury I had enjoyed in my accommodations up to now—even in Gubbio, even at the poor apartment of Margherita Bonucci in Perugia. This was stark, soul-breaking poverty. Yet Ruggero Bruschi and his family were happy, proud even, to be assigned another mouth to feed, another body to shelter, a stranger come suddenly into their midst, destroying any shred of privacy left in their huddled family existence. I wondered suddenly what Amy and Nancy would think if they could see this. I could picture Amy's horrified look, and Nancy's dismay. I was to learn that the layout of the interior of the Bruschi home, while more modest than most, was not untypical of peasant farmhouses throughout central Italy.

"Now you must get some sleep, Signore," said Adalgisa, quietly. I needed no further urging. After the six mile, mostly uphill trek I had made, the wine, and the warmth seeping back into me from the fire, I would have been happy to curl up on the cold stone floor to sleep. Shedding only my coat, my shoes, and my suit jacket, I fell onto Concetta's narrow bed. It felt surprisingly comfortable. I saw the Bruschis all climb into the big bed. Its crossed-rope underframe supported a mattress of coarse linen stuffed with corn husks, which rustled whenever anyone moved. The family settled down, with the two youngsters sandwiched in the middle, heads at the foot of the bed, and the parents one on each side of them, heads at the upper end. I was surprised when they all fell asleep almost immediately. Clutching the worn blanket around me, I followed suit.

I woke in the morning to find myself alone. In the harsh light of day, the place was even drearier than it had seemed the night before. I didn't know how the whole family had managed to get up and slip out without waking me. I shivered, dreading the prospect of washing in water I knew would be not just cold, but icy. Thank God I didn't need to shave. I still sported my "liberation beard," which had waxed quite full and bushy, though still mottled in color.

Ruggero was waiting for me when I stepped into the next room. He had been up for awhile, out doing chores, but hadn't yet breakfasted. Adalgisa brewed a bitter, pale liquid that passed for coffee, and she set a cup of it before us, along with a good-sized chunk of homemade bread that was coarse, but not unpalatable. As soon as we had finished eating, Ruggero took me outside, and showed me several routes leading from the back of the house to densely wooded spots not far away. "These are your hiding places, Signore," he informed me. "You can remain in one of these for as long as you need to, and you will not be seen." He explained that there would be times I would need to hide out, since the "appuntata," the deputized carabiniere, made the rounds of the farmhouses in the district every other week or so. "It is more of a nuisance than a danger," he assured me, "we get plenty of advance warning when he is coming." He then walked me to the minuscule spring which gave the farm its name, "Fontanella."

Dropping down onto a stump at the bank of the narrow stream, he gestured for me to sit on a flat rock near it. I sensed he wanted to talk, and was not surprised when he launched into a tale of his recent wartime experiences. When the Armistice was declared, he said, he had been turned loose from his unit, far from home in the north of Italy. Having no sense of geography whatsoever, he had somehow managed to grope his way back toward Umbria, stealthily evading German and Fascist patrols, sleeping under piles of leaves to stay warm in the bitter cold. He paused in his tale and looked at me keenly.

I sensed that he was curious, and was giving me an opening to follow his lead and talk about myself, but I chose to pass on that. What Ruggero didn't know wouldn't hurt him. "No, no, your story is very interesting, please continue," I urged. When he had finished, I was closer to an understanding of the peasants of Umbria and of how they preserved their spirit of rugged independence. Ruggero's homeward odyssey had taken him three full months, through mind-boggling deprivations, adventures and misadventures, but he had finally made it back to Umbria and Fontanella. When he finished, I praised him sincerely for his bravery and perseverance. From the look he gave me, I knew I had made another loyal friend.

The fact that there was only one entrance (and exit) to the living quarters at the farm house bothered me. The next day, I decided to place a ladder near the bedroom window at the back side of the house. I explained that I'd feel better with a way to get out the back if need arose. Ruggero agreed and helped me, and we carefully arranged the ladder so it looked like it was just leaning there against the house, near the window, but not close enough that it seemed there for a purpose. Then I turned to my next task. I had some important papers on me that I had kept carefully hidden ever since leaving Nice. They were of no use to me for the moment, for they were mostly negotiable stock and bond certificates which I had foolishly brought with me to Nice in case of emergency need. For them to be found in the Bruschi house would endanger us all. I found an old tin box, wrapped the securities and my American passport in a piece of worn oilcloth, and proceeded to bury the box under the stairs that led up into the house. As I dug at the hard, frozen earth with the rusty old shovel I couldn't help smiling in amusement at the thought that neither Ruggero nor Adalgisa could possibly ever imagine how much more valuable their farm had become with this buried treasure. I kept my cash-- the dollars and lire--more accessible. I knew that the poor refugee clerk Michele Franciosi would have a hard time explaining how he came by hundreds, fifties, and even a couple of five hundred dollar American bills, not to mention a small fortune in lire, if he were caught and interrogated, but I decided to risk it for the time being.

By the third day there, I realized that life at the Bruschis was going to be stunningly boring. There was no diversion of any kind — no reading matter, no radio, no writing materials, not even cards to play. I longed for a book of any kind, or an old newspaper to read, to help pass the time. Mostly I paced during the day, or stared out the window. The family retired almost immediately after supper, which was served at about five in the evening. Oil for the single lamp was almost impossible to get, and candles were scarce and expensive. Adalgisa finished clearing up the supper dishes, Ruggero finished smoking his pipe of locally grown tobacco, and had his final glass of wine in front of the fire. Then he would stand, stretching, and announce, "It has been quite a day, time for some rest." At that, the whole family would retire to the bedroom and go to bed. It was an unvarying nightly ritual. I wondered how long I could tolerate such stupefying boredom as this. Fortunately, it didn't last long.

That night, I went to bed just a few minutes after the family. Drifting in that nether land between sleep and consciousness, at first I thought I was dreaming the loud banging that suddenly shattered the silence. With terrifying awareness, I came awake, heart thumping, realizing the banging was not a dream at all, but the door! I leaped out of bed, grabbing my clothes, and was at the window, scanning the back yard, reaching to grab the ladder, by the time Ruggero reached the door to answer it. Then, a touch on my shoulder startled me, but it was only Adalgisa, signaling that all was well. The door-banger was Gigi, who had returned, bringing Lieutenant Mario Bonfigli with him. A single candle sputtered on the table, and Ruggero was pouring out four glasses of wine. Two chairs, for Bonfigli and me, were set in front of the hearth, where the fire was once again blazing. Ruggero and Gigi withdrew to the table.

Lieutenant Mario Bonfigli was about five foot six, and held his slender but wiry frame in erect, military bearing. He was young, probably in his mid-twenties, and looked every inch the career officer. His merry dark eyes, though, revealed a nature ready to enjoy a good laugh and the fun side of life. After our introductions, and a few sips of wine, Bonfigli drew a dark, gleaming Beretta revolver from inside his jacket, and held it out to me. "Signor Bonucci said that you might like this to cover your nakedness, Signor Console."

"Signor Bonucci was absolutely right!" I exclaimed happily. As I took the pistol from him, I glanced toward Ruggero and Gigi. Ruggero's face reflected profound awe. Even Gigi's expression showed more respect than usual. By meriting such a rare and valuable weapon, I had climbed several notches in Gigi's esteem, and the mere mention of "Console," in addition to the weapon, had attained me a stature with Ruggero that was beyond imagining. That Beretta pistol alone represented more wealth than the Bruschi family had ever seen.

We talked for a few moments in low voices. Bonucci was fine, and sent me his regards. There had been no response to our message as yet from the Allies. But then, it was too soon to expect one. We needed help, and quickly, to begin operations. As always, I was short on patience. Then, to my surprise, Bonfigli reached into a jacket pocket and withdrew an envelope. I saw Nancy's handwriting on it, and eagerly snatched it from his hand. Impatiently, I ripped it open, as Bonfigli, noting my haste, prodded up the fire to give me more light to read by. Tears sprang to my eyes on seeing Nancy's fine script—I realized just how much I missed her, and all the others.

Dearest Walter," I read in a blur, "Amy and I are well. We and the family miss you. Please be careful. Your friend will be escorting us to the big church. Everything is arranged very nicely. Love, Nancy."

For a moment I was puzzled. Big church? What big church? Then, slapping my forehead, I muttered aloud, "Stupido! Big church--the Vatican! She means the Vatican! Manfred's taking them to Rome!" Ruggero and Gigi stared at me, dumbfounded. They were no doubt thinking that Americans behave in strange ways. I turned to Bonfigli. "Lieutenant," I inquired urgently, "how soon will you see Signor Bonucci? I need to get a message to Perugia as quickly as possible."

I turned to Ruggero. "I need some paper, and a pen," I said crisply, my tone more commanding than I intended. Ruggero hustled into the bedroom, from whence, after a prolonged conference with Adalgisa, he produced the only paper in the house— a badly wrinkled souvenir postcard. "Um, don't worry about a pen, Ruggero, I'll get mine," I said, mortified at having made such a thoughtless request as pen and paper in a household that had no ability to use, even if they could have afforded them, such luxuries as pen and paper. To spare Ruggero further embarrassment, I thanked him profusely for the postcard, "This is perfect, just what I need—thank you!" I said. "I must get an important message to Signor Bonucci." Ruggero drew himself up with pride at having made such a significant contribution to my mission. "I am pleased to be able to assist you, Signore," he said, with grave formality.

Hastily, I penned a note to Manfred in the limited space on the postcard. "Can you advance money for key necessities? Also, kindly present the enclosed paper to your lawyer in

Trieste." I couched my words carefully to avoid detection if the message was intercepted. I didn't want the money for myself, but for the partisans, —to buy necessary supplies to hold us until we heard from the Allies and an airdrop could be arranged. I also wanted him to have the bargaining paper I had promised for his friend, since the friend had apparently supplied the necessary identification to get Nancy and Amy out safely. I signed the card "Brother Felice at the church in San Faustino," and gave it to Gigi to take to Bonucci. Bonucci would get it to Valentina. I breathed a silent but fervent prayer that my pipeline would get the message to Manfred quickly, and that he'd come through with the interim funds we desperately needed.

Then Bonfigli said quietly, "We are considering some action in two of the presidios in the near future, — in fact, that is what I am going on to discuss tonight. I will talk to them about your wishes. Personally, I see no harm in letting you come along on the mission, but only as an observer, you understand. He was obviously mindful of Bonucci's admonitions that I be protected. "I'll see what can be arranged, and be back in touch with you." Touching his hand to his hat in salute, he took his leave.

We had no sooner closed the door than Ruggero turned to me and said respectfully, "Buona notte, (Good night) Signor Console."

"Ruggero! Never say that!" I admonished sharply. "No one must know who I am! I am Michele. Don't endanger yourself like that! Michele is the only name you should ever use to me!"

"Sí, Signor Console," he nodded agreement. I sighed, exasperated. I felt great at the news I'd just gotten. I was sure Nancy and Amy were already safe behind the walls of the Vatican, thanks to Manfred. I was immensely relieved that they were no longer a burden for Margherita to feed, and that her family was no longer in danger because of sheltering us.

I had no way of knowing that Manfred's scheme had been delayed, and that at that very moment he, Nancy and

Amy were still in Perugia, just beginning to put in motion their dangerous escape plan. I looked over at Ruggero. "Please Ruggero, go on to bed. I'm just going to finish a glass of wine, then I'll turn in too." He nodded, but didn't leave. Instead, he poured me a glass of wine, and one for himself. Then he sat down, across the table from me, watching me quietly. I could only imagine what must be going through his mind. In Italy, the title of "Consul," a carryover from Roman times, carries much more importance than it does elsewhere. Ruggero was overawed. He was determined now to be sure that I was accorded the service, and the respect, to which he believed my rank entitled me. He would not go to bed until I did, I knew — just in case there might be something he could do for me. I sighed again. Well, I thought resignedly, Bonuccio has his Gigi, and now I have my Ruggero. Finishing my wine as quickly as politeness allowed, I got up, and we both turned in.

While it was well past bedtime at Fontanella, it was not so for city dwellers, even with a curfew. Manfred, as I learned much later, was at that moment standing on a corner in Perugia, in a steady, cold drizzle, about a block from Margherita Bonucci's apartment, fidgeting because the vehicle he had arranged for was already late. Amy and Nancy, meanwhile, were still in the apartment, waiting for the signal to join him outside.

To arrange the escape, Paolucci, Manfred's lawyer friend in Trieste, had convinced the questore, and his Sicilian driver Sergio, that one of the two women to be picked up in Perugia and taken to Rome (Amy) was none other than "l'amica" (the mistress) of German Field Marshall Kesselring. The other woman (Nancy) was her companion, he said, — sort of a guardian of l'amica's safety. Paolucci further intimated to Sergio that the Field Marshall was intolerant of indiscretion, or failure, but knew how to generously reward and protect those who did him valuable service. Sweating profusely, Sergio pledged his wholehearted cooperation with the Field Marshall's wishes in regard to the young women.

Meanwhile, in Perugia, Manfred worried. He did not like waiting in the open like this. He had purposely worn only German clothing, which he had purchased in Berlin. His papers bore a variety of official stamps, most of which related to authorizations for the movement of wine and tank cars. These would pass cursory examination by local municipal guards, but God help him if a carabiniere — or worse, a Gestapo officer, — got hold of him. Suddenly, a young German soldier approached. "Haben sie fueur, bitte?" he asked, politely. (Do you have a light?)

"Surely you're not smoking on duty!" snapped Manfred, with authority. The soldier stepped back a pace, discomfited. Then Manfred laughed good-naturedly. "What the hell," he said, drawing out his lighter, "if you have a dry cigarette on a damnably wet night like this, you deserve to smoke it!" He lit the cigarette, declining to have one himself.

Sergio pulled up in the van and Manfred directed him to a parking place in the shadows, then hurried to the house to get the girls. He hurried them down the stairs and hustled them into the van, quickly stowing their hand baggage. "Get going," he said tersely to Sergio, "I'm right behind you." He jumped into his green Willys, swung in behind the van, and they moved out. The heavy rain, a stroke of good luck for them, continued all the way to Rome. There were few checkpoints, and because of the miserable weather, they were subjected to document check only twice. Although their hearts pounded each time they were stopped, after cursory inspection of their papers, the Italian militia guards waved them on. Political prisoners of the Germans being transported to Rome were of no importance on their watch. They had crossed the city limits and entered Rome when they ran into trouble. The control point on the Via Nomentana was manned by German soldiers, not Italians. Manfred's heart dropped, but there was nothing except to continue and try to brave it through.

The van, with the Willys right behind it, pulled to a stop. The senior of the two guards approached the van, obviously in a foul mood. "You Italians!" he shouted at Sergio, "Will you never learn anything?! It is of no consequence to you if your own city of Rome is burned! Stúpido!" Terrified, Amy and Nancy cowered in silence in the back of the van, as a trembling Sergio silently held the sheaf of fake identity papers out to the irate German guard. "I don't want your damned papers, you idiot!" screamed the guard, pushing them away. "You are the third Italian truck tonight in violation of regulations! Hood those headlights! Get the hell out of here and get those headlights hooded! Schnell!"

"Sí, Signore." Sergio slammed the van into gear and roared forward.

Manfred pulled up to the checkpoint. "Trouble?" he said casually to the guard. "I am Herr Hauptmann." He held out his papers, and an open pack of cigarettes. "Danke, mein Herr," said the guard, taking a cigarette. "Take the pack," said Manfred generously, "I have more. Problems with that truck?" He was anxious to know what had transpired. "Pah! It's these stupid Italians!" snorted the German. They cannot obey regulations! The headlights were not properly hooded."

"Well! I will certainly speak to the Italian police commandant tomorrow," said Manfred sternly, "good job that you are so alert. Heil Hitler!" He shoved the Willys into gear.

"Guten nacht, Herr Hauptmann," said the guard, with respect. Manfred gunned the motor and pulled away. The van, followed by the green Willys with New York plates, proceeded with no further incident right into Vatican City. There, Manfred delivered Nancy and Amy safely into the hands of Foreign Service Officer Harold Tittman, who was acting as President Roosevelt's personal representative to the Vatican.

A few weeks later, Lieutenant Bonfigli showed up at the Bruschi's again. He handed me a packet from Manfred. Everyone crowded around to watch while I opened it, despite Ruggero's admonitions to his family to "stand back and give Signor Michele room." At least he didn't call me "Signor

Console," I noted wryly. I was as excited as the family, and quickly tore the package open. "Whoopee!" I shouted with joy when I saw what was in it. Italian banknotes! Two fat stacks of them! There was also an envelope which I tore open, rapidly scanning the note inside. "Your fine packages forwarded safely to the main depot," wrote Manfred. "Returning the enclosed for causes you requested. Good luck."

Concetta and her parents stood staring, open-mouthed, at the stacks of bills. It was more money than they had ever seen in their lives. Handing Concetta one of the packets, I said, "Here Concetta, I need to count this, and I know you are good at numbers, — will you help me?" She looked at her parents, who smiled and nodded, bursting with pride that their daughter was smart enough to be able to help Il Console.

Swiftly, we counted. Each packet contained 50,000 lire — over $2,500! Jumping up, I slapped Bonfigli on the back. "Eh, Mario!" I exclaimed, "A hundred thousand lire! Five thousand American dollars! That's more money than either of us has seen in awhile, right? " Bonfigli whistled. "You bet!" he said, "But I'm glad to see it now."

I turned to Ruggero. Concetta had given them the total, and they were rooted to the floor, eyes wide in astonishment. "Ruggero!" I said. He snapped to attention. "Sí Signore?"

"This calls for celebration!" I smiled. " A glass of wine for everyone!" Adalgisa hastened to get the glasses, as Ruggero brought out the flask of wine. I turned to Bonfigli. "This will give us an operating fund that should hold us for a while!" Ruggero handed us our glasses of wine, then took his, and I indicated that Adalgisa and Concetta should each have one, too. Pepe, who had never fully awakened, was back in the bedroom, asleep.

Hesitantly, they took their glasses. I turned to the group, raising my glass. "To Manfred Metzger!" I said jubilantly. "To Manfred Metzger!" they all echoed, bewildered, stumbling over the unfamiliar words. "And to the liberation of Italy!" I added. <u>That</u> was something they understood, and everyone repeated it eagerly and drank. I knew the Bruschis had never before seen such goings-on under their roof. They would talk about this night for the rest of their lives.

Dropping an arm around Bonfigli's shoulder, I drew him aside. "Can you get this money to Bonuccio Bonucci right away?"

"But of course, Signor Console," he assured me. I sighed. It was hopeless. None of them would ever see me as Michele, the 'sfollato clerk.

"The hundred thousand lire could not have come at a better time," he grinned, revealing even white teeth. "Tomorrow, we'll both go to see Bonucci. But tonight, we have other things to do," he said quietly. "Tonight we go out."

"Tonight? Where?" In my excitement, I failed to lower my voice. Bonfigli froze, and stared at me as though wondering if he had made a mistake in trusting me. Then I realized my blunder. Idiot! I scolded myself. Of course he isn't going to tell me, or anyone else here, what the target is tonight! He started to say something to me, then changed his mind. "Let us go downstairs," he said quietly. "I have something to tell you in private."

At the foot of the stairs, he turned to me. "Tonight we go to a place in the general direction of west," he said cryptically. "The place we go to must have a name, but even I don't know what it is. There will be several men in our party. I don't want them endangered. Can you fire a rifle?"

For a moment, I smarted. I knew his confidence in me had been shaken, so I said, emphatically, "Of course I can fire a rifle! Forgive me, Mario. In the package I received very good news, that two dear friends of mine had made their escape to safety. I wasn't thinking as clearly as I should have been. I'm sorry I spoke imprudently."

"I am glad to hear about your friends, Signore," he said sincerely, "I know that it makes you happy to know they are safe. But now, about the rifle." While we were talking, he had walked us to a mound of straw in the livestock area under the living quarters. He reached down into the straw, and, groping around, pulled out an army carbine. "I left this here the other night," he said seriously, but there was a twinkle of merriment in his brown eyes. He handed the gun to me. I took it and checked it out. I had handled a rifle many times on my uncle's ranch in Colorado, and I was no stranger to using one. Seeing me handle and check the weapon over with expertise, I saw Bonfigli's confidence was restored. "Tonight, at eight-thirty, leave the house and go the those woods there," he said, pointing to his left. The wooded clump was roughly two hundred meters away. He slapped me on the shoulder. "Be on time, my friend." He slipped out the stable door to the back and disappeared into the brush. I was relieved to hear him call me "friend." I really liked Mario.

I examined the rifle minutely, and dry-fired it several times to get the feel of it. There in the empty stable, the snap of the bolt was startlingly loud. I carefully placed the carbine under some boards, where I could easily find it again in the dark, and went back upstairs for dinner. Adalgisa had done her best to produce a special meal. My chipped earthen bowl was heaped full of pasta, and contained more than my fair share of precious sausage. Meat was usually reserved for Sunday only. A glass of wine stood before my bowl, and an extra large chunk of crusty bread was set beside it. A special meal for the warrior, or a good last meal for the condemned, I thought, a bit cynically, then brushed the thought aside. This, after all, was what I had been wanting, what I had been waiting for a chance to do. I ate heartily, complimenting Adalgisa on the meal. She blushed with pleasure, and Ruggero gave her a rare glance of pride and approval before turning back to his bowl and stolidly consuming his meal. The day had been an especially good one, and I felt sure that the night would be, too.

Chapter 6

Betrayal and Despair

As soon as dinner was over, I went into the bedroom and put on my dark green sweater, the least conspicuous one I had. I pulled a second pair of black pants on, over the ones I was wearing. I hoped that would keep my legs from getting too cold. I checked the Beretta over carefully, loaded it, and slipped it into my waistband. When eight o'clock came, I put on my frayed topcoat, my gloves, and my wool peasant cap. God, I hoped it wouldn't be as cold tonight as it was last night! I knew if it was, my butt would be freezing, no matter what clothes I wore. I could feel a knot of nervous excitement building in my stomach.

When I stepped back into the kitchen, Adalgisa pushed a package containing a chunk of bread and some cheese into my pocket, then looked at me. "Dio sia con te" (God be with you), she said quietly, making the sign of the cross. She must have known what I was about to do, but she said nothing more. Retrieving the rifle from its hiding place, I took a bearing on the trees and headed for the cluster at the brow of the hill, the one Bonfigli had pointed out earlier. As I trotted across the field, I thought of Nancy and Amy. Briefly, while still back in Perugia, I had mentioned them to Bonuccio Bonucci, and asked about bringing them into the hills with me. His reply had been an emphatic "No! Absolutely not!" Now, I was glad he had been adamant. They were safely in neutral territory in Vatican City, under U.S. protection again, while I was stumbling across a frozen field in the Umbrian hills, carrying a carbine. God only knew if I'd ever see the United States again.

Suddenly, the brush closed in on me. I tried to find a path through it, to get into the woods. Finding none, I decided to just bull my way through it. I couldn't risk being late for the rendezvous. I had barely gained the trees when I heard "SSST! Sono qui, Signore!" (Over here, Sir!). I peered into the darkness, but could see nothing. "Eccomi qui," (Here I am) the voice repeated. A shadow moved, and I headed for it. Soon I caught up with it. "We will join the others in a few moments," he informed me, and set off, going deeper into the woods. Soon the muffled voices of several other men closed in around us. Once through the woods, we headed down the valley, hugging the brush, going about three kilometers. The cold had intensified, but these wiry partisans set a pace that kept me from noticing it, except for my nose, which from time to time I rubbed with my gloved hand to stimulate circulation. Rocks and stubble cut through my thin shoes, and I knew I would have to find boots somehow, before doing this again.

Finally, after cutting across the valley and up into a wood on the far side, we came to a stand of pine, and stopped. Lieutenant Bonfigli was waiting there. We were a dozen men, including Bonfigli and myself. We were all armed, though only three of us had army carbines. The others carried hunters' guns—sporting guns of varying caliber and age. Bonfigli spoke. "Now is the time to have your last cigarette." He could have rephrased it, I thought, so it didn't emphasize "last". I had not thought to bring one of my cigars—a mistake I vowed not to make again, as I watched the others enjoy their pipes or cigarettes. Seeing I had none, the youth next to me offered me a cigarette, which I gratefully accepted. Otherwise, no one paid me any particular attention.

As we smoked, Bonfigli outlined the evening's plan of action. "When we reach the ambush site," he said, naming a place which brought grunts of recognition from others in the group, "we will divide into two groups of six. One group take one side of the road, and one the other. Stagger your positions so you are not shooting across at each other. The Germans use this road regularly, and we expect a convoy of at least six to ten vehicles will be along sometime tonight." I glanced at my watch, and Manfred flashed into my mind. I wished he were here--he'd have relished being in the thick of something like this. It was ten o'clock. "Okay. No more smoking," Bonfigli commanded, and everyone immediately extinguished pipes and cigarettes. "Let's go!" He waved us on and we headed out, going at the same brisk pace as before. We walked like that for several hours, across a countryside devoid of anything stirring. We scrambled down steep slopes, over convoluted ridges, and across icy streams. We slogged through mud up to our ankles. I couldn't feel my wet and frozen feet any more. Finally, we halted at the crest of the ridge, and everyone threw themselves down on the ground to rest.

"This is the 'ritrovo', (reassembly point) said Bonfigli tersely. "After the 'colpo di mano' (shootout), get back here as fast as you can." One of the partisans brought out bread, sausage, and cheese. I handed him the ration of bread and cheese Adalgisa had put in my pocket, to add to the measure. The food was carefully shared out among us, and then two bottles of wine were uncorked and passed around. Each man took only two swallows, I noted, doing the same. Bonfigli came over and squatted down next to me. "From here on, please stay as close to me as you can. Do not do anything to endanger yourself, Signore." We stood up and moved into place at the road. I looked at my watch again. It was hard to believe, but it was already 3 A.M.! Six men took up their positions on the other side of the road. The ambush site was on the crest of a hill, where approaching trucks, in low gear for the climb, would not be moving fast. Just past us, the road curved away sharply, then dropped down at a fairly steep angle, rising at the same grade again on the far side, to the head of a rocky ridge. Across the road, the brush was fairly thick, and the slope was covered with scrub oak and rocky outcroppings. On our side, an embankment rose steeply about eight feet above the road. The brush was sparse on this side, but there were a few large rocks that provided good cover.

Bonfigli positioned us so that everyone overlooked the road, but each of us was sheltered behind a rock, tree, or outcropping. As he positioned each man, he whispered final instructions. He stationed me last, relatively far down the slope. I knew that Bonfigli was complying with Bonucci's orders,--keeping me away from the action and as safe as possible—but I resisted it. I wanted to be in the thick of things with the others. I hunkered down behind my rock, trying to concentrate and stay warm. Time crept by like an advancing glacier, so slowly that its passing was almost imperceptible. Once, I caught myself nodding off, and countered with a vigorous burst of leg-stretching and face rubbing. To keep myself awake and alert, I mentally ticked off all my resources back home, taking inventory of what Marguerite and Howard would have to live on if I didn't make it back. Then I imagined us in our favorite restaurant, mentally poring over the menu, deciding what I'd order for our reunion dinner. I had settled on a shrimp cocktail for starters, and was debating between a thick, juicy prime rib and a porterhouse steak, when the sound of moving vehicles, like a distant rumble of thunder, reached me. "SSST!" The hiss that signaled readiness went from man to man. I held my breath and strained my ears, trying to count how many there were in the convoy as they shifted gears. One, two, three...I counted four, and only the last two sounded like trucks. Our orders were to stay hidden, and not open fire before Bonfigli did.

The last vehicle had just about cleared my position, when the loud, staccato burst of Bonfigli's Mitre, the only submachine gun in our arsenal, rattled everyone into action. His first burst caught the lead vehicle, a weapons carrier with three soldiers in it. It slewed sideways, and the man in back dived out, and onto the far side of the road. "Sparate! (Shoot!) "Get him!" the partisans yelled. More shots rang out. The second vehicle, a small staff car, tried desperately to steer around the weapons carrier. Rifle fire poured into it from the men on the other side of the road, and the car lurched to a stop, out of gear, its motor racing with a loud, steady whine. Then the first of the trucks, unable to brake in time, rammed into the back of the staff car, completely blocking the road off. "Sparate! Sparate!" (Get them!) Shots poured into the rest of the convoy from both sides of the road. "Colpitelo!" (Kill him!) shouted someone, as a German soldier jumped down and tried to run toward the woods. A quick shot brought him down.

I had wondered if I'd really be able to shoot a man when the time came. Now, as the last truck passed my position, I was up and firing, shouting in my best barroom Italian. "Darlilo!" (Give it to them!) "Non mollate!" (Don't let them get away!) I slammed the second clip home and fired. The fuel tank of the second truck ruptured. Whether it was my shot or not, I couldn't tell—there was so much firing going on. With a roar, it exploded, sending flames shooting twenty feet into the air. The driver jumped out, aflame, then fell to the ground. Down the line, barely visible because of the contour of the hill, another truck had been set ablaze, and the ammunition inside it began exploding with staccato pings-- like hail hitting a tin roof. Then came shouts of "Via! Via!" That was the signal to clear out—fast! Without bothering to load my third clip, I turned and ran as hard as I could for the regrouping point. Later, I couldn't even remember splashing through the small creek to reach it. As I gained the top of the hill, I turned and looked back down at the blazing trucks and the wreckage of the convoy. I knew that the flames could be seen for miles. With the noise of the explosion, and the shots, we had probably alerted every military unit in the area. There would be hell to pay for this.

Almost instantly, the others joined me. Bonfigli slapped my back heartily. "Bravo, bene!" (Well done!) he commended us. Another man gave the thumbs up, "We stuck it to them!" gesture. There was more backslapping, and the partisan who had earlier produced the bread and sausage now surprised us with another bottle of wine, which we passed among us. It barely went around twice.

Bonfigli turned to me. "Vengo con lei, Signor Console," (I'll go back with you). I was glad to hear that, since I didn't have any idea where I was, or how to get back to the Bruschi's. "Give your rifle to Giorgio," he added, "so it won't weigh you down on the return trip. He'll store it with our other arms." A young partisan stepped forward and took the heavy carbine from my numb hands. I was grateful to be relieved of its weight. The lieutenant and I headed northeast along a ridge. He set a fast pace, and this time did not skirt the fields, but moved as directly as possible toward the Bruschi farm.

As we strode along, we discussed the ambush in detail, looking for ways we could improve the next one. We had been lucky this time, we agreed, because there had been very little return fire from the Germans. "But after this, Mario," I said, "we better be prepared. The Germans will undoubtedly provide more protection for their convoys from now on, and it will not be this easy for us." There will also be reprisals, I thought grimly. The Germans are not likely to take a brazen move like ours lying down. But I didn't express that thought aloud. The lieutenant knew the risks, better than I.

After about two hours of nonstop walking, Bonfigli halted. I looked around. The first streaks of dawn were beginning to lighten the sky. "Just over that hill," he pointed to his left, "you will find a cart track. Follow it to the right. After just a few minutes of walking, you will be home." He stuck out his hand, and I grabbed it and shook it. "Perhaps you should come on down to Signor Bonucci's villa on Sunday," he added. "Sunday is a good time for the officers to gather. The farmers won't be working in the fields, and the women go to mass. Everyone is out, so you won't be conspicuous." Then he added, clasping my shoulder, "You did well, tonight, Signore, very well indeed! Go home now, and rest. I will come back again around eight tonight, and together we will go down to Bonucci's and make our report to him." I thanked him, and we parted.

The Consul

What Bonfigli had said about it being safe for me to be out in the daytime on Sundays was true, I reflected, as I quickly wended my way in the direction he had indicated I should go. Sunday was a special day everywhere in Italy, even in the poorest areas, and the Sunday table reflected that. Sunday was the day for a stroll along the pathways and a visit and glass of wine with friends and neighbors. It was the day for sitting around the fire smoking one's pipe, and for everyone to do a lot of talking. Since now the city people were often out foraging for food in the countryside, as Margherita Bonucci had done, it was not unusual to see strangers around during the day, which served to cover the activities of people like us. I found the cart path and turned onto it. I could just make out the farmhouse in the distance. Weariness hit me like a blow. Like a horse scenting the barn, and warm hay waiting, I picked up my pace and quickly closed the distance to home and bed. It was just after seven when I trudged up the stairs. Seeing my tired face, Adalgisa touched my shoulder in compassion, and made clucking sounds, like a mother hen over her chick. She turned to the others. "Poor man, he is tired, and cold," she said. She began issuing orders. "Concetta—get the Signore coffee! Ruggero, a glass of wine!" Ruggero moved with alacrity to bring the flask. I smiled inwardly. Rarely did Adalgisa dare to order him around. But since it was for Il Console, well...! Young Pepe was sent to bring more wood for the fire. "Everyone got back safely," I said, knowing that was their primary concern. "I don't want to tell you much else, except that we were very successful." Ruggero beamed on hearing that. Any success of mine reflected well on him. "For your own safety, I am not telling you more," I added kindly, seeing Adalgisa's face fall in disappointment at the thought that she was not going to hear any good gossip about my night's adventures.

"I have to go out again tonight," I said quietly to Ruggero. "The lieutenant will be here around eight." He nodded. I went into the bedroom and almost instantly fell into a deep, dreamless sleep. I had made it through my first fire fight without a scratch. Moreover, we had dented a German line of communication without any cost or casualties, except some of our precious ammunition. It was a good feeling, and for me especially, it was a big boost in morale. Now I knew that, as a partisan, I could take the gaffe.

I slept through most of the day, and woke in late afternoon. At first, I was completely disoriented. I thought I was back in Gubbio. Not accustomed to being awake nights and sleeping days, my mind was in a state of total confusion. Pain lanced through my feet and licked at my legs with tongues of fire as I stood up. Bending over, I picked up one of my shoes and looked at it. It was falling apart. These hills were murder on the feet. I had to find a way to get better shoes, or boots. Dressed, I limped out to the kitchen. After a bowl of hot minestrone, I felt better, and decided to go out and walk around a bit to loosen up. Promptly at eight, Bonfigli showed up, and we headed down the hill along the tortuous route back to Bonucci's villa. As we approached it, we paused and carefully surveyed the area before going closer to the villa. I slipped behind a tree next to the terrace, Beretta in hand, while Bonfigli went to the door and knocked — three soft raps, then two sharp ones. Gigi opened the door, and escorted us to the library.

I sensed a coolness in Gigi's greeting and attitude, and that puzzled me. In the library, an unsmiling Bonucci awaited us. As he poured out three glasses of wine, he addressed Bonfigli in stern tones. "Word is already out about your 'colpo di mano' last night, and I think you should have been more cautious. We don't want to play our trump card on the first trick," he jerked his head in my direction.

I quickly interceded. "I was in the safest possible position, Bonuccio," I assured him, "and I wanted to go."

He wasn't buying it. "That may be," he retorted angrily, "but that doesn't make it a smart move by either of you! One slipup could have caused your capture, and that would have cost us dearly." Mario looked at Bonucci sheepishly, accepting the rebuke.

The Consul

Well, screw that! I wasn't going to sit around on my butt and stay hidden away until the Allies arrived. "Look Bonuccio," I said hotly, "I damned well didn't come up into the hills just to trade one hideout for another!" Mario shot me a look of gratitude. "Bonfigli was careful for my safety, too careful even, but I have to see some action sometime!" Realizing my determination on this, Bonuccio decided to drop the issue. "Well, enough of that," he said. "Now,—give me a full report. How did it go? Any problems?"

Relieved, we gladly recounted the details of the previous evening's operation. I expressed concern about our dwindling supply of ammunition. "Hand grenades. We need hand grenades, Bonuccio. With them, we'd be able to disable the vehicles quicker, and limit the amount of rifle fire we'd need." Bonfigli agreed with me. " Besides," I added, "they're light, and a helluva lot easier to conceal than rifles."

"Very well, Gualtiero," laughed Bonuccio, "I'll see that some of the lire you gave us goes to procuring grenades, Okay?"

Mario and I looked at each other with glee. "Okay!" I said.

"Now you two get out of here," he dismissed us. "You did a good job last night. Come back Sunday, and we'll make more plans. Anything else you need?" he asked me as we walked toward the front door.

"Yes, I need sturdy shoes, or boots. I can't go dancing around your rocky hillsides in these ballroom slippers much longer." I lifted a battered shoe for his inspection. Bonucci laughed. "You're right, Signore, you certainly need something stronger than that! Come, let's see what we can find for you right away." He led me down a hallway to a back room, and showed me several pairs of boots and hiking shoes. "Try these, and see if any fit," he said. "There is a good bootmaker in Pietralunga, but boots are expensive, and first we have to find leather." Digging around in what was there, I found a pair of hiking shoes that fit reasonably well, and pulled them on. We left quickly and quietly, and made good time going

136

back up to Ruggero's. For me, the boots made a huge difference. They were already broken in, and didn't bother my feet at all. "Thank you, Signore, for coming to my aid with Bonucci," said Mario, as we parted company. "I'll see you Sunday, at the villa."

Sunday dawned, and I awoke to the wind moaning at the corners of the house, trying to get in. The sun barely had the strength to pierce the thick cloud cover. Stepping outside, I scented snow in the damp, cold air. I pulled my collar close, to ward off the wind. Unsure of finding my way to the villa alone, I asked Ruggero to accompany me. He was delighted. Maintaining a brisk pace to keep warm, we made good time. Because of the cold, there weren't many people about, even though it was Sunday. We saw a few at a distance, maybe half a dozen all told, and passed one family on the path. They stared openly at me, which made me decidedly uncomfortable, as they exchanged perfunctory greetings with Ruggero. He did not introduce me. Shortly past noon, we arrived at Bonucci's villa. "Welcome, Signor Console, destroyer of German convoys," Bonuccio greeted me , smiling mischievously.

On hearing that, Ruggero shot me an admiring glance. "The others aren't here yet," continued Bonucci, "but you, my skinny friend, are in time for dinner." Throwing an arm around my shoulder, he drew me inside. Ruggero stopped in the kitchen to talk to Gigi, no doubt to discuss the "destroyer of convoys".

Bonuccio and I warmed ourselves by the fire in the library, and as we sipped our wine, he said, "Already you have gained quite a reputation, Gualtiero. The peasants are saying that the American cowboy Consul blew up and set fire to a convoy of German trucks with one well-placed rifle shot!" "Oh, no, please......" I felt my face redden, and Bonuccio laughed delightedly. "That's not true, and you know it," I said.

"Of course! But it's good for our sake, and for yours, for them to believe it ," he said, becoming serious. "Perhaps we did not play our trump card too early after all."

Crossing the room, he picked up a box, and, returning, offered me a cigar. I took one and lit it, drawing on it appreciatively. Before, I had always taken the availability of cigars for granted. Now, such small comforts, rarely available, were a great treat and a cherished pleasure. "What else can I do for you, my friend, you who have already done so much for us?" I stared at the glowing tip of my cigar for a moment before answering.

"Well," I said, as though about to make a momentous request, "the Bruschis are excellent hosts, Bonuccio, but as you know, their facilities leave a little to be desired. If you really want to do something for me, what I'd like most of all is a hot bath."

He laughed, delighted at my simple request. "That we can provide! But be careful now, you can't go around smelling too clean—that would be completely out of character for a partigiano! " He summoned Gigi. "See that Signor Console gets a hot bath immediately."

We finished our wine, smoking in companionable silence, and then, when my bath was ready, I went upstairs. I luxuriated in the hot water, trying not to think about how long it had been since I had bathed. Months, at least. Not since the hotel Brufani had I enjoyed the luxury of hot water, let alone a bath.

When I rejoined Bonucci, Bonfigli was already there, along with another Italian officer, Lieutenant Vittorio Biagiotti of Perugia. He brought us up to date on war news. I was cheered to hear that the Allies had opened another front to the south of Rome. Then Bonucci made a dramatic announcement. "With the money from Signor Console, we have procured a stock of new carbines and ammunition."

"Terrific! Where are they?" Bonfigli and I asked, almost in unison.

"For now they are safe, and no one needs to know where, yet," he replied. "We didn't dare bring them here, so we buried them nearby until we are ready to distribute them."

"You buried them?" I exclaimed, dismayed.

"Don't worry, Signor Console, " he said, reassuringly, "we doused them in olive oil first, to protect them, and wrapped them well. They'll be fine. And you'll be pleased to know we got some grenades, too." He smiled at me. "They're Italian made, not as good as the American grenades, but they'll do." I was delighted to hear that, and anxious to get my hands on them.

Soon the rest of the band arrived. Everyone reported on their activities. Bonfigli gave a straightforward, factual report of our raid on the convoy. "There have been no serious reprisals by the Germans, so far," he concluded. "Several farms were searched, and one lost its pigs and was set afire, but the family had been warned and cleared out before the Germans arrived, so no one was harmed." I was relieved to hear that. Ramsay then suggested we blow up an important railroad bridge located on the outskirts of a small town nearby. A lively discussion ensued, but we decided against that action, because it would endanger too many families. We all agreed that, to the extent possible, we would avoid endangering civilian life and property with our actions. They had already seen what the Germans could do on that score. We decided our best course of action would be to lie low for another week, to lull the Germans into thinking the ambush was made by a roving band, rather than an organized group in their midst.

Passing through the kitchen on my way out, I picked up two links of dried sausage to take to Adalgisa. After my experience at Margherita's, I was keenly aware of the burden placed upon her by an extra mouth to feed. From time to time, I gave Adalgisa money to buy things at the weekly market, but there wasn't much available any more.

On the walk back, Ruggero said little, and my thoughts turned to Nancy and Amy. I wondered what they were doing, and how they were faring. I wondered if they were still at the Vatican. Then I dwelled on Margherita and her family. Bonuccio had assured me they were well, and safe. Did they have enough food? I wondered. Was Lucia's cough any better? Was Valentina risking her safety in helping the partigiani? There were no answers, and not likely to be any for awhile, unless I heard from Manfred. I wondered how he was doing, too. I kept my thoughts from veering to my own family back home. That would only lead to self-pity and depression, and I had to keep my wits about me and focused on what I was doing in San Faustino.

Mondays were market days in Pietralunga. Adalgisa gathered together a crock of homemade soup, a sack of cabbages, and a bundle of outgrown baby clothes for Ruggero and me to take to market and sell. It was their only source of cash income in winter. When we reached the town, Ruggero directed me to the bootmaker Bonucci had mentioned, and he went on to the marketplace to display his paltry wares.

The bootmaker was pleased to welcome someone interested in buying new boots, instead of having old ones patched and mended. I described the kind of boots I wanted. He gave a low whistle, then sighed and shook his head. "Even if you could pay the price for such boots," he said, looking at me doubtfully, "I don't think I could find enough leather for such a job. And the price Signore, would be high, very high."

"Well," I said with a sigh, "I'm a 'sfollato, and my funds are limited, so please get the best price you can, the lowest. But I need some boots. I'm sheltering with a family in the country, and I'll check with you again in a week." "Sí, Signore," he said. "I will do my best to find the leather to make you the boots you want."

I searched out Ruggero at the market. He had sold the crock of soup for a few coins and exchanged the cabbages for a rusty crosscut saw. The baby clothes had brought twice what Adalgisa expected. I gave Ruggero some lire and told him to buy Adalgisa and the children a small present. He couldn't countenance such extravagance, and started to protest. It wasn't Christmas, after all. But I insisted. "Get some more wine for us, too." I added. That brought a big smile, and he thanked me warmly and went off to accomplish his mission. I wandered around the market. There was little or nothing to buy. By eleven o'clock, everything was gone, so when Ruggero returned with his purchases, we headed back up to Fontanella.

On the walk back, Ruggero assured me I could trust Ugo the bootmaker not to reveal anything about me. "You will have fine boots, Signore, when he finds the leather," he said confidently. I wondered what, if anything, Ruggero had told Ugo about me.

During the rest of the week, we tramped around the local area. I wanted the farmers to know my face, and become used to seeing me around. A time might come when I'd need one or another of them to shelter me. I began to know my way around and recognize landmarks. Wherever we went, we were given a warm welcome and a place at the table. Invariably, we were offered the conventional glass of wine, and, after Ruggero had spoken to the host, usually a second glass. Not only that, but I was accorded rapt, deferential attention that was well beyond normal politeness. "Ruggero, we're getting a lot of wine, and a lot of attention, from these poor farmers on a weekday. You're not telling them who I am, are you?"

"Oh, no, Signore!" Ruggero protested, self-righteously. "Always I protect your name." We walked on for awhile in silence. I was getting used to the long periods between Ruggero's sorties into speech.

I decided to rephrase my question. "Well, everyone has sure been friendly and very respectful. I wonder why they treat me so well after you have talked to them?"

"That is because they have great respect for you, Signor Console. They have never before met an important man who works for Signor Presidente Roosabelta." So that was it! My instructions to Ruggero had been to never use my real name, or my title. I had not anticipated, and therefore not thought to prohibit, this kind of circumlocution. Even the folks in this remote area knew who "Presidente Roosabelta" was. I realized I'd have to learn to live with it, and trust Ruggero and his neighboring farm friends to keep my secret.

Several days later, the Band again attempted a hit on a German convoy, but this time we drew a blank. We waited most of the night, but no vehicles showed up at the ambush point. Disappointed, we trudged wearily home.

Sunday came again, and Ruggero and I headed for the usual meeting at the Bonucci villa. Barely a few hundred meters from San Faustino, a peasant ran out into the road and flagged us down. "No, no, go no farther! Go back!" he called urgently. "What is it? What's happened?" I asked, my skin prickling in alarm.

"Fascisti! A gang of them! They have broken into the villa! You must not go there!"

Damn. Whipping around, we checked the road behind us. There was no one in sight. Scrambling in haste over a low stone wall along the side of the path, we walked as quickly as we could across the open field to a stand of bush, then broke for the trees that led toward the track back to Fontanella. I was winded by the time I felt we had put enough distance between us and the villa to slow to a walk again. My heart was pounding so hard it felt as if it would burst from my chest. I was terrified for Bonucci, Gigi and the others. "This is a helluva fix," I gasped to Ruggero. "How do we get word to the others?" His eloquent shrug gave the answer. If I didn't know, how could he possibly know? Well, I decided, I might as well be patient. The peasant pipeline will get the news out faster than we could anyway. There was nothing to do but return home.

Two days crawled by. Ruggero and I sat and stared at each other, jumping at every sound. Assunta, the girl who lived at the foot of the hill, was alerted to keep a sharp eye out, and to come running to warn us if anyone approached the area. We sent Concetta and Pepe down the road in turns to keep watch, and told them to come running immediately if they saw Assunta coming.

More than that, we could not do. Restlessly, I paced the

concave bowl of the room, down, then up, then down, over and over again. What in the name of hell could have happened? Who betrayed Bonucci? Then, trying to calm myself, I thought, maybe it was just a bunch of thugs—vandals. No, the peasant had been clear. "Fascisti," he had said. Damn and double damn!

Finally, at dusk on the third day, a young boy showed up. The news he spilled out numbed me to the bone. Eight Fascist militiamen had raided the villa that Sunday, thoroughly ransacking it. They were definitely looking for something. I grabbed the youth by the shoulder and questioned him closely. "Did they find anything, that you know of, that would incriminate Bonucci, or any of the Band?" Tears sprang to his eyes. He was clearly frightened. "No, Signore," he replied, "not that day, but there is more."

I sighed. I was afraid of what I was going to hear. "What is your name? " I asked, giving him, and myself, a moment to collect ourselves. Nervously, he twisted his cap in his thin fingers.

"Angelo, Signore." "All right, Angelo," I said, as quietly as I could, to reassure him. "Tell me everything you know. Did you see this yourself?" "No Signore, I was not there, but was sent here to bring you the message of what happened."

He proceeded with his tale. "The Fascisti, they brought a cart with them on Sunday, and they smashed a lot of furniture. "They took all the food in the villa, and put it in the cart and took it away." That news was a blow. Damn! All the effort and expense in acquiring our stockpile of rations — wheat, flour, sausages, wine and olive oil — all down the drain! But the worst news was yet to come.

"That was all they did that day. But Signor Bonucci heard about it and was very angry, and the next day he came to the villa, to inspect the damage himself. He was only there a few minutes, when four young men knocked on the door. They must have been watching for him." "Militia?" I broke in. "No, they were dressed in civilian clothes," he replied. "But they were after Signor Bonucci, no one else, because they let

143

two other officers of the Band come to the villa and leave, before Signor Bonucci got there, and they did not come out of hiding, or bother them."

"What happened to Bonucci?" I demanded urgently. The tears spilled over and slid down the youth's cheeks. "They captured him and took him away, Signore!" I sat back, finally letting my breath out. Christ! This was disaster! "How the hell did that happen?" I demanded. "Why wasn't he warned? Where in the name of God was Gigi? Where were the others?"

"I do not know, Signore," sobbed Angelo miserably. "The minute Signor Bonucci opened the door of the villa, the men whipped out submachine guns and hustled him away, without even his coat. By the time the two partigiani officers got the word, it was too late to help him!"

I calmed the young man down, and thanked him for coming to inform us of what happened. Adalgisa served him some hot soup, which he gulped down gratefully, and, having delivered his staggering news, he left.

I sat in my chair by the fire, stunned and morose. No one spoke. Bonuccio Bonucci, captured! It didn't seem possible. I tried not to think of the implications for the Band of San Faustino, let alone for myself. I worried hopelessly, and helplessly, about what was happening to my friend. My mind flinched at the prospect of what they'd do to him to get information. Where the hell were Gigi and the others? Someone had betrayed Bonucci, I was convinced of that. But who? Everyone for miles around loved him, and respected him. I got up and paced the floor in fury and anguish, smacking my fist into my hand. Ruggero silently poured us each a glass of wine, giving me a sad-eyed look as he handed me mine. Adalgisa and the children had quietly disappeared into the other room. Ruggero touched my shoulder briefly in quiet sympathy, then moved away to sit at the table. He too, was shocked, and lost in thought. If the Fascists managed to torture enough information out of Bonucci, none of us were safe.

Less than an hour later, a second messenger arrived. It was Enrico, a member of the Band, whom I had seen before at the villa. "Bonucci has been imprisoned in Perugia," he informed me tersely, obviously worried. "Paciotti betrayed us. Colonel Guerrizzi was tipped off in the nick of time, and has disappeared, but we have heard that his wife and son have been arrested and thrown into prison." Hell and damnation! Disaster upon disaster!

Enrico left, and I flopped disconsolately into a chair at the table, staring at the dying embers of the fire. We had lost our two top men, all our provisions, and our military advantage, in one quick move! I slammed the flat of my hand down on the table, causing Ruggero to jump in surprise. "No, by God!" I said loudly, in English. "We've still got men, and we've still got a cache of weapons somewhere! I'll damn well find out where, and we'll continue. And I'll damn well make whoever betrayed Bonucci pay for this, if it's the last thing I do!" But I knew there was little or nothing I could do to save my friend Bonucci from his fate at the hands of the Fascists and the Germans. It was already too late for that. God help him. God help all of us.

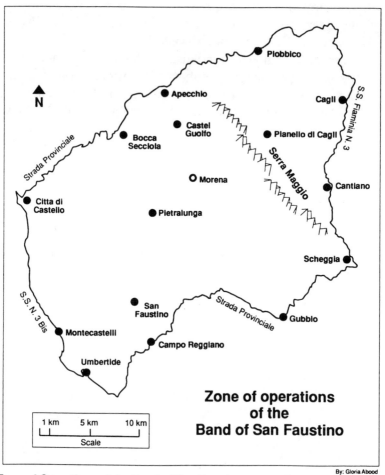

Zone of Operations of the Band of San Faustino

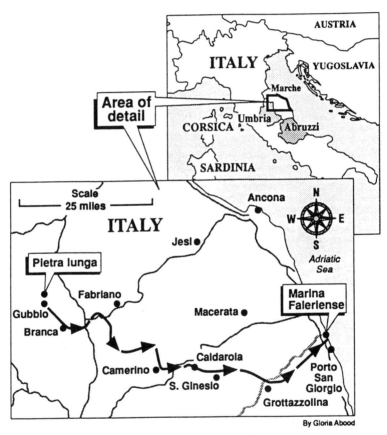

Italy, with detail of Ancona Macerata area, showing Orebaugh-Marioli itinerary

Walter W. Orebaugh

Nancy Charrier

Amy Houlden

Manfred Metzger

Manfred Metzger

Margerita Bonucci and family:
Vittoria, Valentina, Lucia, and
Franco (Francesco).

Valentina and Franco Bonucci, 1942

False identity card carried by Orebaugh when traveling in enemy territory.

San Faustino

Typical farmer's cart

The shed at the Rossi farm in Grottazzolina

Chapter 7

From Diplomat to Guerrilla Leader

The following morning was bitterly cold and overcast. The dark gray of the sky matched my mood. I told Ruggero to go seek out Bonfigli, or find out any information he could about Bonfigli's whereabouts. I feared that perhaps Bonfigli and Captain Pierangeli had also been arrested. After Ruggero left, I spent most of the morning watching the approaches to Fontanella through a narrow gap in the shuttered window.

Up to now, even in my bleakest moments in Gubbio, and in Margherita's apartment in Perugia, I had believed my diplomatic status might help me some in the event of discovery. Watching for the Fascisti to come after me in this hardscrabble, windswept farm hideout in the middle of nowhere, I suddenly felt terribly alone. I was a stranger in a strange land. The U.S. State Department didn't mean a damn thing here. And forget the diplomatic passport being any protection. I knew that only my own ability and determination could help me now. How the hell will you get out of this one, Walt? I asked myself grimly. I didn't have a good answer. A lot of luck, maybe. And the Fifth and Eighth Armies, if they got their asses up here fast enough! But they were stuck in the mud somewhere far to the south, and not likely to arrive in time.

I paced helplessly, puffing furiously on one of my few remaining cigars. It was two in the afternoon before Ruggero returned. Given the situation, the news he brought was good. Bonfigli was safe, and he knew about Bonucci's arrest and Guerrizzi's escape. Bonfigli wanted me to meet with him that night, at the house where he was staying. I decided that on the way, Ruggero and I would stop in Pietralunga and listen to the news on the radio at the home of Giovanni Marioli, one of Ruggero's friends.

Snow flurries began late that afternoon, and I worried that we would leave a trail. But the wind had blown the path clear of snow by the time we set off for Pietralunga. We took extra precautions not to be seen, and detoured around farmhouses, which doubled the time it took us to reach Giovanni's house.

Motioning us to follow him into the unheated bedroom, he crawled under the bed and retrieved the radio from its hiding place under the floorboards. After about a half hour of fiddling with the dials, we finally picked up the BBC in Italian, and got about nine minutes of fairly clear news before the signal became garbled. Sicily, Sardinia and southern Italy had been returned to the control of the civilian Badoglio government, we learned. The Germans were making a major effort to throw back the Allied forces at Anzio. The Allies had bombed the Abbey of Monte Cassino, which was occupied by the Germans. On hearing that, I looked keenly at Ruggero and his friend. Neither showed any overt emotion, but I knew they must be privately grieving at the sad news about the historic old Abbey. Then I suddenly realized that, being isolated and untraveled peasants with little or no education, they knew nothing about the Abbey. The broadcaster exhorted listeners to "support the Allies, resist the enemy in every way possible, and, above all, support the Badoglio government."

We slipped out into the wintry darkness again and took off, following the directions Ruggero had gotten from Bonfigli. At one point, taking a wrong turn, we blundered ankle deep into a stinking, half-frozen pigsty! Muttering apologies, Ruggero got us back on track, and on up to the farmhouse where Bonfigli was quartered. An old crone answered my muffled knock. No lamps were lit, but standing in front of the fireplace was Bonfigli, and, to my relief and satisfaction, standing next to him was Captain Pierangeli, now our highest ranking officer.

We sat before the fire with our glasses of wine. Ruggero had tactfully disappeared. Bonfigli broke the unhappy silence. "I'm no hero, but I'll be damned if I'm going to turn my back on all we've worked for, and all we've done. I say let's take our lumps, regroup, and carry on. I know that's what Bonucci would have wanted." Tears filled his eyes, and he looked away briefly, clearing his throat, then quickly brought himself back under control. "You have a point, Mario, and I agree with you," said Pierangeli, "but we must take into account what has happened. We didn't have the proper security, or the proper safeguards in place. This shouldn't have happened! Bonucci, and we, took too much for granted! We can't let that happen again. But I agree—we must carry on with our mission. We'll know now to be more careful about protecting ourselves as much as we can." I spoke up for the first time. "We need to get that word out to the rank and file, at once! They need to be reassured. We can't let them think, even for a moment, that the movement, and the Band, is leaderless and in danger of disbanding." We prepared a message to be delivered to all components of the movement the next day. It would be signed by Captain Pierangeli as commander.

I brought up subject of the cache of weapons. We exchanged all the information we had about it, which was almost nothing. We agreed that Bonucci had said that he and Colonel Guerrizzi had overseen one peasant dig the hole, douse the cache with olive oil, then wrap and bury the weapons, and cover the hiding place over to disguise it well. We also agreed that we could think of only one peasant Bonucci would have trusted to do that—Gigi. Since I lived the closest to San Faustino, we decided that I should be the one to question Gigi about the location of the weapons.

On the long walk back, I realized that not only did I no longer enjoy diplomatic status, I no longer thought in diplomatic terms! My environment had forced changes in my ethics and my behavior. The guerrilla world I lived in now allowed little room for the practice of striped-pants diplomacy. It was a rough, dog-eat-dog existence, albeit one that was marvelously softened by the compassion of the peasants. The next morning, I made an effort to brush my teeth—having failed to practice that civilized nicety for more days than I cared to think about. After forcing down a mug of the ersatz coffee, I gave Ruggero explicit instructions to order Gigi, invoking the authority of the CLN if necessary — to come to the Bruschi farmhouse for a meeting with me.

Late the afternoon of the seventeenth, Ruggero returned, with a reluctant Gigi in tow. As he drank his ritual glass of wine, I watched Gigi carefully, trying to detect any change in his behavior. He acted no differently than he always had. "These are bad times for all of us, Giuseppe," I began. Giuseppe nodded solemnly, but volunteered nothing. "Not just for you," I went on, "but for all of us. Signor Bonucci was doing a great job for us. You know that, don't you?" Another nod. More silence. "Now we must close ranks and all work together, Giuseppe. You and I." Giuseppe's eyes wavered. I hurriedly added, "I'm not asking you to work for me. You are still Bonucci's man." He nodded again, relieved. "But we need your help," I went on, "Bonucci trusted you with important information. You know things that can help us." Giuseppe looked quizzical at that, but nodded again.

I wanted him to say something, anything, but I knew he was a taciturn man by nature, and now would be even more guarded in his speech than ever. In a way, I understood how he must be feeling. His beloved Bonucci had been arrested. No one knew his fate. Every one of us was in danger.

"Giuseppe, before the Fascisti took him away, Signor Bonucci told me and Lieutenant Bonfigli, about a cache of arms he had buried somewhere. But he didn't tell us where. We need those arms now, so we can continue operations. What can you tell me about them?" Giuseppe turned half away from me. "I can tell you nothing," he stated flatly, without emotion. I felt his reaction—the turning away and the terseness of his declaration—meant he knew something and was hiding that knowledge. If Bonucci had instructed Giuseppe not to say anything to anyone about the weapons, Giuseppe would take those directions literally, I knew. He would not tell me, even though I was Il Console. I adopted a sterner, no nonsense tone. "Surely you understand how important this is! We can't fight the Fascisti and the Germans without those guns! Now please, tell me where the weapons are, Gigi." At my use of the familiar nickname, Giuseppe flashed me a look that warned me against taking that tack again. I repeated the question, addressing him more formally. "I do not know, Signor Console," he replied gravely. "I cannot help you, because I do not know where the weapons are."

Giuseppe was seated at the wooden table. I was standing. I tried reasoning. I tried intimidation, towering over him. He steadfastly maintained he did not know where the weapons were hidden, and, in fact, had never seen them. Exasperated, frustrated, I shouted, "I'll have you court-martialled!"

"But Signore, I am not in the army," he muttered stolidly.

"You are now!" I snapped, infuriated at his failure to disclose the location of our badly needed arms. I whipped out my Beretta and held it to his temple. "Now, damn it, tell me where those arms are or I'll kill you!" By damn, I'd make this man take me seriously! They weren't dealing with any soft city slicker, and they'd find that out quickly! Giuseppe neither moved nor spoke. There was fear in his eyes, but no duplicity. He just looked at me, clear-eyed, with an unwavering stare.

Suddenly, I felt a wave of nausea and self-disgust. "What am I doing?" I asked myself, half aloud. I couldn't believe I had been ready to pull the trigger and kill Giuseppe! Bonuccio's Gigi. I tucked the gun into my waistband. "I believe you, Giuseppe. I'm sorry. Go now." "Sí, Signor Console." Our eyes met. "If I can find the weapons for you, I will," he said sincerely, and left.

I was still shaking when I went to bed. Would I really have killed that poor, simple peasant? I knew in my heart that

I wouldn't have hesitated to pull the trigger if there had been a hint that Gigi was lying to me. I realized there was a side to my nature that had never been revealed, even to me. I kept to myself on Friday and Saturday, wrestling with my conscience and my sense of duty, sleeping little. Ultimately, I made myself recognize that I had made the right decision. I had not pulled the trigger. I slept better Saturday night.

On Sunday, I set out alone for the presidio at Morena, where our staff meeting would be held. When I got there, most of the other officers were already there. Captain Pierangeli sat at the head of the old dining room table. I looked around. Only Ramsay was there from the contingent of British officers in the area. He told me that the American pilot Joe Withers, whom I had liked so much, had left our area to head southward toward the Allied lines. Pierangeli set a businesslike tone, which instilled confidence in everyone around him. Halfway through the meeting, I gave my report about the weapons and my experience with Gigi. There was palpable disappointment. However, no one questioned Giuseppe's integrity. Bonfigli said he would conduct an extensive search for the weapons. We agreed we could probably equip fifty or sixty men for combat, with what we still had, but fights would have to be of short duration, therefore almost a sure thing, until we could find the weapons that had been hidden.

"Not a shot can be fired that is not absolutely necessary," said Pierangeli. "No recruits will be accepted into the Band unless they have a weapon, and ammunition for it." We moved on to a procedure for requisitioning food to replenish our lost stores. To feed the one hundred twenty men we already had was our number one priority.

Although the peasants were, for the most part, more than willing to help, many of them were just not able. Family and guests were already overtaxing their sparse larders. Even in normal times, and these times certainly weren't normal, the average peasant household included several generations.

"Any news of Bonucci?" I asked Bonfigli. "Only that he

has not been publicly executed, and we have heard that he is still alive, but in terrible shape," he said, his eyes reflecting his deep sorrow. My stomach clenched at hearing that. So they were brutally torturing him for information. The discussion about arms and ammunition continued. Lieutenant Soldatini suggested we attack convoys and strip them after they were shot up. We disapproved that as too dangerous, and requiring too much of our scarce ammunition to accomplish. Remeccioni spoke up. "There is a barracks and armory at the garrison at Scheggia, and the force there has been reduced. They must have guns and ammunition."

"Yes, I think a raid on Scheggia would be a good idea," said Bonfigli, "Sunday night, because the guards are more lax then."

I left the meeting feeling more optimistic than when I arrived. At least we were doing something! The will to go on was still there. As I walked back to the Bruschi farmhouse, I rubbed my shoulder, which had been paining me a lot lately.

I'd have felt a lot better if the details in a message being decoded at that moment at the State Department in Washington had been even close to the truth: "Orebaugh now with group approximately 1800 partisans, 80 kilometers from Rome", the cablegram read. Talk about communications screwups!

The next morning, around nine-thirty, I spied a solitary figure coming up the cartpath. Peering through the frost on the window, I could not make out who it was, though his step and cadence seemed familiar. I checked the Beretta, then looked once more before deciding to head for the escape ladder at the back bedroom window. I recognized the slender, angular form and military bearing of Bonfigli. Strange. He had never before come so early, nor in broad daylight. I went outside and hurried down the stairs to greet him.

"Ah, do I have a surprise for you, my friend," he exclaimed, stamping the wet snow from his boots. "Quick, upstairs!" He looked at me slyly and said, "A good Commandante would

offer a poor 'Tenente some real coffee on a morning like this."
"Ma che! Real coffee!" I replied. "Who has real coffee around
here? You're welcome to this brew if you want some, and it's
poor enough, even for imitation!"

"Ah, but look here!" Bonfigli whipped a foil packet from
his jacket pocket, and held it out to me, grinning. "A requisition
from a most willing citizen of Umbertide, who happened, by
the way, to speak German—once too often." I realized that
there must have been a reprisal raid against a German
sympathizer.

Exclaiming in delight, Adalgisa snatched up the packet of
coffee and immediately began dividing it up, to stretch it out
as much as possible. She carefully brewed two cups of
delicious, undiluted coffee for Bonfigli and me, then carefully
wrapped the used grounds to mix with roasted barley
grindings later. Favoring us with a rare smile, she brought us
brimming cups, then shooed the family out to do chores in the
yard.

When they were gone, Bonfigli drew another bulky
package from inside his jacket. "And now, for my second
surprise!" Tearing off the wrapping, he exposed a German
Mauser machine pistol! I gasped and gave a low whistle of
appreciation. Bonfigli smiled happily. Reverently, I lifted it,
turning it over and over in my hands. "Wow! Where did you
get this beauty?" I asked. "It's for you, Signor Console," he
said. "Should make a hell of a noise. Another present from
the man with the coffee. Check it over. Tonight you will need
it."

Picking the gun up again, I asked, "Who is going?" I
didn't need to ask where. It had to be the barracks at
Scheggia.

"Well," he said with a twinkle, "there will be you and me.
We will be, how you say, 'buddies'."

"That's crazy, Mario!" I protested. "Two of us can't take
that on, even with a Mauser!"

He laughed, enjoying his little joke. "No, no, of course
not, my friend. There will be twenty of us. Here, sit down and

look." He produced a sketch of the area around the barracks. "We figure there are about fifteen Fascist militia left there. We'll get in early, surprise them, and try to take a vehicle too, if possible, to carry off whatever booty we 'liberate' from them." He chuckled at the prospect. He was certainly in a fine mood this morning! Turning the paper over, he drew a sketch of what he thought the inside of the barracks should look like. Then he gave me directions to a house where we'd meet between seven and eight that night.

I held out my hand. "Good luck, Mario, and thanks! See you tonight." He brightened visibly at my use of his first name. "So long, buddy," he replied, in English.

I had to smile at that. I walked with him down the stairs, then slipped into the barn area on the ground floor and practiced loading and unloading the Mauser until I could do it with my eyes shut. It would be dark, and I didn't want to foul up. Nineteen other lives might depend on me. Back upstairs, in the bedroom, I checked and rechecked the Beretta, too.

I told Ruggero that I would be gone for a couple of days, and at lunch Adalgisa filled my plate with an extra large serving of pasta. When I was ready to leave, she pressed a fragrant package of bread, cheese and sausage into my hands. Making the sign of the cross, she murmured the ritual "Dio sia con te" (God be with you) as I stepped out the door.

Walking along, I noticed that the afternoon's pale sun had warmed the air slightly, and yesterday's heavy snow was starting to melt. The shiny icicles that descended from the bare branches of the trees and bushes dripped globules of water in steady rhythm. Damn! A thaw, even a brief one, meant the path would be sticky mud beneath the snow. The temperature was sure to drop again after dark, and the mud would freeze, making the going even rougher. I tried to remember what it was like to ride in a car, instead of struggling interminable miles on foot, in the worst weather, over impossible terrain.

Around sunset, I took out the package and ate some of the

meat and cheese. I got up from the cold rock on which I'd seated myself to consume my meal and continued on, shivering from the cold. It was after dark, around seven-fifteen, and I had been walking more than six hours when I passed the cluster of three houses Bonfigli had described. I made a turn, and there, silhouetted against the horizon, faintly back-lighted by the moon, stood the farmhouse where we were to meet. The path that led up to it was at least eight hundred yards long, and the last eighty yards rose so steeply I had to crawl up on all fours. Was there no end to this misery? Suddenly, to my right, the ferocious barking of a dog shattered the silence. My hair stood on end.

"This way, Signore" a strange voice whispered, out of the black silence. "Around here." Groping my way blindly, I followed the sound of the voice. I glimpsed a shadow in movement, but it was too dark to see who it was. We skirted the house, and slipped into a low, lean-to type shed. Mario was there, in the pitch blackness, with four other partisans. We exchanged quiet greetings, then left in pairs, Mario and I last. Cutting across a field behind the ridge, we turned down into Scheggia. It was only another couple of kilometers, but it was torture for me.

We backed up against the tightly adjoined buildings, and, weapons drawn, ducked swiftly and silently from dark doorway to dark doorway. I prayed that no one had dogs. A thick blanket of clouds shrouded the moon, and there were no lights anywhere in the town. Even at Scheggia Barracks, the blackout was strictly enforced.

Bonfigli and I crouched behind the ornate central fountain and waited for Pepe to begin the action. According to what Mario had told me earlier, one of the militiamen from the barracks had been captured by the Band a few weeks back and relieved of his orders, his tunic, and his weapon. Now Pepe, with a substitute name on the orders, strolled casually across the square to the massive wrought-iron gate leading to the military compound, his carbine slung across his shoulder, Fascist style.

Barely daring to breathe, I checked my pistol again, then, as my eyes became more accustomed to the inky blackness, I quickly surveyed the scene around me. The escape route was directly behind me. Mario had positioned me with care. A row of tall trees bordered one side of the piazza. Several of our men were behind those trees, stationed fifty to sixty yards apart. On the opposite side, roughly seventy-five yards across from the trees, the recessed doorways of dark storefronts provided cover for more partisans. I judged the gate of the compound to be about eighty yards from me. From there, it was only a short distance across a courtyard to the barracks itself. We could see six shuttered windows across the front, on the second floor. The wall and gate hid the first floor from view. I wondered about back entrances. If the Fascists were able to get out the back, then come into the square by way of the side street, we wouldn't get a clear line of fire at them. Suddenly, our position at the fountain, right in the middle of the square, seemed extremely exposed. Fortunately, the fountain itself provided substantial cover.

Bonfigli nudged me. Pepe had reached the gate. Everyone tensed for the rush. He reached up and pulled the bell rope. A few seconds later, the shutters on one of the second floor windows opened, and a soldier peered out. Pepe stepped back enough to be seen. He waved his papers at the man in the window.

"Che volete?" (What do you want?) came the voice from above. Pepe coolly shouted his false name and a set of numbers from the orders. "Aprite, per favore!" (Open up!) he shouted. "I'm assigned here!" The shutters slammed closed. It's going to work, I thought. We relaxed a bit.

Suddenly, we heard muffled shouting and running, inside the garrison. What the hell? Then — ominous silence. God, what I wouldn't give for a grenade right now, I thought. I glanced over at Bonfigli, who was watching the building intently. "They know something is up," he muttered. "But they don't know how many of us there are."

"What now?" I whispered.

"Let's shoot them up some—maybe they'll surrender," he replied. I nodded. Bonfigli was already up on one knee, shouldering his rifle. He aimed at the window where the soldier had appeared, and fired. Instantly, a fusillade of rifle fire poured from both sides of the piazza into the barracks.

A woman's scream, from somewhere off to my left, shattered the tranquility of the town. Then the dogs began. A baby howled. All around us, shutters slammed shut. More babies cried, more women started screaming, as we continued to fire into the barracks. It was pandemonium. The militiamen had begun firing back at us. They hadn't panicked at all. They watched for the flash from our guns, and when they had picked a target, they fired.

"Okay! Your turn, buddy!" shouted Bonfigli, above the melee. I propped the automatic machine-pistol on the rim of the fountain and squeezed the trigger. Its loud, staccato rapping startled me, but it had less recoil than I expected. My first burst was aimed low, along the wall. Then I raised up, and to the left, raking a path across the windows on the second floor with my next round. The firing from the barracks all but ceased.

"Let's go! Out!" shouted Mario, and waved toward the church.

Pepe broke from his cover at a full run to join us. Two-thirds of the way across, he lunged forward, and fell to the ground, hit. Mario shoved his carbine over to me. "Cover me!" and he was off, running in a crouch toward Pepe. "The hell with that!" I snarled, kicking aside the carbine, and rammed the second canister home in the Mauser. I covered him with a series of bursts, ten to twenty rounds each, aimed at the windows. A new hubbub of screams and shouts erupted all around me. Scheggia must think that the whole war is being fought on its very doorsteps! Bonfigli had snatched Pepe up and carried him to safety behind the trees. I dropped down behind the cover of the fountain, and slid Mario's carbine over to the nearest partisan. "Take this!" I hissed, "And when I start firing, run like hell for the trees!"

Both men nodded. Shots began again from the windows of the barracks. I pulled back, crouching, and turned to the others, "Ready?"

"Si."

"Now!" They bolted to the left, heading for the trees, and I jumped out from behind the fountain to the right and fired a burst at the windows. Then, I broke for the storefronts to my right. Halfway across the square, I dropped to one knee, swung sideways, and sent off another burst. Then I ran like hell for cover. I saw stone chips flying behind me and thought the Fascists had me targeted, but it was the partisans covering me. I reached an alley behind the church and hustled down it.

"Commandante, is that you?" a voice queried from the shadows.

"Yes!"

"The 'Tenente is down that way, with Pepe." He pointed with his rifle.

I found Bonfigli, with two other partisans, tending to Pepe's wound. "How are you doing, Pepe?" I was gasping for breath and dripping with sweat.

"Ah, Signor Commandante, I'm afraid I have disappointed you," whispered Pepe genially. "I was hoping to play my part well enough to go to your Hollywood!"

"He'll make it all right," said Bonfigli, "but he's going to go around with a big hole in his shoulder for awhile."

I reached down and patted Pepe on the forehead. "You did fine, Pepe, just fine. You had the hardest job of all."

He grinned up at me, teeth flashing white in the darkness. "You didn't do so bad yourself, Signore," he said.

"Nor you, Mario," I said, grasping Bonfigli's shoulder warmly. "That was a brave thing you did. I don't know if I managed to hit anything worthwhile with this thing or not." I held up the Mauser.

"Maybe not," said Bonfigli, "but like I told you, it makes one helluva racket! I bet there is no one in that barracks with constipation tonight! Or in this town!"

He jumped up, giving the signal to pull out, then turned to me, as I slowly rose to my feet. "Or would you rather stay? We'll rent an apartment in the town for you," he jibed.

"No, I thought we were hanging around so your lady friend—the one who was doing all the screaming—could catch up to you," I replied with a chuckle, slapping him lightly on the back.

Everything was quiet. The town seemed to be locked up tight. We withdrew in stages, since there didn't seem to be any danger we'd be attacked, or followed. "Be careful," Bonfigli warned the men, "and don't get caught with that long thing sticking out of your pants." Despite the pun, his warning was sincere, for come daybreak, we were in danger of being seen on the move, toting our rifles and pistols, which would be difficult to conceal.

As each one left, they shook my hand. They were still not at ease in my presence, but their "Arrivederci, à presto, Signor Commandante" (Goodbye, see you soon, Commander) was a heartfelt one. Each gave a lingering look of respect to the machine pistol in my hand.

Bonfigli and I set off, with two partisans helping Pepe a short distance behind us. Two others remained a half mile behind them to cover us in case anyone from Scheggia tried to follow us. We stopped frequently to rest because Pepe tired quickly. He had lost a lot of blood. We dug through our pockets, and managed to come up with a few bits of meat and bread for him to eat.

At about 2 a.m. we arrived at a fairly sizable farmhouse. Compared to most of the others, this one looked downright prosperous. "They raise horses for meat," said Bonfigli. He called out, "Partigiani!" In moments, the door swung open. A very attractive woman, probably in her late thirties, stood there. She was not work-worn, like most peasant women, and had a slender figure, masses of dark curls, and eyes that danced in the firelight. She led us into a moderately comfortable parlor, then stepped into the next room, leaving us alone for a moment.

I cocked an eyebrow at Mario. "And who is this?" I asked. "She's no contadina, that's for sure!"

"She's a nurse," whispered Bonfigli, "a real one." The other two partisans arrived with a white-faced, bleeding Pepe. The woman stirred up the fire, and set water on to boil. Bonfigli poured several glasses of wine. "Now," he said to Pepe, "this is going to hurt worse than your bullet wound."

Pepe stared at him, puzzled. "Why is that, Signor 'Tenente?"

"Because," laughed Bonfigli, "even though you were the bravest man there tonight, you aren't going to get any wine."

Pepe didn't care. That he had our approval was what was important. He couldn't have been a day over seventeen. One day, he would brag about his wound to some beautiful young signorina, and she would tenderly touch the scar.

The nurse shooed all of us, except Pepe, into the kitchen. There, an old peasant woman stood sentinel over the stove, stirring a pot of stew. The aroma was heavenly, and hunger leaped like a flame in our bellies. She handed another flask of wine to Bonfigli, and he refilled our glasses. I marveled that we could feel so lighthearted. Just coming through with our skins whole was reason enough to celebrate. The raid itself had been a complete failure. I wondered if we had enough ammunition to attempt another one. Probably not. One of the other partisans asked Bonfigli where we were.

"About five miles north of Gubbio," replied Bonfigli. The young man thought for a moment, then spoke. "Signor 'Tenente, my cousin lives very close to here. He told me about a factory near his farm. Every day, trucks arrive and take away whatever it is that is made there. He said there are no soldiers at the factory, but there are military markings on the trucks."

Bonfigli and I exchanged glances. Military trucks meant military goods. We turned to young Italo. "Could you find this place? Or could your cousin take us there?" I asked.

"Certainly, Signore," he said, "it cannot possibly be more than a kilometer from here."

Bonfigli and I went into a huddle. Whatever was being produced, we agreed, it was part of the enemy war effort. We hadn't gotten anything from the barracks, so why not see what we could get at this factory? If we succeeded, we wouldn't go back empty-handed. The men could be rounded up quickly—they were sheltered in nearby farmhouses. We decided to go for it, at nightfall, after we'd had time to rest and regroup.

Bonfigli went back to Italo. "What you told us is about to cost you whatever sleep you might have gotten tonight. Do you know your way around here?"

"Sí, Signor 'Tenente," he replied.

"Good! Then go and round up our men. It will probably take you all night. Tell them I want them to meet me here, in the stables. You will need to get word to them before morning, or they'll be gone."

"Sí, Signor 'Tenente."

Bonfigli and I finished our meal and went wearily upstairs to bed.

"Sleep as well as you can, my friend," said Bonfigli, collapsing on one side of the double bed, "this mission is not over, and we are far from being counted out yet!"

I didn't fall easily into sleep. Bonfigli's snoring reminded me of Amy, and I thought of her, and Nancy, and our days in the Bonucci apartment I worried about our ammunition supply. I wondered, for the thousandth time, where Bonuccio Bonucci might have buried our precious cache of weapons and grenades. Then I thought about Bonuccio, the man who had come to be my friend. Was he still alive, I wondered? Could he have possibly survived? Eventually, I drifted into sleep, to the tune of Mario Bonfigli's deep snores.

It was late afternoon when the old woman came to wake us. Pepe, his wound cleaned and dressed, had already been moved to a safe location. Our hostess brought us coffee, better than anything I'd had in awhile. It was already five o'clock, time to get busy and get on with the new plan — it was still a long, tiring hike back to the Bruschi farm.

The nurse reappeared. "Would you like some real English tea, and a cigar?" She asked, with a smile.

I looked at Mario. "Hey...." I said, "To hell with the war! Let's just stay right here and live like big shots!"

"Ah, yes, that would be wonderful," replied Bonfigli, "but, my friend, I don't think you really want to be here when the big shot who owns these cigars returns." He raised his eyebrows, and the nurse laughed softly.

A little later, she served us dinner. Amazing what a difference a bit of influence could make in one's diet! The sausage was meaty, and not mostly fat. The pasta was almost as good, and as white, as pre-war. Our hostess apologized for the lack of a table covering. Table covering indeed! If only she could see my usual mealtimes--snatched on the run, or at the Bruschi's poor table. She had probably used whatever tablecloth she owned to bind Pepe's, or some other partisan's, wounds.

As I spooned up my stew, I thought of Lucia, and the scarf she'd made me. Amazing, these women. They gave all, uncomplainingly, stinted nothing, to protect their men.

Darkness fell and we slipped our packs back on. My shoulder blazed in protest at the burden. The nurse handed each of us a packet of food, and we headed out into the olive grove. "Some woman, Mario," I commented, "much too good for the likes of us!" "You're right, Signor Console," replied Bonfigli, "but I enjoyed looking, anyway."

The night was starry, and the cold crackled like a crisp wafer on the tongue. It quickly cleared our heads. The men were waiting for us at the stables, and Mario briefed them on the new operation. We sent Antonio ahead as a scout. We weren't overly worried—the Germans were usually in vehicles at night, and the Fascists rarely left the safety of the town or the garrisons after dark. Our real danger was from other partisan bands who might not recognize us. With no means to communicate with one another, there was no way to know where other groups were at any given moment, or what they were doing. At night, the Italian countryside now belonged to men like us.

The moon had been up for about half an hour when Antonio returned. "The factory is just ahead, 'Tenente," he reported. "Everything is dark. I didn't see any guards, or any vehicles." "Okay, then let's go," said Bonfigli. He turned to me. "You and I will be point men. The rest of you disperse behind us, about fifty yards off the path on both sides, to cover our backs." We set off at a trot to keep warm and reached the factory in short order.

The building resembled a huge barn. In front was an office area, and what was probably also the living quarters of the factory manager and his family. We inched our way silently around the building, keeping to the shadows close to the walls. At the back was a loading door, and in the small area in front of the loading door were empty barrels and crates. A road big enough for trucks led up to and ran alongside that side of the building. "We'll have to watch the road," I whispered to Mario. "We don't know when trucks or workers might arrive. Put a man a hundred meters out on each side."

As soon as the road was guarded, Bonfigli and I squatted down and quickly devised a plan of attack.

I took four men and we worked our way down until we were deployed opposite the loading door. As soon as we heard anything from the west end of the building, we would rush the loading door. We'd be fully exposed once we left cover, and hard-pressed to shoot our way out of this one.

Mario took the other four men. At his signal, two men scurried across the open space at a low crouch, flattening themselves against the wall next to the smaller of the two main doors. Bonfigli and the other two followed, taking up stations next to the larger door.

He banged on the door and shouted, "Open up!" Then, without waiting, he kicked the door in. We heard the wood splinter. The other two went into action immediately. One smashed the small door in with the butt of his rifle. "Outside!" "Everyone! Outside, now!" shouted Mario.

I leaped up, and, waving my men on, bolted across the open space to the loading door. We jammed at it with boots and rifles, but it wouldn't budge. It was well locked from the inside. We could hear a quavering male voice from Mario's end. "Don't Shoot! Don't shoot!" The owner of the voice, a wailing, sleep-befuddled man appeared, half dressed. He was quickly joined by a disheveled woman in her nightgown, a coat hastily thrown over it, and a young boy of about twelve or thirteen. One of Mario's men herded them against the wall. The manager beseeched the partisans with protestations of innocence and fervent avowals of his loyalty to the liberation movement. The woman, clutching her coat close, sobbed loudly in fright. The boy attempted bravado, but snickered nervously, like a spooked colt. I felt sorry for them.

Mario, meanwhile, had rushed inside and through the building to reach the loading door. "Wait! Gualtiero! It's me, Mario!" he yelled, and flicked on the lights. As soon as he had the door unlocked, we rushed inside. Our eyes slowly adjusted to the light, and we looked eagerly around to see what war supplies we had captured. Huge bins of khaki colored material lined one side of the enormous room. In the middle was a piece of machinery that looked like a giant printing press. Along both far walls were stacks of bundles. I ran over to inspect. Bundle after bundle of.......blankets! I couldn't believe my eyes."

Oh, great! Blankets! We liberated BLANKETS! Maybe we can beat the enemy by taking their blankets,—then they'll freeze to death, and we won't need ammunition to shoot them. I kicked at the stacks in disgust.

Mario and I conferred. It wasn't ammunition, and it wasn't food. On the other hand, it hadn't cost us the firing of a single shot. For the men's morale, if nothing else, we needed to bring back something, anything, to show for two nights of walking and fear. Maybe we'd be able to trade the blankets for something of value.

Bonfigli turned to Italo. "You know this area. Go and requisition two carts, with drivers. Tell the drivers we can't pay them, but they can have whatever they want from here when we're gone." Italo and a companion, probably his cousin, took off at a run. I took Gaetano and went to ransack the kitchen. We found two loaves of bread, several links of sausage, and a fairly sizable hunk of hard, dry cheese. I also grabbed up two flasks of wine. We ate while we waited for the carts. Only about an hour of darkness remained, and I was getting very nervous.

Shortly before sunrise, Italo and his cousin arrived with the carts and drivers. We piled them high with blankets. The manager wrung his hands. "Please, Signori, what will I do?" he wailed. "How will I explain? They will kill me! They will murder my whole family!"

"Just tell them the people who sent us do not like the quality of your blankets, and we are sending them to Germany where they will be better appreciated," said Bonfigli, as we trundled away with the loaded carts. He assigned two partisans to take the manager and his family to an abandoned farmhouse between Morena and Cagli. There, they would be kept incommunicado for twenty-four hours, then released. Bonfigli and I, to avoid risk of being captured together, took separate routes back to the presidio at Morena, which was nearer than the Bruschi farm. The blankets were also headed for there.

At mid-morning, I stopped on a hill that overlooked a cluster of ancient stone houses below, the sun glinting off their scraggly, ocher-color tile roofs. I dropped to the hard, frozen earth for a breather. From the cover of the trees, as I sat slowly munching my meager portion of bread and hard cheese, trying to make it last as long as possible, I spied a group of three peasant women, bundled in heavy coats and scarves, methodically beating wet clothes on the rocks at the side of a small, icy stream. Even from a distance, I could see their hands were bright red from the cold water. How many years, how many centuries, by how many generations of women, had clothes been washed this way, winter and summer, alongside this very stream, I wondered? A wave of affection for the Bruschis swept over me,—especially for Adalgisa, who uncomplainingly bore the extra burden of washing my dirty clothes, along with those of her own family, in this same crude way. My respect and affection for the peasants of Umbria had grown steadily in the past few months. I had learned to trust them implicitly, and although they were clannish, close-mouthed, and rarely opened up about themselves, they showed me great respect, and extended to me without question their very special hospitality.

The noon bell, tolling from a nearby church, pierced the silence. I thought of the priest who must be pulling the bell rope, and of the profound influence priests had in the life of the peasants. They were not only the spiritual leaders of their flocks, but often their real political leader, their psychologist, their doctor, the repository of all the secrets of their lives—the parish priest presided over their ills, hopes, fears, and desires, in addition to their marriages, births, and deaths.

Don Marino Ceccarelli, "il prete bandito" (the bandit priest) of Morena and the San Faustino parish, was an example of the kind of dedicated cleric who looked after his flock and protected them in every way. Tall, thin, gaunt-faced, in flat black hat and long black cassock, he flew amidst his flock like a spindly blackbird, aiding and abetting the partisans. Time and again he helped us when we were at a loss for somewhere to bivouac. His store of knowledge about where we could safely go, who had what, and which families were sympathizers with the Fascists and Germans, was nothing short of amazing. While he never divulged the identities of the sympathizers, it was not difficult to figure out who they were. Those families whose names he never mentioned as places we could go were immediately suspect.

Like many country priests, Don Marino had a good basic knowledge of medicine. There were no doctors in those barren hills. On more than one occasion, we had to turn to him for first aid or medical advice. His love for his people had endeared him to the entire region, and everyone, myself included, spoke of him with great reverence and respect.

With the sound of the church bell reverberating in the clear air, I got up, brushed the crumbs of bread and cheese from my clothes, and continued the long journey back to Morena. By five that evening, I had been twenty-four hours without sleep. I began looking for a friendly farmhouse in which to lodge for the night. I always chose the poorer-looking farmhouses—they were usually safer, and friendlier.

As I stealthily detoured around one I had decided not to approach, my presence set the dogs to barking. I had always liked dogs, but now I would have gladly strangled every canine in Italy. It seemed that whenever I needed anonymity the most, I offended somebody's damned hound!

By dusk, I had reached a suitably isolated farmhouse. Sure enough, as I approached, the dogs began barking. Ignoring them, I strode up the steps and banged on the door. "Partigiano!" I shouted. The door swung open and I was beckoned inside by a man who could have been Ruggero Bruschi's twin. I stepped into the large, rectangular kitchen/family room. The bustling contadina was already setting an extra place for me at the table. I was reminded of Fontanella—this place, too, could have been its twin. It had almost the same long, rectangular wooden table, the same plain, rush-bottomed chairs, several dark pieces of furniture, and, as usual, not a single peg on which to hang hat or coat. The stone floor even bowed the same way the Bruschi's did. And here, like almost everywhere, were countless buzzing flies, and several sons, or daughters, with their respective wives and husbands and children.

With my puritan midwestern American background, and my penchant for personal modesty, I never could fathom how anyone managed to conceive a child in these community-living circumstances, where they often slept eight and ten to a bedroom, four or five to a bed. However, it was apparently no problem, since there were always children in evidence, or on the way. From what the old man told me, I was still about six hours' walk from Morena. "Please, may I sleep here until midnight?" I asked. "I must get to Morena, and I don't want to travel by day." They nodded understandingly and showed me to a bed in the bedroom. At five minutes to midnight, the old woman woke me, with a vigorous shake of my sore shoulder. Pain knifed through me, and I rubbed it, yawning, as I sat there. Damn! I didn't know what was wrong with it,— must have sprained it somehow. There were no doctors around, so I'd just have to learn to live with it, and hope it would go away. I splashed my face with some cold water from the basin, then went out to the kitchen. There was a bowl of hot minestrone and a big chunk of bread waiting there for me. "Mangia! Mangia!" commanded the old woman. "It's no good for you to go out in this cold without something to warm your belly." Noting how eagerly I wolfed down the soup, she went to a back room and returned with a generous slab of cheese. "Here. Eat it all. Then I will give you more to take with you. It is not good to travel hungry."

Is there no end to the generosity and kindness of these people? I wondered. Several generations lived here and had to be fed, yet the contadina fed me, a stranger, from her meager stores. She'd never see me again, but that didn't matter. I was hungry, she gave me food. I thanked her warmly and took my leave.

Five and a half hours later, barely winning the race with dawn, I reached the presidio. As I approached, along the path up the hill, the sentry challenged me. I was pleased that they were vigilant, even at this hour.

Edoardo, the guard, greeted me. "Good morning, Signor Console, congratulations on your successful raid last night!" I looked at him blankly. "The blankets, Signore! Che bellezza! We have thousands of the Army's blankets! The people won't go cold this winter! And the garrison at Scheggia— they got a lesson they won't soon forget, eh?"

I smiled at his exaggeration, but it made me feel good that he was so pleased. The last minute decision to raid the factory and take the blankets had been a smart one after all. They were tangible evidence of success. I staggered in to bed, dropping wearily onto a pallet on the floor, with two slightly prickly, liberated woollen blankets to cover me and keep me warm. Yes, it had been a good raid, after all.

In our wildest imagination we could never have predicted the hit those blankets would be with the countryside. The entire area was seized with "blanket fever". The partisans now had something to use as a bargaining tool. Blankets had not been available in the stores for years, and after the partisans were supplied with them, families who had been helpful and loyal were given them. They became status symbols. They were traded for food. To own one became a flag of pride to the peasants. Many were converted into jackets or overcoats by the talented needles of the local women. In that brutal climate, coats and jackets, even those made from stolen army blankets, were a Godsend.

Food, too, was becoming a scarce item. Procuring enough food to feed the twenty-five partisans garrisoned at the presidio at Morena was difficult. Butchering meat we found was no problem, since the men were all from farm backgrounds. As soon as a beef or sheep was procured, it was strung up from the branch of the nearest tree and butchered right then and there. The peasant donating it got back the hides and tallow, and the meat was easily transported back to the presidio in quarters and chunks. The men did the cooking of it themselves. However, none of the men could equal baking bread the way it was done by the women of Umbria. In truth, the thought of it never even entered their heads. Bread baking was a job reserved exclusively to the women. The men merely brought the wood for firing the ovens.

The rounded brick baking oven was a structure unto itself, usually located out in the back yard of the farm. The men stoked and fired up the ovens, to get them to the proper heat for baking the bread, but their responsibility ended there. Bread was always baked on the same day, enough to last a week. While the oven was heating, the women would knead the bread one last time, and shape it into big oval loaves. When the oven was the right temperature, which the women knew from some mysterious instinct, since there was no thermometer of any kind, they'd rake the coals out of it, and place the loaves in the oven in tiers, using a long-handled wooden paddle. Then the door was sealed, by slapping wet clay around it as a sealant. Depending on the primitiveness of the oven, the door might be metal, or merely a stone fitted into place and held there with the clay.

Once sealed, the oven was not opened again until the bread was done. How the women knew when the heat was right, or when the bread was done, was a mystery to us men. During all the time I was in the hills, I seldom saw a loaf of bread under done or over-baked. The weekly baking was to me like some kind of miracle. By the fifth or sixth day, the loaves were pretty hard and the bread had to be soaked in soup or hot barley coffee to make it edible, but it still tasted wonderful to a hungry guerrilla fighter!

With the coveted blankets as barter money, we spent less time on procuring food, which left us more time for training, gathering intelligence, and planning for the great day when the Allied advance into Umbria would call for an all-out effort from the partisans and the peasants. I could see that the partisans were determined to prove to the Allies that they were as courageous and valiant a fighting stock as any country could possibly produce.

Not long after the factory raid, word came to me that the partisans had arrested Leonard Mills, the young American student from Perugia, as a spy. I was astounded. "Come on, now!" I protested. "Whatever gave you the idea that Mills is a spy?" "We have good reason to believe it," replied one of the officers, stiffly. "He has been behaving very much like one."

Several others confirmed that Mills had often been seen prowling stealthily around the countryside. "Also," added the officer, "he's been asking questions about things that are none of his business, and he's been overheard speaking German fluently!"

In truth, I hadn't given a thought to Mills since I saw him at the organizational meeting in January. He was an intellectual, but I knew little about him, other than that he was doing graduate research at the University in Perugia. His fluency in several languages, all of which he spoke almost without accent, was one of the reasons he had been accepted into the Band, I reminded them. His other behavior was pretty standard for Leonard. He was always nervous, curious, asking questions. It was only intellectual curiosity on his part. "You're making a mistake in this. Leonard Mills is no more a spy than I am." I said. "He is a loyal American citizen."

For the first time, my word was having little effect, and I didn't like what I was seeing. Their minds were made up about Mills' guilt, and I knew that if I didn't do something quickly to stop them, they were likely to just take him out and shoot him. I stood my ground firmly and spoke with quiet authority. "I must insist, gentlemen, that you take no other action about Mr. Mills until I have conferred with Lieutenant Bonfigli." I was a partisan Commander, after all. I gave them a look that said I expected implicit, unquestioning obedience to my authority. Reluctantly, they backed down and acquiesced to my demand.

As soon as the meeting ended, I headed out in search of Mario. He was at least a three-hour walk away. As I trudged wearily along the dark path, I reflected on the irony of my situation. I had never been a night person and hated staying up late. I had always managed to excuse myself early from the endless rounds of diplomatic dinners, receptions, and cocktail parties I was obliged to attend. Now, I spent whole nights up and about, wandering on foot from hill to dale and back again, and my days in exhausted sleep!

When I finally reached Mario, I explained the Leonard Mills' situation as I saw it. "The people involved in the judgment of Mills simply do not understand anyone like him, Mario," I said. "Their backgrounds don't bring them into contact with intellectuals like Leonard, who are always doing research on things around them. Trust me, Mario, Leonard Mills is not a spy."

Bonfigli accepted my explanation. "I cannot release him

yet, though," he said. "First, I must contact the CLN in Perugia for confirmation and permission."

By the end of the following week, Mills had been exonerated and was released. Bonfigli and I then met with him. He was understandably outraged. "Idiots! Cretins!" he raged. "Those fools would have shot me! THEY should be shot! The world would be better off without them!"

"Look, Mills," I said curtly, "in times like these, sometimes individual rights have to take second place to other considerations. I hate to think of what might have happened if I hadn't intervened for you. Like it or not, you'd better curb your curiosity, and keep your German quiet for the time being. Just stick to what the Band assigns you to do, okay? That way, there won't be a problem. I don't know if I could get you off again."

It bothered me that none of the British officers in the area, with the exception of Ramsay, showed any inclination to help with our resistance efforts. Ramsay made himself available for staff meetings, gave us advice about explosives and demolition projects, and was generally cooperative and helpful in every way he could be. His lack of Italian hampered his participation, but at least he tried. The others made no effort at all to help their situation. Several times, I had stopped by the farmhouse where they all gathered in the daytime. They seemed to spend more time in petty bickering with each other than in doing anything remotely worthwhile. They had a deck of cards and had virtually played the markings off them. They were indolent, bored, and ripe for trouble, waiting for the Allies to arrive and "rescue" them, making no efforts on their own behalf. That annoyed me, and I spent as little time as possible with them. Then, early in March, Bonfigli reported some news to me.

"Eh, buddy," he greeted me one afternoon, with a twinkle in his eye, "your British friends have themselves a 'puttana', (a whore) and I hear she is quite something. Whoooeeee." He whistled as he traced a curvaceous female figure in the air with his hands. "Ma che, a puttana! What do you mean?" I asked, surprised. "What are you talking about?"

"A bella Hungarian has taken refuge with the British officers at Acqua Viva, and they have welcomed her with arms open, if you know what I mean." Bonfigli winked slyly, and gave a short, knowing laugh. "Are you sure, Mario?" I asked. "Or is this a figment of your celibate imagination? Beautiful refugee women don't just turn up at remote farmhouses in Italy. No one is that lucky."

Mario looked offended. "Go see for yourself if you don't believe me," he challenged. "They are very cozy there, and need I add, very 'cocky'! They are enjoying their new lady friend, and not about to question what providence has opportunely dropped into their laps, so to speak." Dramatically, he pointed and rolled his eyes heavenward.

"Come on, Mario, you've got to be kidding!" I was still not convinced.

He turned serious. "No, Signor Console, I'm afraid it is true," he said. "The whole countryside is talking about it."

I decided to drop in on the Brits, unannounced, to check this bit of gossip out for myself. The next day, I set out for Acqua Viva, a farmhouse much like the Bruschi's, about an hour's walk southeast of Fontanella. When I arrived, it was about three in the afternoon, and the four officers were, as usual, at one of their interminable games of cards. There was no sign of the woman. I decided to act natural, ask no questions, and see what would transpire. They chatted idly with me about the state of the Allied advance while they continued their game, but I could tell they were ill at ease. I rarely spent time with them, so naturally they were curious about why I had suddenly dropped by to see them. They were behaving very much like little boys caught with their hands in the cookie jar, hoping I wouldn't find out about their new star boarder.

Enjoying myself, and their discomfiture, I sat back and cooled my heels. I didn't have long to wait. When the Hungarian stepped into the room, I almost gasped aloud. Mario was right,—she was a lovely woman! I rose and introduced myself in Italian. "Good afternoon, Signorina," I said, "I am Michele."

Coolly, she returned my greeting in excellent Italian. "I am Marian," she replied, " I'm very pleased to make your acquaintance, Signore." She graciously extended her hand, keeping it clasped in mine a fraction longer than necessary. Tall for a woman, she nearly matched my six feet of height. She flashed me a direct look that was an unmistakable invitation. I felt my throat go dry. Her long, blonde hair fell to her shoulders. She wore a dark, red sweater that was tight enough to draw attention and show off her figure, but not so tight as to be suggestive. Shrugging her shoulders slightly, she brushed past me, and I caught a faint, tantalizing whiff of expensive perfume. She seated herself, in an attitude of languid repose, on the worn divan, patting the empty spot next to her, as she raised a questioning brow to me. I could feel the intensity of the gaze of the four Britishers as they watched this interplay. Their big stake at the moment was definitely not in the game of cards they were playing. Marian crossed her legs and relaxed against the back of the couch, one arm extended casually along the top of it, thoroughly enjoying her little flirtation.

This was no refugee farm wife. This was no frightened damsel, fleeing for her life. She was too well cared for, too sleek and manicured. This Maid Marian of the Umbrian hills was a cultured, worldly woman, accustomed to being pampered, and to having her way. She looked at me archly, in a slightly quizzical way, as if to say "what are we doing here, with all these people?—Come, let's get out of here so we can be alone." I returned her gaze with a level stare, trying to give no sign of the effect she was having on me.

Their card game now fully abandoned, the Brits began to mutter and whisper among themselves, their faces growing more tense with each passing moment. I was fascinated by the woman, as one might be by a snake, but I was more than a bit put off by her act--if it was an act. I sensed it was high time I got the hell out of there, before things got out of hand.

I had seen for myself that what Bonfigli had told me was true, and now I needed time to recover, and sift through what I had just seen. I felt a distinct sense of alarm and foreboding about the situation.

As soon as I could, without appearing hasty, I took my leave. "Goodbye, Michele," said Marian softly , lingering over my name, bestowing me with a brilliant smile. Then, with an air of dismissal, she turned from me to the others, addressing them in English, her accent heavily redolent of Eastern Europe. Her Italian was much better than her English, I decided, as I stepped out into the frosty evening. The officers were more than glad to see me go. No one bothered to show me out.

Taking a deep breath, I began retracing my steps across the drab, gray, winter countryside. After that pulse-quickening blaze of red and gold I had just encountered, my dark, solitary night stretched bleakly before me. I couldn't blame the British officers for being dotty over having her around. Who wouldn't? Still....there was something about her that raised my hackles. I decided to be extremely cautious in the future around Marian, the seductive Hungarian, if I ever saw her again. Surprising myself, I realized I hoped I would. Like a Rembrandt, she glowed with life and light, a masterpiece amidst these lusterless landscapes and dull, still lives. For too many months, I had been restricted to the company of women to whom glamour was as remote as the moon. I wanted to just sit there, staring at Marian for hours on end, enjoying her luminous femininity, inhaling her perfume.

A few days later I ran into her again. I was delivering one of the purloined army blankets to a family which had been very helpful to the partisans. Shortly after I arrived, Marian showed up —ostensibly for a brief visit. I was happy to see her again, and especially glad to have a chance to talk with her without the British officers around.

Apparently surprised to find me there, she greeted me pleasantly, but this time her greeting seemed more sincere, less openly calculating, than the previous time. The flagrant posturing was also absent. "What a nice surprise!" she exclaimed.

"It's nice to see you again too, Signorina," I said sincerely. She pulled two chairs near the fireplace. "Please sit and visit with me for awhile, Signor Orebaugh," she invited softly, indicating the other chair. I froze, almost visibly, at hearing my last name, a name I hadn't heard spoken aloud in months. My heart began pounding like a trip hammer. How could a refugee Hungarian woman, lately arrived to the area, possibly have known my real last name,—let alone pronounce it so perfectly? Fully alert now, my mind raced. I was certain I had never revealed my true last name to anyone since leaving Perugia to join Bonuccio Bonucci. Bonucci knew my name, but I doubted that Bonfigli or Pierangeli did. At the organizational meeting in January, Bonucci had attempted to introduce me by my full name, but had botched the pronunciation badly. Orebaugh was not an easy name. This woman not only knew it, but had pronounced it perfectly! I didn't think any of the British officers knew my real last name, but that was a remote possibility. Or had she come by it, somehow, in Perugia? Had they tortured it out of Bonucci? Or worse, had they gotten to Vittoria, or Margherita, or Valentina, God forbid? A thousand horrifying possibilities crowded my mind in those brief seconds.

I decided to maintain a front of social politeness and do some careful detective work. "With pleasure," I said smoothly, pulling my chair close to hers and sitting down. "But you must call me Michele."

She smiled in acknowledgment. Her sheer physical magnetism still overwhelmed me, even though I was now very wary of her. With their arduous existence of unrelenting poverty and hard physical work, the contadinas, the peasant women of Italy, were almost invariably dumpy and unattractive by age thirty, worn out by forty, and old women at fifty. Marian Heller, though no great beauty, was a refreshing change. She was not only good to look at, she was charming, educated, polished, and very sophisticated. She was a sparkling, verdant oasis in the middle of a vast cultural desert.

Opening her handbag, she pawed around in its contents, finally extracting a small packet of English tea. "Have some tea with me, won't you?"

"Sure, love to." I nodded my assent. The prospect of real tea, along with her company for awhile, was a temptation too powerful to resist.

Marian turned to the contadina, who was, as usual, busy in the kitchen. "Boil some water, please," she commanded imperiously. Ordering others to do her bidding came naturally to her. Yes, I mused, this woman was accustomed to being waited upon. Who is she? Where did she come from? "How did you end up in this part of Italy?" I inquired.

"Well, I was living near Naples. My husband was in business there, and when the bombing began, I was terrified. So I decided to come north, to Perugia, where I thought I would be safer." Ah, so she had been in Perugia. Alarm bells pinged in my head.

"How long were you in Perugia?" "Several months. But then the food situation got so bad in the city, we couldn't get anything to eat." She pouted prettily, looking at me for sympathy. "Yes, I've heard there are terrible food shortages everywhere," I acknowledged. She didn't look as if she had ever experienced so much as an hour's hunger. "And what brought you to this remote area?" I probed.

"I heard about Morena from a friend, and thought I might be safer and more comfortable here, so I decided to 'go to the macchia', and the British officers were kind enough to take me in and give me shelter."

Yeah, I bet they were, I thought. "Kind" is hardly the word! The old peasant woman brought us our tea. We sipped contentedly for a few moments before I spoke up again. "Where did you grow up? In Budapest?"

"No, my father was a businessman in the Pest area, but he died when I was only six years old. My mother was Italian, from near Milan, and she brought me back to Italy to live after

Papa died."

So that's why she spoke Italian so fluently. "I noticed that your Italian is excellent," I complimented her, "that explains it. You also speak English very well. Did you study it in school?"

"Thank you. Not really. I had a Swiss governess who spoke French and English to me, and my mother had attended school in England and spoke it well, so she also taught me a lot." She seemed pleased to be telling me her story, and since she didn't appear to be angling for anything from me, I relaxed a bit. We sat in companionable silence for a few more minutes. Then she looked questioningly at me. "And you, dear Michele, what about you? You are certainly not Italian, although you speak it very well. Where do you come from?" I tensed again, defenses up, though her question was a perfectly natural follow-on to our conversation.

The psychological need to unburden oneself to a sympathetic listener is an ever-present danger in the situation of loneliness and deprivation I was experiencing. I was sorely tempted to just let go, and tell her about myself. I mean, what if she were an innocent refugee, just being polite in asking about me? But I knew better. God, Orebaugh, you don't trust anything or anybody anymore! That was true enough. I couldn't trust anyone—and especially not this woman, at this moment. Her slip with my name was too much of a coincidence to disregard. "Oh, we'll have plenty of time to talk about me later, when we know each other better," I parried. "Like you, I'm just one of those poor unfortunates who got caught in the wrong place at the wrong time." I had purposely peppered my remarks with several words in the dialect of the Trieste area, hoping that would serve to confuse her. "I am a displaced businessman, just trying to survive the war."

Looking at my watch, I got up. "Speaking of business, dear Marian, I could enjoy sitting here over tea with you indefinitely, but unfortunately I have some matters I need to attend to this afternoon, before it gets too late." Lifting her hand, I kissed it in my most continental manner. "It has been a most pleasant afternoon, Signora," I said. "I look forward to enjoying your company again very soon, but now I must be on my way."

Slowly withdrawing her hand from mine, she rose to walk with me to the door. "Please come back, here, again soon, Michele," she said, with slight emphasis on the word 'here.' "I come here often in the afternoon—at least three times a week. Perhaps we can meet again for tea, and share our stories."

"That would be a pleasure. Perhaps we will." I held out hope, but made no commitment. Halfway down the stairs, I turned. She stood at the top, framed in the doorway, watching me. "Arrivederci, " I waved. "Arrivederci, Michele," she waved back, smiling, and closed the door.

For the next couple of weeks, I was extremely busy. We carried out several raids—some were successful, some not. There were meetings, and organizational problems to solve. I thought a lot about Marian Heller, but was unable to get back to the farm to meet her again, and try to find out more about her. Gossip among the peasants, mostly salacious, kept me apprised of her whereabouts and activities. She remained with the British officers, as their house ornament and recreational diversion.

I hadn't spoken about my encounter with her at the neighboring farm, or her mention of my last name, to anyone. I was still turning it over and over in my mind, like a piece to a difficult puzzle.

We began to receive shocking reports, via Captain Pierangeli's partisan network, about the brutal regime in control in Perugia, which under the "Fascisti Repubblichini" had become worse than could be imagined. The notorious Prefect Armando Rocchi and his murderous cohorts, led by Major Carità had brazenly taken over there, and were committing all sorts of atrocities. No one, and nothing, was safe any longer. Along with these disquieting reports, we finally got some scraps of news about Bonuccio Bonucci. He was still clinging to life, but barely, in one of Rocchi's prisons. He had been brutally tortured by the Fascists—whipped, beaten and interrogated almost beyond human endurance, for days on end, during the first weeks after his capture. He had given them nothing, and they finally gave up, but he was reported to be in terrible mental and physical shape.

I was very shaken on hearing that, but glad to know that he was still alive. I worried constantly about Vittoria, Margharita, Valentina, and the children. Finally, I asked Captain Pierangeli to try to check on them for me.

"I will do what I can, Signore," he said, "but we must be very careful,—we don't want to arouse suspicion, if it isn't there."

"Absolutely. Do nothing that would bring any adverse attention to them. I just want to know that they are alive and unharmed." I thought then about mentioning my concerns about the Hungarian woman to him, but decided to keep my silence for the moment. No point in raising flags until I had something more solid to go on. Something solid wasn't long in coming. Just a few days later, a returning messenger informed us that Margherita and her children were fine, to my great relief. Then he reported that Prefect Rocchi, according to rumors circulating in Perugia, was so miffed by the sudden disappearance of his beautiful Hungarian mistress, he was no longer restraining his mad-dog minions. He was letting them wreak whatever havoc they pleased on the populace of Perugia.

I was thunderstruck. "Beautiful Hungarian mistress," the messenger had said. How many beautiful Hungarians could there be, wandering around Umbria, "disappearing?" I went immediately to Captain Pierangeli and told him about my two encounters with Signora Marian Heller, and about her use of my last name. Pierangeli lost no time in dispatching a messenger to Perugia, to ferret out more details. Three days later we received information and descriptions that convinced us that the hated Prefect's absent Hungarian mistress and Marian Heller, reigning 'puttana' of the British officers, were one and the same.

"Signor Console," added Pierangeli gravely, "I have more bad news, I'm afraid. I am fully convinced, from other information the messenger also brought, that Rocchi knows perfectly well where his little chickadee is. In fact, we believe she was sent here specifically to spy on us, and to pinpoint your whereabouts for him."

I sat back, trying to digest the implications of all this. Her knowledge of my real last name was the key. Either they had tortured it out of Bonucci, or the German SS was hot on my tail after our abortive attempt to be flown to Rome following the Armistice. No matter. I was sure now that Armando Rocchi knew perfectly well who and where I was.

I was not present at the next meeting Pierangeli held, but the heated discussion that took place there prompted him to come to Fontanella the following morning, with two other officers, to fill me in and ask my advice on how best to proceed.

We assessed the damage she might have already done us, and agreed that despite the danger that might have accrued from her being in our midst for so long, she probably hadn't picked up much yet to report back to Rocchi and the Germans. I was not surprised to learn that five of the seven officers present at the meeting had recommended leniency for her. I smiled at that, and couldn't resist a barb of my own. "You weren't so charitable when it was Leonard Mills you suspected of spying on us," I pointed out. "You were ready to execute him without a trial!"

"But this is different!" protested one of the officers vehemently. "This is a woman!"

"So she is, but how would this be handled if you were all still on regular Army duty? Shouldn't you follow those rules?"

They stared at me, shocked. "But, but,—Signor Console, she is a woman!" they sputtered.

"Damn it, man, I never said she wasn't! I'm not saying execute her--I'm saying convene a military court martial and hear the evidence. Haven't you ever heard of a court martial?"

"Il Console is right," said Pierangeli decisively. "We will hold a court martial, tomorrow morning. Go and arrest her, and bring her to the presidio at Morena."

Not daring any further protest, they saluted smartly, and left immediately for Acqua Viva, to take Marian into custody. The British officers were predictably furious. "You can't do this!" they raged. "Trying her by military court martial is invalid! She's a civilian. You have no authority to try her. She is innocent of these charges! How could she possibly be a spy? She's just a poor refugee woman!" Nevertheless, the Italians took her into custody, and the next morning, a court martial was convened.

The British officers boycotted it. They'd have done better to attend. As soon as she was confronted with the charge that she was Rocchi's spy, Marian burst into tears, and made a full confession. "Yes, I was Rocchi's mistress," she sobbed. "Yes, he sent me here to spy on you and report back to him! I had no choice! He is an animal," she cried. "What would he have done to me if I had refused? You must understand, and take pity on me! I am only a woman, I had no choice but to do what he said, Signori, "she pleaded tearfully.

She was immediately placed under full arrest.

The news of the Hungarian's arrest, trial and imprisonment flew as swiftly as a trained carrier pigeon from farm to farm, valley to valley. The quip that made the rounds was, "and the Britishers had their hole shot right out from under them!"

I wondered later why Marian Heller hadn't confessed her spy status to the British when Pierangeli's men first came to arrest her. She might have talked them into detaining her themselves—taking her under Allied custody, which might have worked, and might have saved her life. Who knows?

As it happened, several weeks after her arrest by the partisans, it was discovered that she had been imprisoned before, as a spy against Italy. Rocchi, impressed by her good looks and intelligence, had spared her. Then he had packed her off to spy on us and pretended she had disappeared. With this evidence of her former activities, she was tried once again, this time as a spy and a traitor, and was sentenced to death. The following week, Marian Heller was executed by a firing squad.

Chapter 8

The Man With The Cane

The only good that came out of the Marian Heller tragedy was the knowledge that Rocchi's need to spy on the partisans was a tribute to our growing strength and disruptiveness. Although Fascist authority still prevailed in the principal urban centers, it had virtually disappeared in the countryside. Outside of Perugia, Gubbio, and the other urban areas, the maintenance of law and order by any arm of organized government had become a farce, if not a total fiction. By force of long habit, and lacking any other apparent authority, the tenant farmers even began coming to us to pay the age-old tax the government levied on slaughtering a hog. That was another sign of our growing influence. The peasants saw us, the partigiani, as the only real government authority in the region.

For centuries, the peasantry of central Italy had suffered under countless ruthless and greedy masters, while wresting their poor living out of an inhospitable, rocky, over-tilled terrain. Again and again, they had seen the flower of their young manhood conscripted, to leave the farms and go off to fight and die in conflicts and wars in which the peasants had no real stake, or even any mild interest. It is not surprising then, that as a class they held themselves apart from the mainstream of Italian cosmopolitan society, and that they harbored a deep-seated distrust and aversion to government authority. They gathered their few resources about them, and developed a totally family-centered culture, not unlike a return to the safety of the womb, where basic needs like food, shelter and survival were paramount. Worldly or political matters received scant consideration. The only authority to which the Italian peasant family paid nominal to willing obeisance was the Church.

While much has been said and written about the Italians, —often in a derogatory sense in regard to their patriotism and martial spirit—what has not been addressed is the warmth and courage shown by the Italian peasants during that period in World War II when the Germans were dug in, the Allies were slow in advancing, and the government of Italy was in disarray.

Dragged into World War II by Mussolini and his cohorts, they remained stubbornly turned inward, kept themselves closemouthed, and tried to have as little as possible to do with Fascism, —a regime they had never understood nor trusted. That is why the solidarity the peasantry manifested in resolutely aiding and sheltering the resistance fighters and the Allied prisoners-of-war was truly astonishing. Why they risked themselves, and their families, to do it remains a mystery to this day. The fact that their country was occupied by the Germans, and was more or less at war against the Allies, made it an even greater puzzle. History provides us no comparable example of a whole class of society, in any country, acting in this manner.

The thousands of Allied prisoners who survived and were repatriated did so only because they received help in their hour of need from those peasants. They, like I, can attest to that amazing generosity and selfless warmth and courage.

True to the highly emotional nature of the Italians and their fundamental beliefs, there was, even within the partisan movement, continuous political unrest and frequent strong and very vocal dissension,— especially concerning forms of government and extent of government authority.

One afternoon, I engaged in a lively discussion with Ernesto Rossi, the field representative of the Committee for National Liberation (CLN) for the area of Pesaro, who was paying a visit to San Faustino. Rossi was a well-indoctrinated communist, very capable, and highly educated. I was impressed by him, and that only reinforced my concern that the communists were making deep inroads in Italy, biding their time, awaiting the outcome of the war.

During our discussion, I asked Rossi, "How could the Soviet Union possibly support keeping the House of Savoy monarchy in power after King Vittorio Emmanuel showed such wretched leadership during two decades of Fascism?" His answer made sense to me. "As communists, we heartily despise the monarchy, and all it stands for. However, for the time being, we see an advantage to be gained by adhering to the symbolic authority the Royal family represents, and not further weakening the already fragile structure of the Italian government. That is why the Soviet government has reluctantly decided, at the highest levels, to lend its support to the present ad hoc working relationship between the Allied military authorities and the House of Savoy." Given the widely diverse and passionate feelings held throughout Italy, and the difficulty there would be in establishing a government after the war, I could only agree with that tactical reasoning.

During that visit, Rossi suggested that we establish liaison with the Banda di Cantiano, a partisan group operating in the mountains to the north and east of us. We agreed to that, and two days later, Pierangeli met with Colonel Ernesto Tagliaferro, the career army officer who was commander of the Cantiano Band. They struck up a cordial, cooperative relationship, and we were extremely happy to have established contact with another partisan movement. We decided we'd have liaison meetings every two weeks to coordinate our efforts.

Although we had spent a lot of time and effort trying to find the cache of weapons Bonucci and Colonel Guerizzi had buried, their hiding place completely eluded us. What had happened to those weapons was certainly one of the best kept secrets in Umbria. Other attempts to procure weapons and ammunition for our Band had yielded meager results, at best.

In fact, our activities were almost at a halt because of the shortage of arms and ammunition. Then one evening, Bonfigli arrived with welcome news. "I think we might have found some weapons and ammunition, Signore!" he announced excitedly.

I was elated. "How? Where?"

"We had word today, from one of our CLN contacts, that some villagers in the vicinity of Montebello are eager to get rid of a stockpile of weapons and ammunition they are hiding."

"Great Scott, man, this is the answer to our prayers!" I jumped up and banged the table in my excitement. "How do we get them? I'll pay whatever it costs! Where did they get them?"

"Well," he said, "these villagers live down near the Tiber River. When they heard about the armistice, they raided the local garrison and hid all the arms and ammunition from that raid. Now, they want to get rid of them."

After several days of protracted negotiations, a deal was struck. We were jubilant. When Bonfigli came to Fontanella with the good news, I grabbed a stunned Adalgisa and danced her around the room, much to the amusement of Pepe and Concetta. Arms, at last! Now we could plan some real raids against the Germans!

"Easy, my friend," laughed Bonfigli, "don't get too carried away! We still haven't figured out how to get them from Montebello to Morena without getting caught."

"Pah!" I said, "That's the easy part! We'll have that solved in no time."

However, it wasn't all that simple. The weapons were heavy, and mostly crated. We couldn't just send fifty men into the town and have each carry out a few weapons. Besides, the villagers and town officials didn't want the empty crates, with their telltale markings, left there as evidence.

Ultimately, we devised a plan to remove the weapons by donkey cart, two crates at a time, at night. It was a slow and dangerous process. One load came out in caskets ostensibly carrying dead bodies for burial. Another was concealed under a cartload of manure. One load was buried under garbage, and one came out under a pile of rubble from a bombed-out building. Eventually, all the arms arrived safely at the presidio in Morena, and we breathed a collective sigh of relief, then passed around a couple of flasks of wine in celebration. We were in business again—but just barely. We still needed more ammunition than we had.

Making my way back to the Bruschis that night, in the dark, I accidentally stepped into a hole in the rutted path, and fell, spraining my ankle. The next morning, it was badly swollen and black and blue. Adalgisa, fussing over me, put hot poultices on it, but it was several days before I could put any appreciable weight on it without excruciating pain. A couple of nights later, I was still immobilized at the farm, nursing the ankle, when a group of ten partisans from the Banda di Cantiano pulled a surprise raid on our presidio at Morena. Creeping up in the dark, they surrounded the building, and, at rifle point, made off with all of our newly acquired weapons, the best of the few old ones we had, and just about all of our precious supply of ammunition.

When that news reached me the next day, I was livid. Jumping up, I limped in fury around the room, pounding my fist in impotent rage against tables and walls, hurling every Italian insult and curse I knew at the Cantiano Band. Hell and damnation! Those cowardly bastards would pay for this, by God! What treachery!

Ruggero was astounded at my towering rage. Adalgisa was so frightened, she hurried out into the yard with the children. "This," I shouted, "is infamy! The absolute, last goddamned straw! Ruggero! Bring me pen and paper! I'm going to let Tagliaferro know what I think of him and his thieving band!" Ruggero scrambled to obey, producing from only God knows where a musty-smelling, wrinkled half sheet of brown paper. I could barely contain my rage enough to sit and dash off a furious protest to Colonel Tagliaferro. I didn't hesitate for a second over pulling rank, and I added some dire threats for good measure. I vowed to Tagliaferro that if he did not rectify the situation immediately, I would personally make it my business to see that the full wrath of the Allies fell upon him, and every member of the Cantiano Band. With a shaking hand, in a great flourish, I signed "Il Console." Then, somewhat calmer, I asked Ruggero to carry my message immediately to Pierangeli, for transmission to Tagliaferro.

"They will know they are dealing with Il Console," he muttered darkly, as he left.

I didn't have long to wait for a reply. Word came back the very next day that, within minutes of reading my note, Colonel Tagliaferro called the offenders in and gave them a fierce tongue-lashing. He levied heavy punishment duty on them, and ordered other partisans of the Cantiano Band to return the weapons and ammunition to the presidio at Morena "Immediately!" He sent a personal note of apology to Captain Pierangeli and me, vowing that he knew nothing of the raid made on our presidio, and certainly did not order or condone it. He assured us that the offenders were being punished. As it turned out, the incident led to the development of a closer, more cooperative relationship between the two groups than might otherwise have been possible. I limped around the room, leaning on my valuable cane, frustrated at being laid up at this important stage of operations.

Shortly after I arrived at the Bruschis to live, one of the neighboring farmers had fashioned a sturdy wooden walking stick for me. I asked Ruggero to hollow out the lower part of the stick. He had worked carefully, for many hours, to dig a channel deep into the hard wood. When it was finished, I stuffed my American dollars, tightly rolled, into it, then concealed the opening with the wooden plug Ruggero had made. Thereafter, the cane went everywhere with me, and many of the peasants came to refer to me as "the man with the cane."

I was especially glad to have it now, to relieve the weight

on my foot as I recovered from the ankle sprain. And I was glad to have the money with me, in case of need. Selfishly, as I mended, I hoped that something would happen to delay the raid against the Germans that was planned for March 4th, only a few days away. I desperately wanted to be in on the action. As I sat in the Bruschi kitchen, my foot propped up to speed the healing process, I thought about the "Brigata d'Urto di San Faustino" (Shock Brigade of San Faustino)— the official name our Band had adopted, although almost everyone referred to it simply as "The Band of San Faustino."

I wondered why the Germans and the Fascists had made no move yet to challenge our control of the area. Rocchi undoubtedly knew our whereabouts. I was sure they would move when they were ready. In my almost daily inspection visits to the five locations where our men were bivouacked, I stressed the need for constant, unrelenting vigilance. I didn't want another incident like the one that had cost us Bonuccio Bonucci and Colonel Guerrizzi.

For their part, the men never failed to ask me why we hadn't yet gotten the air drop of supplies from the Allies. My credibility and power were in question, and I didn't have an answer. I knew that the message asking for the drop had been transmitted. I knew the partisans were constantly monitoring the radios, ears ever alert for the words "abbia fede" and "puoi gioire" —signaling us that the airdrop was on its way to Morena, and we should prepare the bonfires that would light the drop zone. But the magic words had not, so far, been heard over the BBC. We had no way of knowing that some months earlier, at a summit meeting, the Allies had decided to route roughly ninety percent of all air drops to Tito and his partisans in Yugoslavia. My urgent request for the Band of San Faustino had been put on a back burner.

March 4th arrived, and I could only sit at the farm with Ruggero, drink wine, pace, fidget, and wait for news. It was three o'clock the following afternoon before a partisan who answered to the name of Silvio Conti appeared at the door, bringing me a report on the action. Pierangeli and Bonfigli were both away on CLN business, so none of us had been able to be in on this action. Command had therefore been delegated to Conti, our most senior partisan in terms of both age and experience. I knew him only slightly, but Silvio, whose real name, like those of most of the other members of the Band, will probably never be known, was a veteran's veteran in every sense of the word."

"I took eleven men, Signor Console," he began, "and we arrived at the ambush site, about three kilometers southeast of Città di Castello, just before midnight. We waited about thirty minutes, for the convoy to arrive. I waited until the lead vehicle was only about twenty meters from me, then opened fire with the Sten and nailed it."

"Good work, Silvio!"

"Grazie, Signore. The rest of the convoy piled up behind it, the trucks all hitting one another, and we opened fire and gave it to them good!" His dark eyes snapped, and he drew his short, stocky body up with pride. "We got at least ten vehicles, Signore, trucks, armored personnel carriers, and a command car. Six of them caught fire and burned."

"Any injuries to our men?" "No, Signore. One man got a flesh wound from a rock splinter, but it is nothing. We were out of there in five minutes, as ordered, and took very little return fire from the Germans."

"What about retaliations? Have you heard of any?"

"Not yet, Signore, but I am certain there will be some."

I thanked Silvio for his report. I was pleased that the raid had been a success, but was concerned about what reprisals there would be from the Germans. I told Silvio to tell the men at the presidio in Morena to take extra precautions. Less than twenty-four hours later, a platoon of Germans in squad cars randomly selected and torched four farms, appropriating their livestock, and taking two of the farmers away for forced labor service.

Although a terrible payment was exacted from innocents by the Germans every time the partisans struck successfully, never once did the peasants complain to us directly, or demand that we stop our activities because of their fear of retaliation. To us, it was an inspiring vote of confidence.

Heady with the success of the convoy raids, the Band was ready for bigger and better things. We wanted to make a name for ourselves before the Allies arrived. We wanted them to know the Brigade of San Faustino was there fighting for them. Of the various targets considered, the German arms depot at Gubbio seemed the most attractive. However, to attempt a raid there was extremely dangerous. I urged caution. For a week, we kicked the project around, examining it from every possible angle. My friend Manfred Metzger would probably have jumped at it right away, but I, being more pragmatic by nature, did not like the odds. However, the officers of the Band decided to go ahead with it. They'd make an "assalto lampo"—a lightning strike—at the heavily armed garrison, they decided. A squad of twelve was chosen for the raid. Pierangeli was adamant about not risking me on this one, so I was not among the dozen selected to go, but Bonfigli was, and brought me a complete report on the raid immediately afterward.

Under cover of darkness, the squad slipped into the town of Gubbio, and made it, undetected, to the ancient, massive stone building near the lower town gate that served as the German barracks. There they found the only entry well-guarded by two sentries. Pepe and Vincenzo drew a bead on the two, dropping them with single, almost simultaneous shots, and the others rushed quickly to drag the bodies aside. That operation took less than a minute. The ten men then entered the compound, leaving Pepe and Vincenzo in place of the two German sentries. So far, so good. Then their luck went sour. They heard the sound of running feet coming from every direction inside the compound, and Germans came on the run down the side streets on the outside of the wall as well. They began shooting, and Pepe and Vincenzo fired back. The partisans inside the wall heard Pepe and Vincenzo returning the Germans' fire. They knew it was time to abort the raid and get out of Gubbio—fast. Covering the stairway with several machine gun bursts, they raced for the opening in the wall, where Pepe already had the gate open for them. Gaining the street, they broke for their escape route, zig-zagging along the side wall and then dashing right, into a narrow alley.

"As we ran along the dark street" continued Bonfigli, "seven German soldiers came pounding toward us, firing. The squad split up, ducking into doorways for cover, then individually we dashed out, shooting, and scampered to the next cover. In the melee, Vincenzo and Luigi were hit. We grabbed them, and dragged them along. Everyone made it back safely, and the two wounded men, despite a considerable loss of blood, have been treated and are mending without serious complications."

"Well, we got off lucky that time Mario," I said, "but was it worth it?" He thought a moment before answering me. "I think so, Signore," he said. "Although we didn't pull off the colpo we had planned, Pepe and Vincenzo managed to hang on to the two automatic rifles they took from the dead German sentries, so we have two valuable weapons to show for our effort. And, we did polish off two Germans, and showed them they are not safe any more, not even in their own back yard!"

I wasn't fully convinced it had been worth the cost, but grudgingly allowed as how something was better than nothing. At least we hadn't suffered any major casualties. And the men were proud of their bold attack.

The raid on Gubbio made it imperative that we exercise greater control over our use of ammunition. "Well, we'll just have to do things that won't take ammunition, but will keep us nipping at their heels," remarked Bonfigli a couple of days later, as we surveyed our nearly depleted supply of ammunition.

"Like what?" I said caustically, thoroughly discouraged about the ammunition situation, with no sign of an air drop coming.

"Well, let's see. For one thing, we can change some of the

road signs around and remove some others. Everyone who lives around here knows the roads anyway—the Germans are the ones who will get lost." He laughed mischievously at the thought.

I brightened at hearing that. "You know, Mario, that's not such a bad idea! We should make a list of those kinds of things—actions that we can accomplish, with very little effort and almost no risk, that will confuse or delay the enemy, and try to accomplish several missions like that every week."

Mario, pleased that I approved of his idea, went off immediately to confer with the men and make lists of tasks. For most of March, we engaged in daily activities from the mundane to the significant. The weather was becoming milder, and we sent two or three of our squads out on the prowl every night. We avoided actions that might deplete our remaining supply of ammunition, and prayed daily that our radio monitors would hear the longed-for code words, the words on which our future existence now hung. We desperately needed supplies, but now, we had to get some ammunition, soon, or our clandestine operations would end, and we would become helpless quarry for the Germans and Fascists to hunt down at their leisure.

The night of March 22nd, a loud pounding on the door brought me fully alert. Ruggero hustled to answer the door as I hovered at the back window, ready to bolt down the escape ladder. Adalgisa was already at her station in the doorway, where she could see the front door and signal me to go, if necessary. The children had not stirred.

Adalgisa gave the "it's okay" sign, and Ruggero appeared in the bedroom with two roughly dressed, very agitated partigiani.

"Signore! We have news, big news!"

"Sit," I whispered, indicating my cot. "What is it?"

Ruggero and Adalgisa returned and handed around glasses of wine. The two men drank theirs in grateful gulps, then one said, "A huge force of Tedeschi (Germans) in busloads, maybe as many as fifteen buses, Signore, have come from the direction of Cagli and are heading toward Pianello. They are different from the Germans in Perugia and Gubbio. They are wearing black uniforms, with skull and crossbones insignia. We thought you should know right away." I sat back, stunned. The elite of the German army had been sent to get us. My heart was pounding like a trip hammer. Damn. Fifteen busloads—that meant five or six hundred of them! This was it, the big one I knew would come some day, a sweep of the area to capture me, and the other partisan leaders. "Are you sure there are that many?" "Sí, Signore," Antonio affirmed, with Tullio nodding vigorously in agreement, "we saw them ourselves—there were more than ten buses full, we know. The Cantiano Band has already engaged them near Pianello. They will need our help. We hurried to give you the news."

"Thank you. You did well, very well." I grabbed some clothes and hurriedly threw them on.

If the incursion proceeded on as it had started, the SS troops would enter our zone of operations from the east. They were now well within the Cantiano Band's territory, where a partisan line of defense had been drawn earlier, and that line would at least slow the German advance, and buy time for our reinforcements to reach them.

"Ruggero," I said, "you and Tullio go quickly and alert all five of our combat squads. "Proceed immediately to Pianello, and we'll reconnoiter there." Ruggero nodded and left with Tullio. I turned to Antonio. "Can you show me the way to Pianello?"

Of course, Signore," he replied. "I will be honored to take you there.

I looked at my watch. It was 5 o'clock in the morning. Adalgisa served us hot mugs of ersatz coffee, and some bread and cheese, which we wolfed down. Then she tucked the usual packet of extra rations into my pocket, and, at the door, murmured the ritual "go with God." This time, though, her eyes showed fear as she said the words. I knew just how she felt. Impulsively, I leaned down and hugged her close. Poor soul, and poor souls like her, I thought, always having to stand by, to wait and wonder what their fate would be—a fate determined not by themselves, but by the men they bore, and nurtured, and married. I stepped quickly into the predawn cold.

At the foot of the stairs I groped my way into the dark stall and retrieved my carbine from its hiding place. I would have preferred the Mauser, but there was less than a clip of ammunition left for it. As we set out on the long walk to Pianello, which lay somewhere to the northeast about twelve or thirteen kilometers away, the trees, silhouetted against the pale morning sky, seemed to stand at attention like a forbidding line of storm troopers. I knew we would most certainly be put to the test, and I hoped that I, and all of us, were equal to the challenge.

My companion filled me in with a description of the terrain around Pianello, where we would most likely make our stand. "We will move past Pianello, in all likelihood, Signore, and up the valley, which is set like a tilted bowl against the mountain. Its upper rim is bordered by a line of steep, sharp ridges."

"Do you think we can defend from it?" I asked.

"Probably better from there than anywhere else," Antonio spoke little, but was definite when he did. "From the valley, we can yield ground bit by bit, if we have to, as we work our way up to the ridge. Just on the other side of the upper rim is an old farm track that runs along the perimeter of the ridge. It is so old that it has been worn into a rut, about four or five feet deep, under the rim. It will provide us excellent coverage from anyone attacking from below. That is where we'll make our final stand, if need be. It is a good place. May the Blessed Virgin grant us the chance to defeat the Tedeschi maiali!" He crossed himself.

We had been walking for just over two hours, keeping close to wooded areas to shield us from view, when the first sounds of distant shooting reached our ears. I stepped from the cover of the trees, arm across my forehead to shield my eyes from the sun, which had risen above the hills and glowed like a burnished copper disk through a curtain of smoky haze.

I could just see the rim of the valley, which was laid out exactly as Antonio had described it. The battle was already joined. As we neared an outcropping of rock, two partisans jumped out from behind it and motioned to us. There we found eight of our men waiting, and to my relief, Bonfigli was with them.

"Well, good day, Signor Console," he greeted me. "Now, finally, you will see some real action! Probably more than you bargained for, but that's war, no? Let me know if you want to check out early, eh?"

"Hell, me check out?" I answered, acting properly indignant. "You with your skinny legs could make a run for it now and get away, but I'm too old for running far! So just tell me where you want me, and give me my orders. I'm ready for action, and you're wasting my valuable time."

Mario pointed upward to a spot about halfway along the rutted road on the right side of the ridge. "Choose good cover, and tell your men to make every shot count. If we're not careful, we'll run out of ammunition before noon."

I took eight men and, keeping low, we made our way to the old farm road and followed it along under the cover of the rim to the spot Mario had indicated. Finally, sheltered behind a large rock, I saw that Bonfigli had positioned me as far out of harm's way as possible.

Farther down the valley, to my left, I could see the points from which the Germans were firing. There were small mounds of dirt and rock where they had dug in, after their first, almost suicidal charge up the steep slope. Dead bodies of SS troopers littered the slope, mute evidence of the devastating storm of fire that had rained down on them from two heavy, water-cooled machine guns the Cantiano partisans had positioned above them, just behind the rim, with only the muzzles protruding over it. From time to time, a German would leap from cover and heave a grenade, but invariably the grenades fell short of the mark. They were also firing mortars, but the trajectory was difficult, and very few landed near the rim where the partisans were sheltered. A good choice of location, as Antonio said.

A runner came out of the woods to my right. "Signor Commandante!" he said, "Commandante Tagliaferro would like you and your men to go and occupy those positions over there." He pointed over to the left side of the valley, which was sparsely defended by a few of the San Faustino Band.

"Okay," I said, grabbing up my carbine, "but how do we get over there?"

The runner grabbed my arm and led me back up and over the crest of the ridge, then went back to bring the rest of my men to join me.

As we crouched there in our new position, still on the periphery of the battle, Bonfigli arrived. He had twenty or so men with him. "Good work, Signor Console," he said, in greeting. I breathed a sigh of relief. I was afraid he might be angry that I had changed positions without first consulting him.

Bonfigli took charge. This was his kind of fight. He directed our men to positions on the western third of the line, which permitted the Cantiano Band to reinforce gaps in the middle and at the eastern end of the line. "You, Signore, over there," Bonfigli directed me. He placed me to the far left, right below the notch that was our withdrawal path. As I dashed to my position and flattened myself down onto the ground, swinging my carbine into position, I realized I wasn't as nimble as I had been just a few years back. As I looked around me, I was pleased to see that my rocky nook formed a natural gun port. To fire on me, the Germans would have to draw a bead through a narrow gap between two rocks, whereas I could direct my fire to a wide area that extended from the center of the valley to the extreme left. Our orders were to carefully pick our shots to conserve ammunition.

By one o'clock, the Germans had advanced enough to make a rush on the road to the far right, where the Cantiano

Band was defending. Tagliaferro had realized the possibility, and had ordered all remaining grenades shifted to that sector. When the rush came, grenades fell like a giant hailstorm onto the SS troops, exploding on contact, and driving them back with heavy losses. From then on, aside from another minor, unsuccessful rush, the situation remained at a standoff. By three-thirty, it had become critical for us. Although we hadn't been severely pressed, we had expended a lot of ammunition in containing the sporadic rushes by the SS troopers, and we were running dangerously low. Our San Faustino force, though not as heavily engaged as our Cantiano comrades, was down to its last cartridges.

Bonfigli summoned me into the huddle of officers to decide our next move. I could sense that the officers felt that to withdraw now, besides being dangerous for the Bands, might give the populace the impression that once again the Italians had "snatched defeat from the jaws of victory." Too often they had been ridiculed as the "world's worst soldiers." Though we were forced by the numerical superiority of the SS troops into a defensive stand, the officers did not want us to be the first to disengage.

"Look, we don't want to get into a siege situation, either," I said tersely. We were vastly out-armed and outnumbered, but even so, we had managed to inflict heavy losses on the enemy. "How many German dead are there? Do we know?" I asked.

One of the Cantiano officers spoke up. "My men counted over 100 German dead. There are at least 40 wounded."

"What about the partisans?" I asked.

"We have had only minor losses so far, Signore," said Bonfigli. "Two or three of the Cantiano Band have been killed, and there are about twenty-five wounded from both bands."

"Ammunition?" I asked." We have almost none left," said Bonfigli, dejectedly.

"We're almost out, too," said Tagliaferro, "and we don't have any more food for the men, either."

"Well then, I think we should devise a sensible plan of withdrawal," I said. There is no sense in us taking unnecessary losses. We'll just have to take our chances on getting as many of the men as we can out safely. There's going to be hell to pay! They'll hunt us down, but it has been a big victory for the partigiani. We'll have to go into hiding, and lay very low. You have taken on the most elite force of the German military, and inflicted heavy losses on them, with very few men and almost no arms. The Allies will surely commend you for this."

"Grazie, Signor Console," said Tagliaferro. "We hope the Allies, and our countrymen, will agree with you."

"I assure you, they will. But now, we must try to live to tell the story."

We decided on a plan of withdrawal that would have the area cleared of partisans by within the hour.

I returned to my place on the line and gave instructions to my men. Three of us shared our remaining chunks of bread and a couple of swallows from my water bottle. I noticed that fire from the Germans was diminishing along with ours. Even so, they were firing ten rounds to our one.

Shortly after four, I motioned to three of the men to leave. Like us, the Germans must have seen enough action for one day, because suddenly they began to withdraw, too.

Then it was my turn. I slid my remaining three cartridges over to the man on my left and began slithering backward up toward the lip of the hill. I didn't realize how stiff I had gotten from lying on the hillside, until I tried to get up and into a running crouch. My thirty-fourth birthday, just a few days ago, has made its mark, I thought ruefully.

As we made our way toward the woods, my group stayed close together, in box formation, but once we reached the safety of the woods, we split up. Each man was on his own.

The slight warmth that the sun had provided was absent in the dank, cold muskiness of the pine woods. I was exhausted, I realized. Gritting my teeth, I plodded along, knowing full well I had ten to twelve kilometers of rough hills ahead of me before I would reach shelter. I decided to head for the presidio, which was closer than Fontanella. That way, if the Germans happened to pick up my trail and follow me, they would be met by armed partisans, instead of a family of unarmed peasants.

Still concealed by the woods, before heading out into the open fields, I flopped down onto a rock and drew the remains of one vile, incredibly strong Italian cheroot from my shirt pocket. The hell with the risk of someone seeing smoke--it might be my last cigar. Shielding the flame as I lit it, I sat quietly smoking for a few minutes. Some reward! I thought cynically, staring at its glowing tip as the acrid smoke curled into my nostrils.

By the time I reached the presidio, my feet were a swollen, purple mass of congested blood. As darkness fell, the ground froze, and the muddy route turned into rough and uneven ridges, which bruised my feet through my boots and tripped me up again and again. I could give no more than a tired, perfunctory nod to the sentry, as I passed him on the way into the building. I had no sooner stepped inside than I was surrounded by my comrades, all of whom were congratulating me and clapping me soundly on the shoulder. The sore one, of course. But I was as glad to see them as they were to see me. They were telling their tales to the men who had remained behind, and their accounts, still burning fresh in their minds, needed no embellishment.

The men who remained behind had not been idle. Scouring the countryside, they had foraged flour, meat, and a pile of firewood. They had even procured three demijohns of vintage red wine. The beef stew they had prepared for us was delicious, the roaring fire they had built warmed my frozen body, the wine relaxed me, and before long, disregarding my exhaustion and my aching feet, I, too, was beaming, as I added to the tale of how our own San Faustini, together with the Cantiani, had fought the elite German Waffen SS troops to a standstill.

The next day, I had to pry my body from the pallet. I hurt everywhere! I was sipping coffee in the mess area when

Bonfigli appeared, looking as worn as I felt. "Well, Mario, that was certainly something yesterday! We can all be proud of ourselves."

"Yes, Signore, none of our men were seriously wounded. Two got flesh wounds and have been treated by Don Marino." We were on our second cup of coffee when a messenger from the Cantiano Band arrived.

"Did the machine gun crews get out safely?" we asked anxiously. "Si, Signori," he replied, "the disengagement went exactly according to plan. The Germans pulled out about fifteen minutes after we did. We tried to go back later that night to retrieve any German weapons we could, and make an accurate count of the casualties, but the Germans had taken their dead away with them. The peasants of Pianello report that many fewer men got back on the buses than had gotten off."

We knew that we had killed at least a hundred SS troops. (The official report from the Germans, much later, showed that German losses in that engagement were 170 killed, 63 wounded.) We had inflicted heavy casualties on them. Our own losses were a mere 3 fatalities, 10 wounded.

We had barely digested the Cantiano report when a second messenger arrived with an urgent summons from Captain Pierangeli. "He wishes to see you, Signore, and Lieutenant Bonfigli, and the other officers, immediately. He said that it is a matter of great urgency."

I groaned aloud. It would be nearly two hours of walking to get to the meeting site! Seeing the look of anguish on my face, the messenger added, "The captain sends his apologies. He knows you must be tired."

An hour later, feet protesting every step of the way, I set out. It was on that walk that I vowed to myself, that if ever I got out of this mess alive, I would never take an extra step, or go any distance on foot again. Little did I know what lay ahead for me.

Pierangeli congratulated us on the previous day's success, then queried each officer as to the ammunition situation. The responses made him shake his head sadly.

"My fellow officers," he said gravely, "we couldn't possibly be in a worse situation than we are now. Just when we are in a position to make a real contribution to the war effort, and just when we might desperately need to defend ourselves against the Germans, we cannot put together the ammunition for even one small raid. I'm afraid we'll have to disband." He sat down, almost tearfully. There was silence for a few minutes. Then Bonfigli spoke.

"Yesterday, our concerns were for the immediate battle, and the ammunition we needed to sustain it and get out of it alive. Now we must face the future. If we cannot continue our efforts, we will lose the confidence and support of the peasants. They have learned to count on us when they need us. And we on them. If we don't continue, this whole zone will fall back under the control of the Germans and Fascists within a matter of a few days, and many of us will be captured and imprisoned, and probably shot. We simply must figure out a way to carry on! "

Everyone nodded assent, but after a half hour of discussion, no one had advanced a feasible plan. It seemed that what the Germans had not been able to accomplish by direct confrontation would be theirs by default. The partigiani of Umbria had run out of the wherewithal to continue further resistance. I stewed in frustration that my message to the Allies had not been heeded. One of the officers said, "We need to send someone through the German lines to the Allies, to appeal to them directly for help, and to send us an air drop." All eyes turned to me as one. I knew what they were thinking. Who else but me? I was certainly not safe any longer in Pietralunga, since the Fascists and the Germans now knew my whereabouts.

I didn't relish the thought of wandering across hundreds of miles of Italy, through enemy territory, hoping against hope I'd make it back to friendly lines. But I also realized it was the partisans' only hope. I cleared my throat. "You're right, of course. Reaching the Allies is our only chance. I'll go."

If a bolt of lightning had struck in our midst, it couldn't have had a more galvanizing effect. What had seemed a hopeless cause suddenly took on new life. Everyone crowded around to shake my hand. The air of excitement in the room was electric. Pierangeli took control again. "All right, now. It is decided. Il Console will try to get through to the Allies and get us an air drop of ammunition and supplies. He cannot go alone. We must send someone with him who knows the countryside, who can protect him, and help him get there alive." He looked around at the circle of faces. They nodded. Then he turned to me. "Il Console, you are free to choose any member of the Band you wish, to go with you."

Names and faces flashed before me. "I'd like a day to think it over, while I make preparations to leave," I said.

"Of course," said Pierangeli. "How about if we meet here again day after tomorrow? At noon?" I agreed.

Leaving the meeting, I suddenly felt light-headed, as though I had drunk too much wine. The prospect of leaving the Band and having to cross enemy lines was a powerful intoxicant to a mind and body already strained to the limits of physical endurance. I decided to go back to the Bruschis to ask Ruggero's help in choosing my traveling companion.

I started to fantasize about life back home, if I got through to the Allied lines. I would be with Marguerite again. Would little Howard even remember me? Would Marguerite recognize me? For eighteen months now, I had been running from either the Italians or the Germans. I hadn't had a hot bath in over two months, and it was a good five months back before that to the previous one! I stroked my scraggly beard and tried to imagine a barber shop shave, with hot towels, and aftershave lotion. Holding a woman in my arms again, and making love to her. Lying in bed on a Sunday morning and talking together—in English.

For the first time in months, loneliness and a wave of homesickness washed over me. Chiding myself, I blinked back tears and strode resolutely up the path to Fontanella.

The whole family welcomed me back enthusiastically, and I realized just how much of a family they had become to me. I cared deeply about each and every one of them. I didn't know how to tell them I'd be leaving them for good, and very soon. As Ruggero poured me a welcoming glass of wine, I made no effort to hide my excitement.

I told them all about my experiences of the past two days, including what had transpired at the officer's meeting I had just attended. Everyone suddenly stopped whatever they were doing and turned to look at me, wide-eyed. "When will you leave, Signore?" asked Ruggero.

"In two or three days, at the latest." On hearing that, Pepe burst into tears, and ran from the room. Then Adalgisa started to sniffle, and I almost followed suit. "I will need someone to go with me, Ruggero, and I'd like your help in deciding who it would be best to take."

"I will go with you, Signore," said Ruggero instantly.

"Yes, Signore," added Adalgisa, "Ruggero should go with you, to see that you get there safely. We will be all right here until he returns."

I was deeply touched by their generosity and willingness to sacrifice for me, but I needed someone with more of a sense of the cloak-and dagger-nature of this mission. Someone strong of body, yes, but also someone who had a more outgoing personality, and plenty of imagination, cunning and daring. But who?

Suddenly Ruggero's eyes brightened. "Giovanni...." he began, "Marioli!" I finished, slapping my hand on the table with a big smile. Ruggero beamed. Giovanni was definitely the man. Even Adalgisa was smiling and nodding her head in agreement, although I'd have never believed we'd find anyone that she'd agree was acceptable.

Giovanni Marioli, a man about my own age, was a childhood friend of Ruggero's. He was a lot like Manfred Metzger, but certainly from a vastly different background. He had dark coloring and a slender, wiry, athletic build. There was always a merry twinkle in Giovanni's steel-gray eyes, and like Manfred, he got a big kick out of pulling off a practical joke. In my dealings with him in the past, he had impressed me as nimble-minded, but able to make calm judgments, daring without being reckless, gregarious, and completely unpretentious. He was just the kind of man I needed. My only concern, though, was that he was married, and had two young children. It was a lot to ask of him to leave them and go with me on such a dangerous journey.

I asked Ruggero to go to Pietralunga and tell his friend only that I wanted to talk to him about an "avventura rischiosa," (dangerous mission) and if he was interested, he should return to Fontanella with Ruggero in the morning. "See about my boots while you're there, too." Ugo the bootmaker had somehow gotten the leather and hopefully had my boots finished by now. I'd sure need them for this trip. I gave Ruggero 3,000 lire, roughly $100, the amount that Ugo had quoted me.

While Ruggero was gone, I began my preparations. It would mean hundreds of miles of working our way through dangerous country and high, mountainous terrain. We'd need to travel as light as possible. I dug up my cache of documents from under the stairs, took out my United States diplomatic passport, and the rest of my dollars, and reburied the securities and papers. I stuffed the dollars back into my cane.

Just before lunch the next day, Ruggero returned with Giovanni. Before we sat down, Giovanni reached slyly inside his jacket and, with a grin and a dramatic gesture, whipped out my new boots. I grabbed them from him, exclaiming in pleasure, and immediately tried them on. Medium-high and beautifully crafted, they gave me a thrill of pride and possession — a real feeling of elation. And best of all, they fit my feet perfectly. Now, at last, I would command "rispetto" —respect. I had noted, on entering a farmhouse for the first time, that glances were instantly directed toward one's feet, not the face. That was not surprising. In the rocky, mountainous countryside of Umbria, with no vehicular transportation, one's shoes were more indicative of status than anything else. We finally had enough of admiring my boots, and turned to our lunch.

As we ate, I outlined the problem and the plan. Giovanni listened intently, saying nothing. Ruggero looked alternately at me, then at Giovanni, head swiveling as if watching a tennis match. I could tell he was dying to see what his friend's answer would be. When I finished, Giovanni sat quietly, turning it all over in his mind for a few moments, occasionally running his hand through his thick, chestnut curls. Finally, he spoke. "I am honored you have chosen me for this mission, Signore, and I am ready to go with you, whenever you say. I ask only that you write a statement for my wife and children, in case I don't get back, so that when the Allies come, they will be properly taken care of."

That response assured me that we had chosen the right man for the job. "Of course I'll do that, Giovanni," I replied.

Giovanni carefully folded his document, placing it in his jacket pocket, and left. "I will return in two days, Signore, with a detailed plan for the first leg of our journey." I shook his hand. "Grazie, Giovanni. The Band and I will be forever indebted to you and the Marioli family."

The officers were unanimous in their approval of Giovanni Marioli to accompany me, and we immediately turned our attention to things to request for the air drop. Naturally, ammunition, grenades, explosives, and automatic weapons headed the priority list. Pierangeli, after some deep thought, said, "I think we need to ask for a radio-transmitter, and if at all possible, a man to operate it." We agreed that should be next on the list. Then came a fairly long list of medical supplies. I smiled at the fourth request. Not wishing to appear demanding, they asked for leather, rather than boots.

Bonfigli stood up. "Well, buddy, it is not all take and no give, as you say," he said in English, smiling. Reaching into his pocket, he pulled out a silk aviator's map of Italy. Spreading it out on the table, they conferred for a few minutes among themselves—not without some heated and emotional disagreement—and finally traced on it the route they felt would be the best, and safest, for me to follow. I looked, and my heart and spirits fell. It meant slogging southward through steep, tortuous, country, over high mountain passes, down through the Appenine Mountain chain to somewhere near Anzio. A brutal, almost impossible, itinerary. I folded the silk map and pocketed it.

Pierangeli then produced a rare and valuable bottle of Stock brandy. He poured each of us about half a glassful, and we all raised our glasses in a toast. "To the safe return of our leader, Bonuccio Bonucci!" he said, and we all echoed "Sì! To Bonucci!" and drank a sip. We'd had no further news of him, and could only pray he was still alive. Bonfigli raised his glass. "To the safe journey of our friend, Il Console!" "To Il Console!" came the echo, and I felt my eyes misting over as we drank again. I raised my glass. "To my dear friends of Umbria, and to the liberation of Italy!" I said, my voice breaking slightly. "To Umbria, and to Italy!" they shouted, and Pierangeli added, "And to the Allied victory!" as we drained our glasses.

Each man came to me in turn, to solemnly shake my hand, and give me an "abbraccio" (embrace). Finally, as spokesman for all, Pierangeli said, "Good luck, Signor Console. We have been fortunate, and honored to know you and to have you with us. You have been a good leader, a good soldier, and a good friend." Mario Bonfigli walked with me out the door, his arm across my shoulder—or rather across my back, since he was a good four inches shorter than I. As I turned to leave, he grabbed my hand and shook it repeatedly. "So long, buddy," he said, in English. I could see tears standing in his eyes. It struck me that it was unlikely that I would ever see him, or any of them, again. I turned away, and headed blindly down the path.

For the next two days, I spent my time making preparations for the journey, and in planning meetings with Giovanni. I wanted to get to know him very well. My life might depend on him.

In going carefully through my things, deciding what to take and what to leave behind, I turned up an envelope. I realized with a start that it had been hand-delivered to me some time back by a CLN agent, and I had put it aside to read later and then forgotten it. It was still unopened. I tore it open. It was a letter, at least ten pages long, handwritten in a cramped, European-style longhand. I shuffled to the end for the signature. The writer was a Mr. Foster, a name that rang not the slightest gong of memory with me. I began reading.

Foster claimed he had met me once in Trieste, where I had been of service to him in some diplomatic capacity. He rambled on and on with details of his personal and financial problems. Impatiently, I plowed on through it. He claimed he was being held under house arrest near Ancona on the Adriatic Coast, was in danger of a nervous breakdown from the stress piled on him, and wanted me to contact the Swiss Legation on his behalf. I laughed, shaking my head in wonder as I read. I was about to toss the letter aside, as nothing more than the frustrated ravings of a deranged mind, when the footnote,—a page-long "P.S." in the same handwriting,—caught my attention. In it, Foster had written:

"You might want to try contacting an agent known as 'Quinto,' the British A-Force agent for the Le Marche region. Quinto has direct contact with the Cingoli Band, the major partisan movement in the area. He can be contacted through a peasant family named Rossi, whose farm sits at the base of the hill, about 600 meters west of the road, on the outskirts of Grottazzolina. The Rossis can put you in touch with Germano, who knows how to contact Quinto. Quinto arranges for resistance supplies to be delivered behind the German lines by Mas boat, and sets up the transport of military escapees to the Allied lines on the return trip. If you could arrange for Quinto to get me out, I'd be most grateful."

I sat, thunderstruck, after reading that part. If even remotely true, it was very valuable, and highly sensitive intelligence, and Foster, whoever he was, was foolhardy for putting it on paper. Or else someone was desperately trying to get critical information to me. And how had Foster known who I was, that I was in Italy? My heart lurched. Could it be Manfred? Was Foster's use of Trieste, where Manfred and I had met, a clue? I knew from my initial meetings with Bonuccio Bonucci that "A Force" actually existed.

Excited now, I pulled out my map and searched for Grottazzolina, a town I had never heard of before. There it was, a dot on the map in the Le Marche region, just as the postscript had said. I studied the map carefully. It would be much shorter to go across to the Adriatic coast, where we might get a boat, and go by sea down the Adriatic to the Allied lines at Ortona, than to go south along the mountain chain, on foot, over the route Pierangeli and his men had indicated. This information, if true, could shorten our journey by weeks! With the current ammunition situation, any time gained was precious. Could "Foster" be Manfred?

If the letter was from Manfred, as I suspected, I had to trust it, and use the information in it. Not that getting to the Adriatic would be easy--we'd have to cross the mountains on foot to get there from here, too. But fewer mountains, fewer miles. That meant fewer days.

Just then, Giovanni arrived. I carefully reread the footnote. "Foster," whoever he was, could not possibly be making all this up. It was worth checking out. If this Quinto person existed, he was the answer to our prayers. I hoped that the crazy sounding "Mr. Foster" was really Manfred. I looked up at Giovanni. "My friend," I said, smiling, "it looks as if there has been a big change in plans!"

Ruggero and I set out on the Monday evening following Easter Sunday, in the gathering dusk. Under my coat, I wore my good luck charm—Margherita Bonucci's white dresser scarf, the one little Lucia had embroidered with the American Eagle. In my knapsack were provisions for the next day's meals, prepared by Adalgisa and Concetta. Pepe had scrubbed and polished my cane, and at the last minute, had shyly offered me his wool cap, which, though much too small for me, was now clapped jauntily atop my head. Ruggero was at my side, carrying the knapsack. He had insisted on accompanying me as far as Pietralunga, where I would pick up Giovanni.

As we left Fontanella, I handed him my Beretta, and indicated he was to lead the way. He stepped out in front, the Beretta in hand. As we started down the worn and rutted path, I stopped for a moment to turn and look back at the place that had been my home these past three months.

Framed by the dilapidated old farmhouse, the baking oven in the yard, and the trees beside the little stream, stood a tearful Adalgisa, hair blowing in the wind. Concetta stood like a young colt at her side, hugging a sobbing Pepe. When I turned, they all gave sad little waves. "Buona fortuna, Signore, vada con Dio!" called Adalgisa.

Like the moment when Lucia Bonucci reached up and put the scarf around my neck and hugged me, and that first taste of the Christmas goose at Margherita's, with everyone gathered around the table, I knew I would carry the image I was seeing, a treasured photograph in my mind's eye, for the rest of my days. I waved back, then reluctantly turned, and left Fontanella.

What would it be like for these people, I wondered, when the devastating turbulence of war swept through here like a howling, raging tornado? Here, everything seemed peaceful, and timeless. And here, as elsewhere, everything was relative.

It was well after dark when we reached Giovanni's house. He swung the door open on the first knock. After the obligatory glass of wine all around, Ruggero stuck out his hand, ready to leave, and I shook it. Then we embraced warmly. I couldn't allow him to leave with such a sad face. "Ah, Ruggero," I teased him, "you came with me only so you could sample the wine of the Casa Marioli!"

His round face creased into a warm smile, though tears

glistened in his eyes. "No, no, Signore Console—I had to come along, so I could taste the wine first, to see if it was good enough for the likes of you!"

And so, laughing, we parted for good—he to return to life at Fontanella, and I to go on with Giovanni to whatever unknown adventures lay before us.

Chapter 9

The Long Trek to Grottazzolina

Giovanni's wife set out huge bowls of rich minestrone. "A journey should never begin on an empty stomach." I showed Giovanni how to use the Beretta, which Ruggero had reluctantly relinquished to him, and checked over my own recently acquired Colt automatic. I asked Giovanni if he knew how to use Italian grenades, six of which I had managed to cajole out of Bonfigli. He said yes, he had used them before. We concealed the grenades on him, since I wasn't sure I would be as good with them as he would. "If challenged, we'll use grenades for a group, pistols if there are only one or two of them, okay?"

"Okay." Giovanni grinned with pleasure, like a small boy, as he repeated his first word of English.

Neither of us mentioned the obvious—that it would be certain death, for him at least, if anyone caught us out, armed, after curfew. My diplomatic passport might, just might, save me from a firing squad—but only to be subjected to God knows what else.

"I have a nice surprise for you Signore," said Giovanni, with a smile, as we got ready to leave Tuesday evening. "We'll be going by bicycle for the first leg of the journey! A trusted friend of mine will be here with them shortly."

"Hey, that's great! How did you manage that?" I was pleased. My feet, and my ankle, were still not completely healed, and any relief from walking, given what lay before us, was welcome.

Promptly at nine, Giovanni's friend Oreste arrived, with

two extra bicycles. I insisted on paying him for the use of them. In turn, Oreste insisted he would accompany us as far as Branca, a town about forty kilometers away. Initially, I was against it. It would be hard enough for two to be inconspicuous, let alone three. And on bicycles, at that.

"But Signore, I think it might be a good idea," said Giovanni. "Oreste knows the route to Branca, and the terrain, like the back of his hand, and can get us there safely by skirting Gubbio and taking less traveled secondary roads. He also has a cousin in Branca, who will give us lodging the first day. Then Oreste can bring the extra bicycles back here, one at a time."

"Okay, but only as far as Branca."

After quietly handing some money to Giovanni's wife, I suggested we get on our way. Oreste and I waited outside while Giovanni said his private farewells to his family.

The moon, which by then had risen high, shed a pale, silvery light on the hills as we pedaled toward Gubbio. At first, I had difficulty balancing all my gear. On the steeper hills, I barely had the strength to keep up with Oreste and Giovanni, who were obviously more used to this. After what seemed like an eternity, with my calves and thighs on fire from the strain, we crested the last hill, and began the long, easy coast down to Gubbio. After a short stretch, Oreste slowed, signaling us to stop.

"About two hundred meters ahead, at the road to Umbertide, bear left and ride hard. Stay close together. After about eight hundred meters on the highway we'll cut right onto a smaller road. We don't want to stay on the highway any longer than we absolutely have to."

We hit the highway pedaling like mad. The two shadows I was following suddenly darted right. I followed suit, and before I knew what was happening, I was hurtling head first over the handlebars, landing in the grassy ditch next to the road. Unaccustomed to European hand brakes, I had grasped the handlebars too firmly as I made the turn, locking the brakes. My two companions, hearing the commotion behind them, stopped. As I remounted, embarrassed but unhurt, I heard Oreste laugh softly and mutter to Giovanni, "Behold! The next Campione d'Italia (biking champion of Italy) has been found!" I laughed too.

"Let's put you in the middle," said Giovanni, "so we don't lose you along the way."

We set off again, and about an hour before daybreak, we arrived at the outskirts of Branca. Oreste's relatives, the Panfiglios, welcomed us with open arms. Out came bread, and the inevitable wine, while a pot of ersatz coffee was prepared.

Oreste, as he left for Pietralunga, said, "Take good care of my important friends here, eh?" He needn't have worried.

I explained the general direction, and the purpose of our journey, without giving them too many specifics. "I will help," said Signor Panfiglio. I wondered what he meant. As soon as breakfast was finished, Panfiglio left for work. His wife shooed the children out of the house, and showed Giovanni and me to the bedroom. Within minutes, we were sound asleep.

When we woke that evening, in time for dinner, we found all the Panfiglios gathered at the table, dressed in their Sunday best. We did Signora Panfiglio's delicious meal justice, but I winced at the thought of the dent she must have put in her larder, and her finances, to lay such a magnificent table for us. First, there was a rich minestrone, with meat in it—probably chicken. Then a decent egg pasta, like fettucini, dressed with a sauce that actually had pieces of meat in it. I savored each mouthful before swallowing. The bread was crusty and not too coarse. For dessert, Signora Panfiglio produced "cenci", a sort of cruller made of dough, rolled, twisted, fried lightly in oil and sprinkled with honey. With it, Signor Panfiglio served us glasses of vinsanto, the beautiful dessert wine of Umbria. The meal was holiday fare—a very special treat. Giovanni said he thought it was probably the best meal the family had eaten in years. I could almost say the same. I rose to express our thanks, telling them I had never been shown a higher or more generous order of hospitality than I received from them that night.

"I have arranged for a horse, a cart, and a driver to take you on the next leg of your journey," announced Signor Panfiglio, as though it was the most ordinary thing in the world. "He will be here before daybreak in the morning."

In our conversation that morning, I had remarked that I wished we could ride a cloud over the mountains instead of walking. Signor Panfiglio had undertaken to find us a cloud to ride, over the first mountain peak, anyway.

"Grazie, Signor Panfiglio, you have no idea what a great help this is to us."

"It is nothing. Do not think of it," he replied politely.

When bedtime came that night, they insisted that Giovanni and I take the one bedroom. Where they, and the six children, spent the night remains a mystery, but they would hear of nothing else.

Shortly before dawn, we piled into an ancient, straw-filled wooden cart, in whose peeling paint we could discern faint traces of the colorful, whimsical artistry of its youthful coat. The tired, old horse matched the cart in age, as did the cantankerous driver of the dilapidated outfit.

After embracing the Panfiglios and saying our farewells, Giovanni and I clambered in, covered ourselves with some loose straw and a smelly old blanket, and enjoyed the novelty of being transported, jouncing about, over the rough road across the Marchigiano spur of the Apennines, the mountains which divided Umbria from the Le Marche region. As we bumped along, Giovanni and I chuckled more than once at the running stream of colorful and imaginative curses the driver rained down upon his poor old horse.

After five hours of mostly uphill travel, he drew up and dismounted. "This is it," he grumbled. "I go no farther. Get out, and be on your way." We got down, stretched, and looked around us. We were at a crossroads, somewhere in the general direction of Macerata, probably near the little town of Cancelli, I figured, consulting my silk map. We had no idea of which way to go. The driver was no help. Anxious to be gone, he turned the cart around and bid us goodbye in the same surly tone of voice he had used to curse the horse. Then, just as he reached the first curve, he turned around in his seat and shouted, "Buona fortuna!"

Giovanni and I looked at each other and broke out laughing. "See, I told you he was a softie," Giovanni remarked dryly. We set off at a brisk but comfortable pace. The warm sun felt good on my aching shoulder. It was a pain that didn't go away. Since I hadn't injured it in any way that I could think of, I decided it must be some sort of bursitis, or tendinitis, and I'd just have to live with it.

Shortly after two, we saw a group of men filing down the mountain to our left. As we neared the base of the mountain, we encountered one of them. He looked tired and disheveled, and we learned that he, and others of the local partisan band, had engaged the Germans the day before, and had suffered a number of casualties, including several killed. The men we had seen coming down the mountain were carrying their wounded. They quickly dispersed, not wanting to risk further retaliatory action by the Germans.

Now on the alert, we bid the partisans farewell and continued on our way. We began looking for a likely farmhouse in which to shelter for the night. It was dusk, and we were still searching, when suddenly, from behind us, came a soft, but insistent "ALT!" We halted. "Now, very slowly and carefully, put your hands on your head." These words were spoken in a dialect that I barely understood. They came up to us and patted us down, relieving us of our weapons and Giovanni's precious grenades. "All right, now, lower your arms, and turn around."

"Don't try anything," another warned, unnecessarily. I knew that these men had to be partisans.

I ventured a question to our captors. "Who are you? What are you up to?" I ventured.

"More to the point, who are _you_?" snapped the older of the two. "And what we are up to is placing you under arrest."

"Why would you do that to two fellow partigiani?" I asked mildly. They looked startled. "I am an American diplomat, recently a member of the Banda di San Fa......" "SILENZIO!" (Be quiet!) Then, more calmly, "have you any identification to prove it?" I produced my passport and my forged identity card. Giovanni produced his identity card. The partisans examined our documents.

"The beard is not much of an improvement," the younger one commented, looking from my passport photo to my face. I didn't dare laugh. "Come," he ordered, and with one leading the way, and the other covering us from behind, we left the road and set off down a narrow path.

"Where are you taking us?" I asked. No answer.

After about twenty minutes, we reached a cluster of farm buildings. There were a good many partisans around, all equipped with Sten guns. This was no insignificant, poorly armed partisan force. We were led into the house, where we were able to quickly establish the truth of our identities to the officers billeted there. They questioned us closely about what we had seen on our trip, and what was happening in the San Faustino area. I filled them in as frankly and fully as I could.

"I envy you your equipment. How did you manage to get so many Sten guns? We had almost no arms to work with."

"This is the headquarters of the Garibaldi Division of the Cingoli Band. We are one of the largest partisan movements in Central Italy, so we have gotten Mas torpedo boat shipments of supplies and arms from the Allies." I was impressed by that, and my heart lifted on hearing the words. They were the Band Foster had named in his letter! And the boats he spoke of also existed! The Cingoli Band was, without a doubt, a formidable guerrilla force. The San Faustini were country cousins by comparison.

We were comfortably housed and fed that night in the old farmhouse that served as their local headquarters building. Giovanni enjoyed a new gastronomic experience —he had his first taste of American "Spam". To eat meat from a can was a novelty to him, and afterward, he extolled the virtues of Spam to me, and anyone else who would listen.

The next day, our weapons and grenades were returned to us, and we were escorted back down to the road leading to Camerino.

"Give Camerino a wide berth, Signori," advised Vincenzo, our escort. "There is a large garrison of Germans there. Also, the town is on a major highway, and German convoys are constantly passing through. It is wise to avoid the area completely if you can." He turned, saluted us, and took off.

We walked all day, following the twisting path of the Patenza river, down the valley in the direction of Camerino. Giovanni was a pleasant and good-natured companion. At lunchtime, giving me a wink and a sly grin, he drew from his shirt a can of Spam he had filched from the partisans' supply. He was intrigued with the metal key that peeled the can open. Although I had never particularly favored the stuff, I was delighted now to have it with our dry bread and bit of cheese.

A few hours later we came to a crossroads, and a short distance from it was a farmhouse. It was much too close to the intersection to serve as a refuge for the night, but we thought we might at least get some directions from there. Giovanni went to the house to make inquiries, while I stood back in the shadows, out of sight. As he raised his hand to knock, the door suddenly swung open. Giovanni froze for a moment, then he turned and broke into a dead run. Seeing that, I took off on a run, too.

Running with a knapsack flapping and slapping at your back is no way to run for your life, but my feet were pounding the road as fast as I could move them. Giovanni quickly caught up and passed me. "What the hell is going on?" I shouted as he whizzed by me. I could hear yelling from the house, and risked a quick look back. Four armed men had emerged from the front door. "Militia!" panted Giovanni.

I found strength I didn't know I possessed, and ran faster, but after a few moments, I knew I wouldn't be able to keep up the pace. "Run!" I called to Giovanni. "Don't wait for me! Just keep running!" "What the hell does it look like I'm doing?"

Giovanni shouted back. Behind me, shots rang out. Three of them. What a hellish time to be wearing a light tan raincoat! A bullet zinged by my left ear, so close the concussion was like a blow. The firing continued as we dashed around a curve. Then I saw Giovanni dive off the road, into some bushes. I followed, and together we slithered and wriggled away from the road for about a hundred meters. The firing had ceased.

We lay there panting, listening for any sounds of pursuit. Motioning for Giovanni to follow me, I slunk along behind a row of trees, following a shallow ditch, until we were far enough away from the road to feel relatively safe. Stripping off my knapsack and throwing it down, I announced, "Now, I need to take a leak!" Giovanni doubled over in laughter as I calmly relieved myself against a tree.

"Run!" he mimicked. "What did you think, I was taking an afternoon stroll down the road, while those Fascist bastards were shooting at my ass?" At that, I started laughing too. Soon we were both howling.

"Hah!" he pointed at me, "You with that pack flapping and your long legs churning—you run like a camel in sand!"

"Well, you should have seen your face when they came to the door! 'Scusi'" I mimicked derisively, in a high falsetto, and that set us off again. It was a long-overdue nervous reaction, and a hell of a lot better than not being able to laugh at all.

The sky was beginning to lighten when, through the swirling dawn mists, we saw, atop a nearby hill, the chocolate-frosted wedding cake tiers of lofty Camerino.

Giovanni suddenly stopped, and pointed over to his right. A lone farmhouse stood about two hundred meters away. He raised a questioning brow to me. We had been on the road since six the previous morning, and we were both ready to drop in our tracks. I nodded yes, too tired to even speak. "Back in a minute," he said, "but if I turn and run, you head for that stand of trees over there."

"Okay. Be careful. If it looks good, just signal for me to

come on in." I dropped down into a shallow ditch by the side of the road, from which I could cover Giovanni and watch the door to the house. Thank God no dogs started yapping! I could see him talking earnestly with the person who came to the door, turned and gave a short, piercing whistle and a quick arm wave. I breathed in relief. It was safe.

I loped across the field and met him at the top of the stairs. We had to brush past several people to squeeze into the crowded kitchen. I looked around in amazement. There were at least two complete families gathered there, including grandmothers, aunts, babies , and children of all ages. It was a mob scene. Clouds of flies were buzzing around. Everyone was talking at once, and no one seemed to be listening to anything that was being said by anyone else. They were like a barnyard full of chickens, all cackling, darting here and there, pecking and scratching.The welcome warmth of the fire thawed our weary bones. "Are you hungry?" asked one of the old ladies. "Si, Signora," replied Giovanni. "We have not eaten since yesterday."

"Ma, poveracci! Che disgrazia!" (You poor things! How terrible!) she said, turning immediately and yelling, to the room in general, "Eh! some food for these poor men. They haven't eaten since yesterday! Angelina! Qualcosa `a mangiare, per favore!" (Some food, please) This had the effect of doubling the decibel level in the room, if that was possible. It also sparked a frenzied renewal of activity from two of the women—one of whom, presumably, was Angelina.

"Here, Signore," said the other one, "Sit, sit,—rest yourself. You must be tired near to death." That was closer to the truth than she could have imagined. I dropped gratefully into the seat. One of the men jumped up, signaling that Giovanni should take his place at the table. Cups of hot coffee were quickly brought and put in front of us, and we sipped, dunking chunks of bread in the hot liquid, and wolfing them down.

The old woman watched us, hawklike , nodding as we ate and drank, punctuating our every swallow with a cooing murmur of satisfaction, like a nurse with two very sick patients to be coddled. Then Angelina set a "frittata", the Italian version of an omelette, before us. Saliva rushed into my mouth at the sight and smell of it. Besides never wanting to walk an extra step, I hoped that once I got out of this, I would never in my life feel so hungry again either!

Everything goes into a frittata except, as the saying goes, "the kitchen sink." This one was about an inch thick, round and puffy, made of peppers, onions, potatoes and cheese, bound together with eggs. We tried, unsuccessfully, not to bolt it down in huge bites, like starving animals. It was the most delicious thing imaginable. "Grazie, Signora," I said to Angelina, laying my fork down after consuming every last morsel on my plate, "you have made life worth living again, with that delicious frittata." "Think nothing of it Signore," she replied modestly, beaming with pleasure.

I glanced around the room. How in hell she fed this mob, I couldn't imagine, let alone strangers who wandered hungry to her door. An older man, who seemed to be the master of the house, approached us. "Signori," he said apologetically, "I am sorry there is no space here for you to sleep. But you are welcome to sleep in the barn."

Inured to dirt and farm smells though we were, the stench that assaulted us when we opened the stable door was overpowering. The stalls must not have been cleaned for a week or more! Scrabbling around, we searched out some fresh straw, and, strewing it around, each prepared to bed down next to a cow. Pointing to the largest of the three animals, I said, "You take that one, Giovanni, I can see she has eyes for you." Patting the cow on the head, he rejoined, chuckling, "Yes? Well, she'd better let me sleep, and not expect any action from me tonight!" He settled in beside her. Snuggling deep into the straw next to my own cow, I was soon warm, if not exactly cozy. The bitterly cold wind whistled around the corners of our haven, and although I didn't want to think about what we'd smell like later, I was glad to be in here with our warm, bovine companions, and not outside somewhere, where the temperature was below freezing. Soon, we were both fast asleep. Giovanni snored loudly.

Although I was vaguely aware of my "bed mate" stirring from time to time as she was watered or fed, I never really woke, and we slept most of the day that way. Late in the afternoon, one of the youngsters came sidling into the barn to wake us. "Mamma says you should come up now,—there is dinner ready for you." We washed ourselves as best we could in the icy water of the stock trough. Giovanni entertained the children by juggling hand grenades, something he had enjoyed practicing in our rare quiet moments. "All right, Giovanni, put your toys away and let's go eat!" I said, and we trudged upstairs—he still juggling grenades, a gaggle of awestruck children following him. Several people wrinkled their noses when they caught a whiff of us.

Angelina urged us to "Mangia!" as she dipped into the giant pottery bowl in the center of the table and spooned out huge helpings of the piping hot fettucini, cheese, and tomato dish the women had prepared. Once more, the old woman hovered nearby and watched us, clucking and nodding in approval as we ate. We needed no urging! Not knowing when, or if, we'd see another hot meal, we obligingly stuffed ourselves. Then, sated, we toasted the assembled group with our remaining few sips of wine. They all smiled genially and joined us in the toasts.

At the door, Angelina handed me a wrapped package, which I knew contained bread and cheese, and her husband gave Giovanni a flask of wine. The old woman then made the sign of the cross over us, saying "Va con Dio" (Go with God), and I felt a wave of nostalgia for Fontanella and the Bruschis. Thanking them for their hospitality, Giovanni said, with a merry twinkle, "My girlfriend for the night, your cow, was very simpática, (charming) dear friends." Everyone laughed uproariously at that, and we made our way out into the frigid night, their laughter echoing down the stairs behind us.

The night was damp and chilly and I knew there would be snow as we moved higher up. Even worse, the drizzle that had fallen during the day had turned the trail into a muddy mess, which meant that all the back roads and trails would be impossible to negotiate—even more so in the dark--as they froze over. Giovanni stopped and stared at the steep, slippery, quagmire of a trail that stretched before us. Then he shook his head and sighed, turning to me. "We cannot do this, Signore. No way! Even in summer it would be difficult, but now—I'm afraid we'll just have to risk staying on the paved highway."

"Yeah, it looks that way, doesn't it, but I hate the idea. It's a main highway." On the map, the portion of paved highway that would take us through the mountain pass, where we could then branch off onto a less traveled secondary road, was at least eight or nine kilometers long. Calderola lay just west of our route, a bit off to the side of the secondary road.

"We'll have to move fast," said Giovanni. "Can you run most of the way to the pass?"

"I'm sure going to give it a try." I didn't want to be on that damned highway one minute longer than we absolutely had to. As the road became steeper, we were forced to slow down, though fear urged us on. The snow became crusted with a thin, brittle layer of ice as we neared the summit, and I prayed the road would not ice over completely until we were through the pass and down the other side. To my right, out of the corner of my eye, illuminated by the moonlight reflecting off the snow, was an unprotected sheer drop down to the river far below. One slip, or misstep, and we'd be over the edge, plunging hundreds of feet down to the river's icy waters. We were close to the summit when we stopped for our first break. We leaned against a spindly tree, panting. We wasted no energy with words.

Suddenly, we heard the unmistakable drone of motors below us. Trucks were laboring up the pass, in low gear! We scrambled off the road, and took cover in some bushes, under an outcropping of rock where the roadbed had been cut through the sheer face of the mountain. We pressed ourselves flat to the icy ground, clinging to the thickest branches of the brush to keep from sliding down the slope. I prayed our handhold would not give way under our weight. Giovanni whispered, "Don't worry, the Germans won't need to see us, they'll smell us long before they get here!" He chuckled softly. I grunted, too cold and frightened to respond. Gingerly releasing one hand, I tapped a finger to my temple, then to him, to indicate he was nuts. Hell, at least he could laugh at a time like this! "But it is no big problem," he concluded irrepressibly, "one whiff and they'll pass us right up, figuring anything that smells so bad has to have been dead for at least a week!" He laughed aloud at that, and I winced. "Shhh!" I was sure whoever was coming would hear his laugh echoing in the night air. Finally, the convoy passed us. We stayed well out of sight for at least five minutes afterward, then scrambled back onto the highway. Soaked with perspiration from exertion and fear, and from pressing our bodies against the wet surface of the rocks and snow, the biting cold wind quickly froze us. We broke into a run. By the time we were over the pass and had turned onto the secondary road, I was lathered in sweat, and my lungs hurt so badly with every icy breath I was sure I had pneumonia.

"Giovanni!" I gasped. "Look for shelter—I have to rest—can't go on!"

"Haystacks...over there!" he panted. We veered off and jumped into the nearest haystack, burrowing deep. We thought the hay would shield us and keep us warm enough to cool down gradually. We learned a quick and miserable lesson to the contrary. Shivering and shuddering, and we huddled close for warmth. We stuck it out for fifteen minutes, but could take no more. "Let's go, the hell with this, we'll freeze to death here," I said. We set off again at a run. After trotting along for another half hour, we rounded a turn and found ourselves smack in the center of the town of Calderola. From the map, I had expected it be off to one side.

"What the hell...?" Skidding to a halt, we jumped off the road and hunkered down behind a cypress tree, peering down through the center of town. There was no sign of life. "We'll have to chance going through," I whispered to

Giovanni. "Stick to the shadows." Slowly, we began working our way through town. The moon hung like a lighted globe above us. I was convinced I could have read a newspaper by its stark, cold light.

We were facing a tiny piazza. A double row of small trees ran along one side of it, but they would afford us very little cover. Cautiously, we sidled along between the trees. A movement to my right caught my attention. I froze in my tracks, so suddenly Giovanni bumped into me from behind. "What is....?" the question died on his lips, as five uniformed men hove into view.

They caught sight of us at about the same time we saw them. Moonlight gleamed on white Sam Browne belts that marked two of them as carabinieri. The other three were Fascist militia. All were armed. Fear prickled along my arms and ran up my neck like the legs of a thousand spiders. "Get a grenade out—quick!" I hissed. "Done!" Giovanni whispered back. Slowly, carefully, I drew the Colt, and held it ready at my side. Giovanni moved his right hand, with the grenade, close to his mouth, where he could quickly pull the pin with his teeth, and heave the grenade into their midst. Watching them intently, we continued quietly along the length of the piazza. They stood like statues, staring at us, as though seeing an apparition. We passed not fifteen feet from them,— two ragged, unkempt strangers who had materialized out of nowhere—and they never challenged us, or so much as moved a muscle!

Gaining the opposite end of the piazza, we quickly slipped behind a large building, and I let my breath out in a whoosh. Without a word, we broke into a dead run, and didn't pause until we were a good half mile out of town. We came upon a small mountain stream, in a deep cut below the road. Clambering down its steep bank, we hid in the bushes beside it, weapons at the ready. We waited about five minutes, but nothing happened. There was no alarm, no pursuit. Why had they, with the odds in their favor, not reacted? Were they moving ahead of us to set up a roadblock? It was long past curfew, so we had no right to be out, let alone armed, strolling casually through their town.

"Let's leave the road and head for the fields," I whispered. "It will be safer." Giovanni nodded agreement, and we took off across a field and up and over the top of a small hill. The bright moon seemed to be guiding us, following along, lighting our way, so that by the time dawn peeked over the hills a few hours later, we had put several kilometers and several steep ridges between ourselves and Calderola. "Time to find some breakfast and a bed, Signore." The friendly moon had scampered for cover and disappeared. Daylight, our biggest enemy, was arriving in a great burst of orange fire. "Look for a farm,— a poor one," I said.

"That should be easy enough to find," said Giovanni dryly, "I doubt that there are too many rich villas or palazzos around here."

After about fifteen minutes more of walking, we found the kind of poor, isolated farm we were looking for. Giovanni came back to report to me. "I listened with all my ears, Signore," he said, shaking his head in frustration, "and I could hardly understand them, but it seems to be safe there, and at least I know we are welcome." Wearily, we made our way to the house. Once again, the greeting we received was warm and sincere. After bowls of hot minestrone, we were shown to the family bed to sleep. Again I was struck with amazement at the generosity of these poor folk of the Italian countryside. Giovanni and I were served heaping bowls of pasta, some cheese, and a link of sausage cooked with onions and peppers.

When we asked directions, spreading our map out on the table, the woman exclaimed in delight over the silk, touching it with gentle fingers, as her husband's stubby, work-worn finger traced out the route we should take. "What a rich country America must be," she commented softly, fingering a corner of the map. "Even your maps are made of silk! Imagine!" After supper, she wrapped a small package of food for us. "Stay out of trouble, and make your mothers proud," she admonished us, like we were small boys.

Near midnight, we paused to rest a bit, near a small stream. Giovanni, always hungry, suggested we eat, so we took out the bread and sausage the woman had given us and ate it as we sat on a large flat rock in the cold night air. "I wish we had some wine to wash this down," said Giovanni, but no genie appeared before us to grant his wish. "Well, you'll have to be satisfied with water from the stream here," I said. "A quick drink and we'll be on our way. I want to make San Ginnesio before dawn." "Well, I just hope that San Ginnesio doesn't send out a welcoming party like the one we saw in Calderola! My heart can't take that twice in a row," said Giovanni, and putting his hand over his heart in a dramatic gesture, he dropped to the ground next to the little fast-moving stream. In the moonlight, his grinning face was mirrored in the shimmering water. Standing behind him, I smiled down at the image, and was startled to see my own unkempt, almost unrecognizable visage reflected above his. We were certainly a frightening looking pair! "Look at us, Giovanni!" "Would this sight make our mothers proud?"

"My mother would scream and faint at the smell, before she even saw me," replied Giovanni, his white teeth flashing as he laughed.

I'm so glad I have him along, I thought, as I stared at our two faces, mine bearded, his with several days growth of whiskers, wavering there in the water. I shuddered to think of what this trip would have been like alone. Giovanni abruptly plunged his fist into the water, sending our reflections undulating away, in wider and wider circles, until they disappeared completely. Scooping up a handful of the clear, icy water, he gulped it down. Dropping down beside him, I did the same.

"We'd better get moving, Giovanni,—it looks like we're in for a weather change."

A few hours later, wet and miserable from a steady, cold drizzle, we stood facing San Ginnesio. The road ran right through town, as it had in Calderola. We edged our way in, cautiously slithering up and down the narrow, cobbled streets, groping along in the darkness. Suddenly, above me, a gust of wind caught a shutter and banged it against a wall, sending me jumping in fright, my hand automatically clasping the butt of the Colt. Not even a dog barked.

We were about ten minutes past the town, when Giovanni finally spoke. "Whew!" he said, "that town gave me the creeps! I think everyone must have been dead there."

"Well, lucky for us if they were. But, never mind them,— we're still very much alive, and I'm wet and hungry. We better start looking for a place to sleep the day away!" I shivered miserably, the icy rain dripping steadily from my cap down onto the back of my neck. Would this misery ever end, would I ever enjoy a normal life again, I wondered? A life where nights would be for sleeping, and I could awake and be out among people during the daylight? Happy daytime person that I was, I had turned into a silent, solitary creature, who moved about only in stealth, in the dark of night.

Our next lodging wasn't the type of isolated farmhouse that we usually chose, and it was near enough to town to make me apprehensive about it, but there seemed to be nothing else around. Assunta Lombardo was tiny and cheerful, around fifty, I judged.

"Phew!" she said frankly, as we stepped through her front door. If she was frightened by the appearance of these two rough-looking strangers, she didn't show it. "You certainly need some dry clothes, and a bath." She bustled to the fireplace and filled the cauldron there with water, swinging it over the fire to heat. When it was warm enough, she left the room, and we took turns sponge bathing as best we could. Then we changed into our only other set of clothes, which miraculously had stayed pretty dry in our knapsacks.

"I'll wash these while you sleep," she said briskly, returning with some food. Scooping up our filthy, wet clothes, she dumped them into the still warm cauldron of water. "I think the sun will come out, and I can dry them in a sheltered place in the back yard, where they won't be seen by anyone."

"Grazie, Signora," I said gratefully. "Clean clothes are a big luxury for us poor 'sfollati." Sipping the hot barley coffee she served us, I looked around the room. It was a well-furnished little place—several cuts above the average poor farmhouse. Massaging my bruised and aching feet before pulling my boots back on, I decided to chance a question.

"Signora Lombardo, is it possible, do you think, for us to hire a horse-drawn vehicle, a cart of some sort, to take us for the next portion of our journey?" She thought a minute. "Hmm! I don't know, Signore. Let me think about where you might get a horse and cart. That is not an easy request. "

She went over to the fireplace and began vigorously scrubbing our clothes, twisting and wringing each piece. There was no soap, of course, but a good dunking in hot water would help rid them of the worst of the dirt and smell we had accumulated.

Suddenly, she straightened up, murmuring, "Forse, il Dottore!" (Of course, the Doctor!) She turned to me. "Perhaps il Dottore can help you about your cart," she said.

I brightened at that, thoughts of sleep gone. "Give us directions to his house, Signora, and we will go right now and ask him," I said. As we left, I told her to expect us back in an hour or so.

Leaving Giovanni to guard the front door, I was shown into a large, well-furnished parlor. The old woman motioned me to a big overstuffed chair. Clutching her hands together nervously, she said, "Scusi, Signore, but my husband has been very sick. It will be a few minutes until he comes down to see you."

With that, she left the room and didn't return. Strange. Minutes dragged by, and there was no sound in the house except the ticking of a clock on the mantel above the fireplace. Our reception by the lady of the house had not been very cordial. My instincts had always warned me against asking favors of anyone in the upper classes. They didn't have the same generous attitude toward those in need as the poorer folk did. Just as I decided to forget the whole thing and bolt out the front door, I heard a slow tread on the stairs. A few seconds later, il Dottore entered the room, leaning heavily on a cane. He didn't offer me so much as a greeting, or a handshake. "Assassini!" (Assassins!), he snarled, hoarsely, his voice barely above a whisper. "You have abandoned all semblance of civilized behavior, you English!" He lifted the cane a fraction of an inch to point it toward me, a look of loathing on his face. "You bomb populated areas, even peaceful Macerata—an offense that even the Russians, those barbarians, are not capable of! We know what you are doing—you are determined to destroy, to obliterate, the great heritage and culture of Italy!" His eyes grew wild and his voice rose an octave. "You cannot stand it that it is OUR art, OUR music, that the whole world celebrates! Yes, great art and great music are Italian, not English!" As he ranted on, his face flushed a mottled red, and his eyes, wide and furious, bulged from his head.

I jumped up to leave. The doctor grabbed my sleeve. I jerked my arm away. "To hell with you, and this nonsense!" I gained the door, and was reaching for the handle. "Wait!" he thundered, "I am not finished with you, Inglese!"

"Well, I'm damned well finished with you," I retorted, and whipped out my Colt, pointing it at his head. "Now, go over there and sit down!" I ordered. He quickly obeyed, his tremors becoming quite pronounced. "Look at the clock," I said. His eyes swiveled from the gun to the clock on the mantel, which read 10:15. "If you so much as move a muscle for fifteen minutes after I'm out that door, I will come back here and blow your head off! Depend on it! Not a word to anyone about our little visit, understand?"

Terrified, gasping for breath, he nodded mutely. I headed for the front door. I hope the bastard has a heart attack, I thought spitefully. Then I caught sight of the telephone, an antiquated wooden affair, attached to the wall. Damned if he'll call the carabinieri down on us. I ripped it out of the wall and flung it across the room. It landed near the old man's feet, and he jumped in fear and whimpered. "Signore," he quavered pleadingly, "my horse is lame, and could not possibly pull a cart."

"What do I care about your damned horse? " I retorted, livid. "And another thing, I'm not English, I'm American! And you'd be damned lucky to have the Americans liberate you, you horse's ass! The uneducated farmers of this country have more brains than you!" With that, I flung the door open and stormed outside.

Giovanni jumped in alarm on seeing me. "Signore! What is it? Put the gun away! What the hell happened?" I strode down the little path between the gardens, fuming. "Just walk calmly, Giovanni, and smile. We're two guys on our way to visit our sick aunt." I filled Giovanni in on what had happened. "Accidenti!" he said malevolently. It was an oath that has no real translation, but I knew what he meant.

The widow Lombardo had been watching for us, and she admitted us immediately, wringing her hands, obviously distressed. "Oh, oh, Signori, I'm so glad you are back safely! I made a terrible mistake! The recent bombing at Macerata destroyed il Dottore's big house there! Now he hates the Allies!" That explained it.

"It's all right," I said. "I don't think the Dottore will do anything." With that, we fell into bed, and slept most of the day.

Since it was a Sunday, and we wouldn't arouse suspicion by being out, I decided to use the afternoon daylight hours to cover most of the remaining distance to Grottazzolina, which looked to be about a six hour walk from Assunta Lombardo's cottage. Our freshly laundered clothes were dry, and after a hot meal and our farewells, we again headed down the road.

How good it felt to be out in the pale afternoon sun, with full bellies, dressed in clean clothes! I had even trimmed my beard a bit, so I didn't look so bedraggled. "Eh, Signore, we sure smell good, now, no?" smiled Giovanni. "The Signorine will all be happy to see us coming, two such handsome

Signori as we are. They won't turn their noses up and make faces any more!" He laughed and began whistling a sprightly tune.

We made good time, and it was just before midnight on April 10th when we reached the area we sought. We had no difficulty locating the farm of Francesco Rossi. It stood isolated, a prosperous looking stone edifice, in good repair, at the foot of the steep hill whose crowning glory was the ancient, crumbling town of Grottazzolina.

Excitement surged through me. All the information in Foster's letter so far had proven true. It meant that the contact named Quinto probably existed, too. "This is it, Giovanni!" I exulted. "This is our link to the Allies! We made it! The worst is over!" Clapping him jubilantly on the shoulder, I strode ahead up the path, climbed the stairs, and banged confidently on the farmhouse door.

Chapter 10

Airdrop at Morena

No one answered. I banged again. I could hear sounds from within, but the door didn't open. Finally, from behind it, came a muffled voice. "Who is it? What do you want?" "I am here to see Francesco Rossi. We need shelter." I waited. Nothing happened. "I am an American officer," I added, "and I have an Italian companion with me."

Someone else must have joined the person on the other side of the door, because I could hear voices raised in discussion.

Exasperated, I called, "I have come to meet with Quinto!"

More voices from within, but the door remained shut. An old man's voice quavered, "Go away! We will not open the door! Go elsewhere for shelter!"

"Signori!" I shouted in Italian again. "You MUST open the door! I am an American officer, with an Italian partigiano friend, and we were sent here to contact Quinto! I have a passport and papers to confirm our identities! Please let us in!" I had cast my lot with Foster's directions. If this contact failed me, I didn't know where we could turn, or what I would do. Another voice, a younger man's, came through the door. "We will not open the door tonight, but if you come back in the daylight, we will speak to you. Go away now."

My endurance snapped. "If you don't open this door, I'll throw a grenade through your window!" Giovanni gasped, horrified. "I wouldn't do that if I were you, Signore! Return at daybreak if you need food. If you need shelter, go to the shed in the back and sleep there."

Furious, I turned away, and Giovanni followed. At the back of the yard was a small wooden shed. Double doors creaked on rusty hinges as I lifted the wooden door latch. We stepped inside, pulling the ill-fitting doors shut behind us, and peered around in the dark, looking for some straw to bed down on. There was none. The bitter wind that whistled in around the door and through the chinks in the wood made it impossible to lie down on the frozen earthen floor. Crouching in the farthest corner, we huddled together. It was like sitting in a large, empty refrigerator, with a fan blowing on us. For the next five hours, we were two of the most wretchedly miserable human beings on earth.

We shook and shivered uncontrollably, teeth chattering, as the temperature plunged and the minutes and hours to daybreak ticked slowly by. From time to time, when the cold became unbearable, and we were in danger of falling asleep and freezing to death, we'd jump up and stamp around the shed, blowing on our hands, trying to keep circulation going.

As that interminable night wore on, I turned the incident at the door over in my mind. I had been foolish to admit that I was an American officer, that I wanted Quinto. To have opened the door after that would have been tacit admission of association. What if it had been a trick? Their fate would have been sealed. They were pretty sharp. At no time had anyone on the other side of that door admitted anything— not even that it was the Rossi farm.

Giovanni couldn't resist giving me a couple of verbal jabs—" 'This is it? The worst is over'? Hah! If the 'worst' is over—I don't want to see what the best is!" I couldn't feel my hands and feet anymore. Our bellies growled with hunger. We were half dead with cold, exhausted, and starved. We weren't sure we'd get a welcome, let alone a meal, in the morning. Hell, we weren't sure we'd _live_ until morning! "This is pure hell, my friend, but we can't give up. It will be better in the morning. Please, dear God, just get us through the next few hours!" I prayed fervently. I wondered if God could even hear my prayer, my teeth were chattering so loudly.

When the first pale rays of light filtered through the cracks in the walls, I was up and shaking Giovanni, who had dozed off. "Let's go!" I said, tersely. "That sonovabitch said daybreak, and it's daybreak, and I'm not waiting another second!" I fumbled with numb fingers for my passport, while Giovanni, yawning, stamping like a horse, dug in his pockets for his identity card. He limped to the doors and opened them. Swirling mists of cold, gray dawn swept in. We stood in the doorway and stared upward at the farmhouse door. There was no sign of life. "I'm going up there and wake them," I said. "It's daylight."

As I started to cross the yard, the door opened, and a sturdy old man wearing brown pants and sweater, and a wool farmer's cap, stepped out and beckoned to us. "Ah, Signori, 'scusi, 'scusi," he called in the quavering voice I recognized from the night before. "My apology! It is so dangerous now, we must be afraid of people who come in the night. 'Scusi, per favore!" I held out my passport and began again to explain who we were. "No! No," cried the old man, "much too cold out here! Venga! Come inside." He waved aside our documents. "Inside! Not so cold."

There was a roaring fire in the fireplace, and we made a beeline for it and held our hands out to warm them. It was a large kitchen, even for this prosperous looking farmhouse. We turned our backs to the fire, to warm our backsides a bit, and the old man began introductions, starting with himself. "I am Francesco Rossi," he said, with dignity. My heart skipped a beat. So it WAS the Rossi farm! "And this is my wife Giulia." He then presented his two sons, Gino and Carlo, and their families, and Graziella and Mariana, his two "zitonelle," —his unmarried daughters—and more than a half dozen grandchildren.

Signora Rossi motioned for us to sit down. "Poveracci! You must be starved!" The kitchen was obviously her domain, and she ruled it smoothly and easily as she directed members of the household to their assigned tasks. "Mariana,

per favore, some hot coffee and bread for our guests."
Immediately, we were served. "I am sorry to have had to put
you through such a terrible night, but you must understand—
if it was the Fascisti, or the Germans.....we knew they would
not stay the night in that shed!" That was true enough. No
human that didn't have to would have opted for that torment!
"Now, please tell me what you need me to do to help you,
Signori," said old Signor Rossi.

"I need to get in touch with Quinto, either directly, or
through Germano, as quickly as possible," I said, briefly
explaining who I was. "Can that be done?"

"Yes, it can be arranged, Signore. I don't know how
quickly, but we will try."

"It's very important that it be soon—as quickly as
possible."

"Yes, Signore, I know. But now you must rest. You are
exhausted." Calling one of his daughters over, he said,
"Show our honored guests to a clean bed, so they can sleep.
I'm sure they didn't sleep much last night." He looked
apologetically at me. "Si, Papa," she replied, and bustled off
to prepare our sleeping arrangements. Then he turned to the
younger children. "We have important guests who need
rest—you will be quiet while they sleep."

"Si, Grandpapa," they answered respectfully, and fell
silent. The two sons, and most of the others, had already eaten
and gone. I looked around the cheerful kitchen. Francesco
Rossi was not a wealthy man, but he had managed his
resources well, and was more comfortable than most farmers.
The house was large, its furnishings a cut above the norm.
The floors were tiled, and the place was very clean, with no
flies in evidence.

"Before you go to sleep, Signori," said Francesco, rising,
"I will show you our hiding place. The Fascisti sometimes
send patrols out for food, and sometimes they come here."
He led us into one of the bedrooms, which I assumed was the
one we would be using. There was a massive four-poster bed
in it, which he indicated we were to move. It took all three of

us to do it. Then, slipping one gnarled finger around a bolt-head embedded in the floor, Rossi swung open an ingeniously designed trap door. Taking a kerosene lamp from the sideboard, he lit our way down into a large underground hideout. The area was spotlessly clean, with whitewashed stone walls, and a hard-packed dirt floor. It had two cots aligned along one wall. The other three walls were lined with sacks of flour, and jars of olive oil, and large, raffia-sheathed flasks of wine. Hanging from the rafters were dried sausages, salamis and hams, and clusters of dried grapes. Francesco Rossi and his wife were prudent, thrifty farmers. They also were crafty and imaginative. Back up in the bedroom again, with the trap door carefully closed, I eyed the area critically, but its outlines were virtually invisible.

"You are clever and resourceful, Signor Rossi. You should be proud of what you have accomplished."

"Grazie, Signore, but this I do not only for me and my family, I do it for the Church. We must always remember to repay God for His goodness to us." I soon discovered that the Rossis were the most devoutly religious family I'd ever met, or ever would meet.

In less time than it takes to say it, we were snuggled under the warm blankets, and sound asleep. I was roused by a soft knocking on the door. Giovanni, deep in slumber, hadn't stirred. I went quickly to the door and opened it a tiny crack. "Yes?" I whispered.

"A man is here to see you, Signore," said Simonetta softly.

I looked at my watch. We had already slept the day away—it was five o'clock in the evening. I splashed cold water on my face, then hurried along to the kitchen.

A stocky, dark-haired peasant awaited me there.

"Buona sera, Signore," he said, with deep respect, cap in his hands, "Mi chiamo Germano." (I am Germano).

A quiet man in his mid-forties, Germano didn't look much like a seasoned resistance fighter, I thought. But then, neither did I.

We shook hands, and I beckoned him into the next room.

"Io voglio Quinto" (I want Quinto). It was the phrase that was supposed to unlock access to Quinto.

"Not possible." Germano stated flatly. My heart sank. "Quinto is not here. Two days maybe, he should be back."

I let out a sigh of relief. "Germano, it is very, very important that I see Quinto as soon as he gets back. It is important to Italy, and important to the Allies. Tell him the American Consul wants to see him."

On hearing the words 'Il Console', Germano's eyes widened. "Do not worry, I will personally get your message to him, Signor Console, and I will say it is most urgent."

"Thank you, Germano, you are doing me a great service."

"Grazie, Signore, but it is nothing." He took his leave.

Supper was served promptly at six. The men were seated and served first, which was the custom in many Italian households, especially where several generations were housed under one roof. After a long, sincere grace, we were served heaping bowls of hot pasta with garlic and cheese, followed by a delicious rabbit stew. Signora Rossi, with her daughters and daughters-in-law, waited on us. After the meal, we retired to another room to smoke and talk about the war, while the women and children ate dinner and cleaned up the kitchen. The household operated in perfect harmony, with Signor and Signora Rossi as benevolent rulers of their respective domains—farm and household. No one, from the eldest son to the smallest grandchild, would have dreamed of questioning their wishes, or challenging their authority.

I enjoyed my few evening conversations with Francesco Rossi. Although nearing eighty, he had a keen intelligence, and wanted to know what I thought Italy's role in the world might be after the war. He was current on the news, and very interested in America and "Roosabelta." I was deeply impressed with the man's sincerity, with his profound faith, and with the solid values he taught his family. As I fell back into the warm bed that night, I thought deeply about the truly good men in the world. In my experience, men like Francesco Rossi were few and far between. Sadly, they rarely held, or manipulated, the levers of power.

The next day, Germano returned. Beckoning me into the next room, he nodded toward his companion. "Ecco Quinto. (This is Quinto)." Quinto, solid-looking, dark-haired, was nearly six feet tall. He was in his thirties--about my age--and nothing special in looks or bearing. It took a bit for me to accept that this was the redoubtable Quinto. Later, I realized that part of Quinto's success was that he did not appear different, or special, but there was no question of his toughness and fearlessness as a partisan fighter.

"Could I see your identification papers, please?" he asked me politely.

"Of course." I went to the bedroom to get them. "Quinto's here," I muttered to Giovanni, at his questioning look. He gave me a quick, thumbs-up gesture. Quinto examined my passport and Foster's letter, minutely.

I stated my case to him, as emphatically as I could. "Many lives, and many partigiani, depend on me getting back to the Allies quickly—by the first available boat."

"I understand perfectly, Signore," Quinto was respectful, but noncommittal. "I don't decide who goes out first, but I will do my best to get you there and see that you get out as quickly as possible. More than that I cannot promise." "I know that, Quinto," I said, "and I'm grateful for any help you can give me." "Signore," he said, "since a dark moon period is coming up, the Mas boats will be making more contacts, so your chances of getting out quickly should be pretty good." At my hopeful look, he added, "I say this because one, you have relatively high rank, and two, you have strong reasons for needing to reach the Allied lines faster than the others." Feeling reassured, I grabbed his hand and shook it warmly. "Thank you, Quinto. Tell me about this Mas boat evacuation program."

He filled me in, confirming that there had been ups and downs during the seven months since the Armistice. Throughout the fall of 1943, Mas boats, as the Italian motor-torpedo boats were called, had been used effectively to evacuate released Allied personnel from points along the Adriatic coast. However, as winter set in with its bad weather, some of the boats and their crews had been diverted to other military uses. The Mas boat evacuation program had been virtually at a halt since mid-December. "Now, with the coming of spring, more boats are available again, so your chances of getting out are much better than they would have been a month ago," he concluded.

Germano, who had not spoken a word since introducing Quinto, now jerked his head toward the door. Quinto turned to me. "Now, I must go, but I will be back in a couple of days. Be ready to leave on very short notice."

"Don't worry about that, I have lived that way for over a year now."

"Good, then you understand how it is. Do you have any more questions, before I go?"

"No, none that you haven't already answered."

"Quinto Silenzi, at your service," he shook my hand. "I'll be back for you very soon. Be ready."

"Grazie, Germano, for bringing him so quickly," I said, shaking Germano's hand. Then they were gone.

Giovanni and I now had our first chance to talk, in a leisurely way, about things beyond our immediate needs and concerns. His formal education was very limited, but he had managed to acquire, through observation and astute questioning, a sound understanding of how to deal in a complex environment, and had mastered the art of getting along with a variety of people. He questioned me about America. "Where is America, exactly, Signore?"

"Pretty much due west of here, Giovanni, about six thousand kilometers," I replied. "If you left where we are, and headed due west, you'd probably hit New York City."

"Six thousand kilometers! Eh! That's a long way!" He thought for a moment, then asked, "What is there beyond New York?" I tried to think of a simple way to answer such a broad question. "Well, America is a big land mass, Giovanni, big! From east coast, say New York, to west coast, say San

Francisco, about five thousand kilometers of land. Then another big ocean, the Pacific, even wider than the one between here and New York."

"But then, what is beyond that?" he persisted, childlike. It dawned on me that here, in the year 1944, four and a half centuries after the days of Magellan and Christopher Columbus, this man was still grappling with the concept of the world as a vast, flat expanse, with an end—a dropping off point—somewhere, rather than as a sphere! Giovanni couldn't read, had probably never seen a globe or map of the world, so his understanding of the world's physical shape was no different from that of his ancestors, several centuries back! I was astounded. I explained the world, and the universe to him, in very simplistic terms. Then, I told him stories of America, and about spending my boyhood summers on a ranch in Colorado. Since cattle did not roam the range in Italy, he had no real concept of what a cowboy was, or what he did.

Giovanni Marioli was quite a man, I discovered. Courageous and loyal to a fault, he could be devious with strangers, but not with friends. He had gotten me safely through, and now that I had established contact with Quinto and A Force, his mission had ended. It was time for him to return to his family. On April 14th, we said good-bye. Solemnly, he handed me back the Beretta. Alone and unarmed, he could travel easily and without suspicion, a simple countryman caught far from home and family, due to circumstances of war. A weapon would be a death warrant. I offered him some money, but he refused. "I am friend and partner to you, Il Console."

As he left the Rossi farm to make his long way home, I vowed that some day, somehow, I would find a way to repay this man the debt I owed him. The next day, a messenger—another peasant farmer—came to tell me I should be ready to move that night.

The close-knit Rossi family had achieved a level of peace and well-being, even in the midst of war, that I deeply envied. Nothing in these chaotic times, or in this broken land, I reflected, could vitiate this family's deep-rooted faith, its love and respect for the land, and its ability to live in harmony and hang together in adversity. Francesco and Giulia had achieved a higher order of life than most mortals can ever aspire to. I prayed fervently with them on that last afternoon, not only for myself, but for all of Italy, and the Italians. No one, I reflected, and nothing, should have the right to interfere with fundamental goodness like that of the Rossi family. In my room, I carefully packed my knapsack, and thought about my own family.

I vowed that some of the life values I had witnessed and some of the lessons I had learned at the Rossi's would be values I'd instill in my own household, if God allowed me to return safely. I thought warmly of Marguerite and little Howard, and of our parents. I was so deep in my thoughts of home, the soft knock on the door startled me. Eight year old Isa had come to escort me to dinner. "Look!" she cried, clapping her hands delightedly, laughing up at me. "It's a party!" And what a party it was! The table groaned under its load of meats, pasta dishes, all kinds of vegetables, and, of course, desserts. Even the children had done their part--they had scoured the countryside for mushrooms and fresh greens. We all sat down, men and women and children together. We were at table, eating, for more than two solid hours. Each adult proposed a toast to me, and to my success. When it was over, I wanted to succeed in my mission as much for the Rossi family, and their faith in me, as for the San Faustini. Shortly after eight, Germano and another partisan arrived, and I took my leave. Tears flowed on all sides as we said goodbye.

Germano was armed to the teeth, with a Sten gun in hand, a bandoleer and several grenades slung around his neck. He led the way, and his buddy, also armed with a Sten gun, guarded my back. The hills bordering the Tenna River valley area are like a tangled nest of serpents slithering steeply down to the Adriatic Sea. The coastal highway and coastal railroad line had been hacked out of the rocky shoreline. Dotting the riverbanks were tiny towns and fishing villages, clinging like so many hungry parasites. It was where the Tenna River met the Adriatic that I would be making my attempt to escape by Mas torpedo boat, explained Germano, as we struggled along.

Suddenly, he stopped and pointed to a dilapidated farmhouse. "That is where you will stay tonight. There are other Allied military there, also waiting to be evacuated."

Crammed into the main room of the farmhouse were half a dozen or more British officers, and one American flyer. As I greeted each one, the others looked me over, frankly staring, and whispered comments to one another. The first to greet me was Brigadier E.W.D. Vaughn, the nominal leader of this coterie. He was a big, imposing figure, who radiated confidence and command, and had the build, bearing and look that most men only dream of achieving. His clear, hazel eyes swept over me, his well-trimmed mustache twitching slightly at the sight of my ragged appearance and scraggly, unkempt beard.

I shook his hand. "Good to see you, Brigadier."

"Same here, I'm sure. You'll want to meet Brigadiers Combe and Todhunter here," he said, maintaining the strict order of rank and precedence as he handed me off to Generals J.F.B. Combe, D.S.O., and E.J. Todhunter. Both were of average height and build. They greeted me, and in their turn presented Captains J.G. Kerine and G.E. Ruggles-Brise. Kerine's hair was almost a golden wheat color, and he had the patrician look that comes from a background of private schools and the right clubs. Ruggles-Brise was about thirty, the shortest in stature of the bunch, but also the most cheerful and outspoken. "How d'ye do?" He said, with a grin, his pale blue eyes gleaming with mischief. He held out a square, stubby hand. "Welcome. Bloody boring lot, we are, but we'll have to do."

They were all so in character, I felt like I had walked into the middle of an English film. Ruggles-Brise, in his turn, presented a young lieutenant who out-titled them all— Lieutenant the Earl of Ranfurly. A wiry, sandy-haired man of about my own age and height, his Lordship greeted me with a quick smile and a firm handshake. "Hullo, Orebaugh," he said, "Glad to have you join us." He had a pleasing voice, and his accent was very cultured. They sported an assortment of garb—probably whatever they had been able to scavenge since being turned loose to wander on their own. However, with the possible exception of Ruggles-Brise, they all managed to look as though they were still in full military uniform. "Where were you captured?" Ranfurly asked. "Monte Carlo, in late 1942." His eyebrows rose. "Monte Carlo! You mean...? You can't be serious," he said. I nodded yes. "I should like to hear _that_ story!"

"I'm sure you'll get plenty of opportunity to hear it, " I laughed. "It's quite a story. How about you? Shot down?"

"No," he said, "they got most of us in the North African campaign. Brought us back here, and when the Armistice came, they turned us loose. Same with you?"

"Not quite," I answered. "I've been fighting with the partisans in Umbria." Up went the eyebrows again, and he looked intrigued.

At that point, the young Ameri can interrupted. "Hey Ranfurly, enough bull! I can't wait to talk to another Yank!"

"Same here! " I said happily, shaking his hand. "Walter Orebaugh, Wichita, Kansas--State Department."

"Jack Rieter, Chicago, Army Air Corps, Lieutenant," he said, mimicking my shorthand introduction. "Good to see you, Walt! It'll be great having another American around to defend the boorish ways of the colonists! These English blokes are convinced we Yanks are all untutored savages." We all laughed.

Two Italians in khaki uniforms arrived, and announced we'd be moving out immediately. All conversation ceased, as we scrabbled for our gear and headed for the door. "Who are they?" I managed to ask Rieter, amid the hubbub. "A Force, Bari Command," he replied, as we shouldered our packs and followed them out. "They're in charge of the exfiltration operation in this area. They're very sharp, and _very_ well-trained, from what I've seen."

With the Italians leading the way, we worked our way down toward the Adriatic. It was shortly after three a.m. when they stopped at a remote farmhouse. "You'll stay here for now, " said the senior of the two Italians, in fairly good English. "Figure a way to sleep. There are many of you, little room." An understatement. The family was already asleep in the one bedroom, so we bedded down on the floor of the kitchen. We pushed the table against the wall, and Ranfurly and Rieter promptly set up under it. I ended up close to the banked hearth, sharing a pallet with Brigadier Vaughn. It was warmer there, but if I slept at all that night, it was no thanks to the Brigadier, whose stentorian snoring outshone even Amy's.

The next evening we went back up the river a short distance, walked up a long path, and although it was dark, I could tell that on both sides were well-tended gardens. Our destination was a well-to-do country villa. Two more officers had joined us during our march up from the last house, bringing our number to ten, a sizable number of house guests for even this large villa. At the soft call of our guide, the front door was thrown open, and we were greeted, in English, by a tall, very striking woman, who looked to be in her early sixties. "I am Helen Salvadori," she said, giving me a brilliant smile, "welcome to our home." Her slightly graying blonde hair was swept up, and pinned to the top of her head. She was an imposing figure, dressed in a modish lavender wool dress. Two other women, younger, but as stylishly dressed and coiffed as our hostess, directed us to a cheerful dining room. We seated ourselves at the long table, whose dark wood gleamed with the patina of years of polishing. It was centered with a silver urn filled with fresh flowers. "First, some warm breakfast, then off to bed with the lot of you," ordered Signora Salvadori. Breakfast was a marvel in itself. Copious amounts of food were presented in charming, well-appointed surroundings, and the conversation at table was conducted entirely in English. What a novelty that was for me. Professor Salvadori, master of the house, was a highly regarded writer and teacher, well-known in intellectual and academic circles in Italy. I had heard of him while stationed in Trieste. He had earned quite an international reputation for his acerbic criticisms of Fascism. It was very dangerous for them to help us. Nevertheless, they were determined to help the Allied cause, and had given the Cingoli Band free access to their villa. Situated on a hill overlooking the river, with clear views all around, it was particularly well-suited for use as a way-station.

That evening, after a solid sleep and a most welcome hot bath, we gathered in the parlor for a glass of sherry before dinner. I sat on the couch and chatted with Helen Salvadori. "I am pleased to be here, Signora," I said, "but concerned about you taking this chance, and endangering yourselves to harbor fugitives like us. Aren't you afraid of what will happen to you if you're caught?"

"Oh, piffle! The Fascists are afraid of my husband. They don't want to enhance his reputation for verbally hitting the mark on them, so they leave us pretty much alone." Just at that moment, the man in question diverted our attention. He was venting his spleen against the Fascists, the Germans, and the Allies, too. Although in his late seventies, Professor Salvadori had not lost his talent for the well-placed barb, and now the British were his target. "Tell me, is there something in British genes that adversely affects the eyesight?" he inquired. He fixed his piercing brown eyes on Brigadier Todhunter.

"Not that I know of," replied Todhunter warily, "Why?"

"Why? Hah! Your futile attempts at knocking out the bridges, and the coastal road, have become a bore! Even with the whole area lit up like daylight with those infernal Bengal flares of yours, you've not been able to score a single hit! You must all be half blind! Your men couldn't find a volcano if it erupted up their noses.!" The professor cackled, enjoying his taunt.

The Britishers had gone red in the face."Now see here..." sputtered Brigadier Vaughn angrily, leaning forward in his chair. "That's what I'm saying," interjected the old man. Your English pilots <u>can't</u> 'see here'! That's the whole problem!"

Everyone roared with laughter at that, and Vaughn subsided good-naturedly.

The next morning I finally met the A Force agent in charge of our evacuation, Lieutenant Cagnazzi. A South African, of part-Sicilian parentage, "Cag" was a lean, dark-haired bundle of energy and a crack intelligence agent. His specialty was behind-the-enemy-lines activity. I took an immediate liking to him, as did almost everyone who met him. He had been dropped off near the port of San Giorgio a few weeks earlier, and had promptly established an incredible communications network, with the help of the partisan guerrilla bands. "My main mission," he said, "is getting the top brass among the Allied, like you, out of here--quickly and safely."

"I'm glad to know that, Cag." Briefly, I out lined my situation, and my mission, to him. He looked at me with new respect.

"I'll do my best for you, Signore Console," he said. Cag was also involved in getting weapons and supplies to the resistance movements operating in the area. "You know, I knew you were on your way here," he said, grinning, "even before you met Germano." At my surprised look he added, "I have a pretty good communications network set up with the partisans."

"So <u>that's</u> why Quinto showed up so quickly after I contacted Germano!"

"Yes. Germano didn't know that we were waiting for you to make contact. I heard about you from the Cingoli partisans who detained you overnight. Had they gotten word to me before you left them, I'd have made contact with you there."

"Then you know that a lot of lives depend on me getting through to the Allies, as quickly as possible," I said.

"Yes, Sir. I'm honored to meet you, and we appreciate all you've done for the partigiani, and to help the Allies. Tell me, how did you found out about Quinto, up there in the middle of nowhere in Umbria? Has our communications network extended that far?

"Well, it was very strange, actually. Someone sent me a letter that told me exactly how to contact Quinto."

"A letter?" He was instantly alert. "Who sent you a letter?"

"I don't know. It was signed by a Mr. Foster. I don't remember ever meeting him, but he claimed in the letter that he had met me several years ago, in Trieste, when I was with the U.S. Consulate there."

"Oh. Yes, I know Foster," Cag nodded. " In fact, I saw him just a couple of weeks ago, in Cagli."

"You did!" My heart began a trip-hammer rhythm. I tried to stay calm. "I'm trying to place him.....how old is he? What does he look like? What does he do? I have absolutely no recollection of the man." I wanted to see if the description Cag gave me fit Manfred, or anyone I knew.

"He's an older man, balding, kind of strange. Tall, very skinny. Always complaining." Cag grimaced, his dislike of the man obvious. Definitely not Manfred. I felt a twinge of disappointment.

"What's this Foster person, whoever he is, doing in Cagli? His letter sounded like he's a borderline nut case. And how did he know to write me through the CLN?"

"He was a manager for Shell Oil, with all kinds of connections. Got detained when the war broke out. I don't know how he knew how to get a letter to you, but he's certainly a big whiner, and he knows about us. "

"Well, Foster is a potentially dangerous security leak. Somebody better muzzle him before he blows your cover, and gets Quinto and Germano killed," I warned.

"Don't worry, Signore, we'll take care of that little matter immediately. Foster won't write any more letters, I assure you."

I was champing at the bit to get on with my mission, and was not an easy person to be around. I had long ago ceased being a reserved, polite diplomat with infinite patience. I was not an officer and a gentleman, like these others. I was a partigiano, a guerrilla fighter, and not accustomed to lolling around a villa exchanging polite chit-chat. The British officers, especially the Brigadier, chided me for my open impatience. For my part, I couldn't understand their complacent, uncomplaining acceptance of delays. With every day's delay, the Band of San Faustino was more exposed. It was my responsibility to get them resupplied, to assure their safety.

The afternoon of April 18th, Cag called us together. "We are coming into a 'no moon' phase on the calendar," he said. "This is the safest time to try to get you out. We'll make our first attempt tonight. Be ready to leave as soon as darkness falls. By then, we'll have intelligence reports on German and Fascist patrols in the area, and can take routes to avoid them." He briefed us on alternate routes, rendezvous points, hideouts, and signals to the boat. Every man was to memorize the recognition signals—a pattern of flashing lights—in case called upon to be a signaler to bring the Mas boat in.

"During the hours you are out tonight, as you know, you'll be at considerable risk. Stay close together, and follow your escort's instructions to the letter."

We moved out in darkness, following the course of the Tenna River, heading for the coastal highway. In single file, we made our way laboriously, up and down and around the twisting hills, dropping to the ground at a hand signal, or a whispered command. It was slow, tedious going, and it took more than an hour to cover two or three kilometers. Several of us had weapons, and Quinto and the other partisan were armed with Sten guns, but given the large number of enemy troops in the area, it would be little protection if we were discovered. Finally, we reached the steep embankment above the highway and railroad line beside the beach. Carefully we slithered down it. Then, like a herd of clumsy deer we bounded across the highway and the railroad tracks, leaping into the protection of the deep brush that grew a few feet below the railroad bed—in the narrow strip between the rail line and the beach.

Crouching low in the tangled scrub, we worked our way silently toward the water. When I reached the outer edge of the brush, I was surprised to find the beach so wide. Getting across it without being seen would be extremely risky,-- boarding a boat undetected, fully exposed like that, almost impossible. I checked my watch—it was already close to midnight. A cutting, icy wind blew in off the water, and we hunkered down as best we could to ward it off. Peering out to sea for signs of a boat, our ears strained to pick up any stray sound. We positioned Aldo and Mario as lookouts to guard our rear. After what seemed like an eternity, we heard a low, throbbing rumble from out at sea. No one spoke, or even breathed. Quinto advanced a little and began flashing the signal out toward where we'd heard the boat. Eyes aching with the effort not to blink, we watched for a return signal. Seconds ticked by. No lights or recognition signals came from the sea, though the engine noise increased, indicating the boat was coming in closer to shore. We waited, hopes high. Then, incredibly, the sound of the engines began moving away, and slowly faded in the distance. There was no sound except the waves--the steady, rhythmic swoosh and slap of their unending assault on the shore. For some unknown reason, the Mas boat had decided not to come in for the pickup. Quinto gave us the signal to pull out, and slowly we retraced our tortuous route, stopping only when we reached the prearranged rendezvous point. "You can smoke now, if you like," whispered Quinto. Dejectedly, shielding the light of the flame with cupped hands, we lit up, and sat silently smoking. A voice, barely above a whisper, suddenly broke the deep silence. It sounded like Ruggles-Brise.

Well, dammit all to hell!" he swore. "Just plain dammit!" Another voice responded with a terse, clipped "Right-O!" That about summed it up. The disappointment was almost palpable.

We trudged all through the night again, arriving back at the villa just before first light. Within minutes, Helen Salvadori was up and in the kitchen, brewing pots of tea, and making toast. "Have to take the chill off my boys," she said, cheerily. She seemed almost happy to have us back. "Nine o'clock tonight again. Be ready," announced Quinto. He and his buddy slipped noiselessly out. Exhausted, we tumbled into our beds and were quickly asleep.

The next night was a replica of the first. We couldn't believe it! Back at the rendezvous point, some began to wonder aloud about the ability and courage of the Italian crews. "Look," said Ranfurly, "it's no cakewalk to navigate one's way into a specific point, in enemy territory, with no lights and no moon." I agreed. "The boats may have been warned off for a reason." Others, less charitable, vented their feelings with liberal profanity, asserting that it was sheer cowardice by the Mas boat crews. "I'll hear no more of that, now," said Vaughn sharply. They were immediately silenced.

I forced myself to remain optimistic. I felt sure the third night would be the charm. "It will be the lucky night, when everything will go right for us," I said. When darkness fell that third night, not only was there no moon, there were no stars. "That's a good omen," I commented to Ranfurly. Finding our way was difficult, and we tripped and stumbled and cursed eloquently in the pitch black. Once again we reached the beach at midnight. Sometime around one-thirty, we heard a boat. This time it was closer in. We flashed our signals, and the engines grew louder. Even though throttled back, their roar seemed to fill the night. It was definitely coming in. This is it, this time we're going to go, I thought exultantly. Vaughn signaled us to move out to the edge of the water, so we'd be ready to board. We left the cover of the brush and started across the expanse of sand. Out of the corner of my eye I caught a quick flash from the direction of the railroad bridge. Then a rifle crack. Angelo screamed and grabbed his face, then fell to the ground. I dropped flat, too, and scuttled on all fours, crab-like, toward him. More shots rang out from the bridge to the north of us. "Angelo's hit," I called hoarsely.

"Abort! " yelled Vaughn, and we broke for the bushes.

"We've been spotted! Clear out!"

There was no chance of getting to the boat. We heard its engines rev to full throttle as it turned and roared away. Quinto grabbed up Angelo as we left the beach, dragging and forcing him along with us. Zig-zagging across the sand, I chanced a quick glance back, and saw the gleaming phosphorescent curve of the boat's wake break the inky darkness. The shooting continued, but luckily was still directed at the beach. We worked our way back across the railroad and highway in silence, clambering up the embankment into safer territory. I figured it was probably a German work party that had heard the boat, and maybe saw shadowy figures on the beach, and began shooting.

When we finally regrouped, stopping only for a quick rest and a smoke, we were out of breath. We had come so close! "Go back to the villa. We'll try again, but not tomorrow." Quinto and Aldo disappeared with a bleeding Angelo to get medical help. I couldn't believe we were back here at the rendezvous point again. Just one minute...one more minute!....and we'd have been on that boat and headed for the Allied lines. Dammit all! My morale fell to rock bottom. I'll never get out of here, I thought despairingly. The war will be over, my San Faustini comrades will all be dead or captured, and I'll still be wandering around these hellish hills all night!

Cag arrived early the next day. "Sorry about last night." He brought us the welcome news that Angelo would be all right. "He is lucky it was his nose and not his brains," said Cag, with a philosophical shrug. "He can live with a stub of a nose. It could have been far worse. You were ALL lucky. " We knew he was right. "Do not despair, Signori, " he said. " We'll try again on the twenty-third. This time, though, we'll have a new pickup point, on the beach north of the mouth of the river." He went on to give us new recognition signals and rendezvous points. Then he drew out a map, marked with the location of a dozen or more safe farmhouses within a five mile radius.

"If this next attempt fails, do not return here. It is too risky to keep all of you in one place for very long. We'll split you up, and billet you in pairs, or in fours, from now on. As one big group, you make too lucrative a catch for the enemy." I fully agreed. Three British Brigadiers, a member of the British House of Lords, and an American Consul, along with four other Allied officers, would make quite a nice haul for the enemy!

On the night of the twenty-third, there were reports of German patrols in the area, so we reached the beach later than planned. I was sure we had missed the Mas boat. However, shortly, out of the black, came the welcome chug-chug of a boat engine. Our spirits soared. We hadn't missed it after all! To my ear, this engine sounded different from the others we had heard, but no one else seemed to notice it. Quinto wasn't with us that night, and Gino, our man on the beach, was sending the signals. Flashes came back almost immediately, but the return signals were the same ones Gino sent. Gino didn't seem alarmed, so I overcame my anxiety. The thump-thump of the boat's engines grew louder—it was coming in!

"Okay, let's move to the water," ordered Vaughn in a hoarse whisper. We scampered across the sand and drew up with the waves licking at our boots. As the boat drew near, Aldo, peering into the gloom, was able to make out the shape of the craft heading for us. "Damn! That's no Mas boat! That's a damned German boat!"

As one, we turned and ran pell mell for the brush, flinging ourselves down in it, trying to disappear into the earth. Suddenly, we could hear voices in German, and the beam of the boat's big searchlight swept the beach, brilliantly illuminating the spot where, only seconds before, we had been gathered. We slithered backward through the brush, inching farther away from the shoreline, praying we could get out of range of the relentless searchlight as it swept a wider arc along the beach, looking for whoever had flashed the signals.

The light swept the beach three or four times, then, finding nothing, finally flicked off. We waited, not moving a muscle. Finally, we heard the boat turn, its engine roar, and away it went, churning a wake. Silence still reigned. Thankfully, I let my breath out, and once again Vaughn gave that all-too-familiar signal that we were to retreat to the rendezvous point. This time we ran almost all the way. Reaching relative safety, we flopped down like a school of beached fish, audibly gasping for air. Eventually, out of the dark came the voice of the irrepressible Ruggles-Brise. "Well, feather my britches! Nothing like signaling the bloody Jerries in for tea!"

"Hey, old boy," replied Todhunter. "Don't complain! At least we got the chance to find out the difference between an Italian Mas boat and a bloody German coastal freighter, and lived to tell about it, thanks to Captain Aldo's sharp eyes!"

Wearily, we picked up our gear and began retracing our steps. It was early daylight by the time we reached the first of the safe farmhouses.

Two nights later, Jack Rieter and I were awakened by the sound of a German motor patrol passing by on the road near the farmhouse where we were staying. That was too close for Vaughn, who decided we'd move further inland, where there would be fewer German patrols, and we'd be safer. That day, we dragged ourselves about six kilometers upriver. I could no longer feel my feet. We had barely reached our new locations when a messenger from Cag arrived. There would be another sortie to the beach that very night! We all groaned. Even the stalwart Vaughn grimaced at the thought of the long walk ahead of us. "Sorry, gents," he apologized, "I guess I should have waited another day before moving us."

This time Quinto was our escort, along with another A Force agent I'd never seen, who introduced himself as usual with only his first name, Fabio. As we neared the bridges close to the mouth of the river, we found there were other dangers besides the Fascists and the Germans. This time it came from our own guys—the British bombers, bent on another attempt to knock out the Tenna railroad bridge. We were sitting ducks—smack in the middle of their target area!

"Jaysus!" I heard someone say, "we'll go out bashed by our own blokes!"

"Shut up!" said another, "Get down, and say your bloody prayers!"

Suddenly Bengal flares, dropped by one of the planes, lit the landscape in an eerie, lime-colored glare. All thoughts except survival fled, as the deafening concussions of bombs falling all around us filled our world. My body was plucked into the air by unseen fingers, then slammed unceremoniously down again, breath forced from my lungs, and I thought my eardrums had burst. Finally, all fell silent. The planes had gone. Slowly, painfully, I struggled to my feet, and checked myself over to see if anything was broken, bleeding, or missing. There was a terrible ringing in my ears, and I was bruised and shaken. I was grateful to be alive.

One after another, we all reported in safely. Miraculously, no one had been killed, and our injuries were only minor cuts and bruises. Professor Salvadori would have had a field day. The bombers had missed their target again, and by a considerable margin. At that moment, no one among us, even their own countrymen, had a kind thought for the Royal Air Force. I remarked, "Well, I don't see why the Allies don't just send some explosives and some sappers up to the Cingoli Band by Mas boat, and let them knock out the bridges, instead of all this stupid hit-or-miss bombing!"

"You know, Orebaugh, that's not a bad thought," said Reiter. "It would be a lot easier and cheaper, and probably the only way those damned bridges will ever be hit, from the looks of it!"

"Hell, yes, " Ruggles-Brise chimed in. "Cag and Quinto could handle a job like that in ten minutes. Maybe five. Those blokes up there can't find their own arses with both hands. Let's tell 'em that when we get down there, what?"

"Right you are!" snapped Brigadier Vaughn vehemently. I could tell from his tone that there would be hell to pay for this when he saw the British commanders. He was royally pissed off at having missed this rendezvous, and to have almost been killed by his own Air Force. However, such were the risks of war. But to have been eyewitness to such a poor show, confirming the Professor's earlier criticism, really stuck in Vaughn's craw.

The moon moved into its waxing phase, and with its increasing light our chances of getting off the beach by Mas boat grew dimmer. The others were not gripped by my urgency, but neither were they anxious to stay in danger longer than necessary. No one was happy about sitting around, risking discovery, waiting for the next moonless phase.

Rieter, Ranfurly and I, billeted together, talked a lot about our situation. To reach the new pickup point, we'd passed through the tiny fishing village of Marina Faleriense. "Weren't there several good-sized fishing boats pulled up on the beach there?" I asked. The Germans had banned all commercial fishing in the Adriatic north of the battle lines, so the Italian fishermen had been thrown out of work. "Why don't we try to buy one of the boats, and use it for our escape? I have some money I'd be willing put up for that."

"Hey, that's not a bad idea! " said Jack.

"Yes," agreed Ranfurly. "It sounds good, but how could we do it? We can't just go strolling up to them in broad daylight and ask to buy one of their boats! But they must hate the Jerries, and they must need money. The boats aren't bringing them any income, beached. So buying one might be a possibility. We can ask Brigadier Vaughn to talk to Cag about it. Maybe A Force can negotiate with them."

"Okay," I said, "Let's go over to meet with Vaughn tonight, right after dark."

"Orebaugh the Impatient," teased Rieter, good-naturedly.

That night we went to see Vaughn and outlined our idea. He agreed it was a good one. "I'll send for Cag for a meeting."

"It's a possibility we hadn't considered," Cag agreed. "It might not be as chancy as the Mas boat. Let me explore it a bit with A Force."

Three days later, Vaughn told us, "Cag bought us a

twenty-four foot wooden fishing boat, for 70,000 lire." (About $6,000 U.S.) "It has a sail, but no motor, and is in pretty rough shape. But it's ours. A Force paid for it, so we don't need your money, Orebaugh."

"Don't get your hopes up all that high," cautioned Ruggles-Brise. "Cag says the bloody thing's a stinking mess, and will take bloody what-all to make her seaworthy".

When we got back to our farmhouse, I was too wound up to rest. "Let's go look at her tonight! She can't be all that bad." Dusk had barely fallen when Rieter, Ranfurly and I sneaked down to near Marina Faleriense. My heart fell. Cag was absolutely right,—she was a mess. What a scow! It would take one helluva lot of patching just to get her to float again. Beached for months, the sun and wind had taken their harsh toll, and had rotted the sails, beams and ropes. Her wooden hull had dried out, leaving wide openings in the seams that I could put my fingers through as I felt along her ribs. "Damn, what a lousy tub!" said Rieter. "This thing will never float! Cag must be crazy."

"Never mind. It's a boat, isn't it? We'll just have to do whatever it takes to make her seaworthy again, because right now she's our only hope for getting out of here," I said.

The next day, we heard that Cag had already hired two partisan villagers to work at night, patching up our boat.

On May 2nd, Cag sent word that we could try one more time, tonight, for a Mas boat connection, but this would be our last chance. I had met Quinto in Grottozzalina on April 12th, and thought then that I'd be headed for Allied lines within the week. Now it was May, and I was still cooling my heels. We decided to go for it. I winced at the thought of another long walk that might end in a blank. My feet had become a permanent mass of bloody, purple bruises. Pain knifed through my right shoulder whenever I moved my arm. Carrying the knapsack was agony.

That night, once again, we made our way to the beach. Two hours past the pickup time, the Mas boat had not appeared. There wasn't even a rumble of engines in the distance. Finally, we were forced to give up. "Well, that's that," I said, as we worked our way back. "Looks like our 'yacht' is our only chance." And that became her name among us--The Yacht.

I drew Ranfurly again for my billet-mate. We peeled off from the rest of the group when we reached the farmhouse assigned to us. Our sleeping arrangements—the sheep stall— were a bit rougher than usual, and we exchanged a few jokes as we pushed and prodded the sleeping animals to clear a comfortable place to sleep. "Well, it ain't Buckingham Palace, but it'll do," joked the Earl of Ranfurly, chuckling. Pillowing his head on a clump of straw, he promptly dropped into deep sleep. I was not long in doing the same. We slept so soundly that the first passes of the British bombers failed to rouse us. However, when the anti-aircraft batteries at Porto San Giorgio opened up, and the hail of bombs began exploding near the bridges, we were jolted awake. We scrambled out of the sheep stall and into the open field, momentarily dazed by the daylight.

The RAF bombers were making another pass at the target, coming in at low altitude, right above us. We looked up, shading our eyes against the dazzling early morning light. Two planes came zooming in, making a run toward the bridges. As we watched, two round dark objects, trailing smoke, detached from one of them, and came tumbling down at us. We dived behind a nearby hedgerow and cowered there, arms over our heads, awaiting the horrendous explosion of the bombs. We heard two thuds as they hit the newly-plowed ground of the adjacent field and we cringed, but no explosion followed. Must be unarmed, or duds, I thought. Relieved, we got up, brushed ourselves off, and walked the few steps up to the farmhouse.

The contadina welcomed us. "Buongiorno, Signori," she said as she hastened to set out something for us to eat. She was a fairly young woman, with a cherubic, curly headed little girl of about two toddling around the kitchen. We were enjoying our meal, engaged in idle conversation with the woman, with me acting as translator for Ranfurly, when another little girl of about six came running from the adjacent field, yelling "Tedeschi! Mamma, Tedeschi!" (Germans! Mamma, Germans!) I jumped up and raced to the window. Four German soldiers in an open car were already turning into the yard.

The woman and I exchanged terrified looks. It was too late for us to leave—we'd be seen. She pointed to the next room. The bedroom was our only hope. Frantically, we crammed ourselves down between the bed and the wall, concealed by the bedclothes. We heard the woman scoop up our dishes and mugs and drop them in a bucket. We could hear the scrape of chairs as the Germans seated themselves in the kitchen. My hair stood on end, and neither of us dared breathe.

The murmur of voices rose and fell. Then, suddenly, a piercing shriek from the toddler rent the air. I jumped, and heard Ranfurly draw in his breath. Then the soothing voice of the mother came, and the child quieted.

Several more minutes dragged by. Suddenly, we heard a soft, insistent tapping at the window above our heads. Screwing up my courage, I turned to look, and there was the woman, up on a ladder, looking in, her finger to her lips for silence. I got to my knees, and she was already backing down the ladder again, making signs that we were to climb down and head for the trees. I nodded. Her skirts flew as she raced around the corner of the building, returning to the kitchen. I heard her enter again, and she began speaking in a somewhat louder tone. Then she began making noise with dishes and glasses, to cover any noise we might make getting out.

Slowly, cautiously, we pushed the window up, barely enough to squeeze through. Then we scrambled rapidly down the ladder, expecting at any moment to hear "ALT!" in German, or feel bullets ripping into us. Once on the ground, we quickly dropped the ladder and shoved it under the foundation of the house, then turned and dashed across the short yard, sliding down the gentle slope behind it, into the safety of the brush. I peered back up to the yard, and saw newly washed laundry hanging out to dry. She must have used that as her excuse to go outdoors, so that she could put the ladder up and get us out. What quick thinking! The woman's courage was astounding. She knew that her life, and her children's, was as much at stake as ours.

My watch told me that only an hour had passed, but it seemed more like four. Finally, the six year old came down to the stream looking for us. "Signore," she called, "The Tedeschi are gone, la mamma says you can come back to the house now."

We found the young woman in the front yard, calmly throwing feed to the ducks and chickens. "Grazie, Signora," I said fervently, "you saved our lives today!"

"Who were they? What did they want?" asked Ranfurly. I translated his questions to her. "It was three Germans and an interpreter," she said. "They were interested in what fell from the plane. It landed in our field. They looked, but it was only half empty oil drums. They took them and left." Ranfurly had wandered to the far side of the yard. He spotted Ruggles-Brise and Brigadier Combe heading our way, coming across the fields from a nearby farm. "Hullo! Here are two of our blokes."

"What? Are they nuts, wandering around in broad daylight like that? What the hell are they thinking of?" I waved for them to head into the safety of the trees, indicating we'd meet them there. They had come to investigate what had happened to us. "That wasn't very clever. It's dangerous for us to be out in the daylight like this right now," I warned.

"Well, never mind that now," said Combe, "Tell us what happened! We saw the duds hit in your field, you were lucky not to be hit."

"They weren't duds," I said, "They were just...." A farmer came running, waving his arms. He was trembling. "Militia! A squad is coming! They are here!" He pointed.

Six black-shirted Fascist militiamen, weapons in hand, had just jumped the stream about 400 meters below us, heading our way. They had seen us.

We took off at a run. The militiamen gave chase. In this terrain, it was up one hill and down the other, which gave our pursuers only an occasional glimpse of us. Resolutely, we raced on, alternately appearing, then disappearing, as we traversed the mosaic of hilly wheat fields and hedgerows. Frantically, I looked from side to side for a hiding place, but there were none. We were in open fields. The wheat was only about eighteen inches high, not tall enough to conceal us well, and the trees were all cut back short to allow sun to reach the grapevines. For everyone, there comes a time when he can physically do no more, and I had reached mine. The others, though younger and more conditioned by military training, were reaching their limits, too. "Go on! Leave me!" I gasped, and dropped to my knees. I flattened myself and wiggled, snake-like, toward the thickest, tallest stands of wheat.

Seconds later, I heard our pursuers nearby. I wished myself into the dirt, but I had my Colt out and ready, so I could come up firing, and get in at least one good lick before they got me. I knew the Colt would be no match for a submachine gun. Then a voice, so close it seemed to be speaking to me, called, "Guardi nel mezzo del grano!" (Let's look there—in the middle of the field!) Another few paces, and he'd have stepped on my head! I could hear wheat being trampled down as they searched the middle of the field. Holding my breath, I waited to be pounced on, sweat trickling down my face, the wheat dust choking me. Fearing I'd sneeze, I pressed my nostrils tightly together with my left hand, breathing through my mouth.

Agonizing seconds ticked by. Then their voices receded and all sound stopped, but I didn't dare raise my head. They were probably just standing there, waiting for us to pop up so they could blow our heads off, or capture us. For a half hour or more, I remained as I was, perfectly still. Finally, I could stand it no longer. I raised my head to where I could just peep through the tips of the wheat stalks, and looked all around. The militiamen were gone. The wheat field was deserted. In the next field over, a couple of young peasant farmers were working the soil. Slowly, I got to my feet, ready to run again, and they beckoned me over.

"Rallagrementi, we are glad to see you in one piece, Signore," said one. "We saw what happened, but we did not dare interfere. They would have killed us all."

"That's okay, " I said, "You people have risked enough for us already today. They're gone?"

"Yes, and we were glad to see them go," said the other, and spit disdainfully on the ground, to show how he felt about the Fascists. "There are so many in the macchia these days, the militia give up chasing them. Anyway, they were here for something else--those tanks that fell."

"Lucky for me. What about my friends? Did you see what happened to them?"

"They're gone, too. But they eluded the bastards," said the first farmer. "They got away. The stupid Fascisti had to leave empty-handed!" They both laughed, and, clapping me happily on the back, hurried me along to a nearby farmhouse. "This is an occasion for celebration," said 'Renzo, whose farm it was, as he poured each of us a glass of wine. I was parched, and gulped mine gratefully. Several hours, and several glasses later, I bid them farewell.

I walked back to the farm where I was sheltering, enjoying the pungent smell of the budding bushes and trees, and the newly plowed earth. I was weary, but God, it felt good to be alive! Today had been the closest call yet. It was dark when I arrived, and the contadina and her husband were happy to see me. Ranfurly was there, too. "What a relief to see you, Orebaugh! We were worried about you. We hid out in the wheat too, but we were a pretty good distance away from where you stopped. We didn't hear any commotion from back your way, so we figured you probably got away."

"Yeah," I said, picking up the little one and sitting her on my lap. Curious, she tugged at my beard. "Stupid of them, but lucky for me, they only searched the middle of the field."

The oil drums had been seen by many eyes. The Fascists,

always eager for booty, thought it was an airdrop of supplies for the partisans. Like the Germans, they had come to investigate, and see what there was for the taking. We knew we couldn't stay around any longer, so we bid our thanks and farewell to our hosts and shifted billets again, to some farms farther away.

Then a soggy weather front settled in, and we anxiously waited for it to pass, hoping there would be a northerly wind following it—the wind we needed to push us down the coast in The Yacht. Finally, on May 9th, the weather broke somewhat, and a messenger came from Cag. "Be at the assembly point at nine o'clock tonight," he said. "We'll be leaving at 9:15." My excitement over the prospect of actually making another attempt to get out was tempered by the nagging fear that this, too, could prove fruitless. With Giorgio, our A Force escort for the voyage, and three other Allied officers we had picked up along the way, our number had swelled to fourteen. The night was plenty dark, with cloud cover. Promptly at 9:15, Giorgio gave the whispered order, "proceed to the boat, and get it into the water as quickly and quietly as possible."

The Yacht—all twenty-four feet of her, carvel-planked, with solid oak knees for the ribs, was no light racing affair, to be lifted easily and tossed quickly into the water. While Todhunter and two of the new group stood guard, Giorgio and the rest of us worked to get her cumbersome hull into the water. "Okay, LIFT," came a hoarse command, and we lifted. "Stern up more!" came another whisper. "Now PUSH!" We pushed and prodded mightily, sweating and straining, not daring to speak except for necessary commands. Foot by agonizing foot, we pried her loose from her mulish foothold in the sand. Slowly, painfully, we prodded and tugged and shoved her stubbornly resistant bulk toward its natural home—the sea. A full forty-five minutes of struggle were spent before The Yacht dipped her pointed prow, like a bird's beak, into the river, and took a sip. She must have found it to her liking, for with the water buoying part of her weight, and all of us heaving mightily from the stern, she obligingly slid in the rest of the way. We dumped our gear into her, and clambered aboard, two at a time, as quietly as we could. Giorgio gave one last mighty shove, then swung himself in as she floated seaward. Nothing broke the sound of the waves lapping at the sandy shore, not even a dog's bark. We were away!

Then, "Sweet Christ!" from Reiter, "There's water coming in everywhere!" "Yeah, over here, too," said Ranfurly. "Here, too!" from someone farther astern. She was taking on water from at least twenty leaks. "Grab those pitch buckets and bail! Hurry!" Feverishly, we bailed. We were fast drifting out to sea, and water was already ankle deep. "God help us," swore one of the men, "this thing's going to sink!" The two fishermen Cag had paid to caulk the boat had been able to work only at night, and without lights. They'd missed a lot of holes.

The only buckets aboard were the two empty pitch buckets they had left behind, which still had pounds of half-dried, heavy black pitch stuck to them. But we bailed as fast as we could with them. The added weight of the water made bailing an arduous task. After a half hour or so, I was spent, and lathered in sweat. I turned my bucket over to Ruggles-Brise.

"Hell's fire, Orebaugh, this damn thing weighs a ton!" he complained on the first toss. "How the hell did you do this?"

"Just shut up and keep bailing or we'll sink," I groaned, "don't waste energy talking. It's a damned long way from here to the Allied lines!"

Giorgio was on his knees, soaking wet, plugging leaks with raveled hemp and globs of black tar. He worked methodically, silently, emitting only an occasional grunt as he pushed and pressed the stuff into the leaks, then moved on to the next. Occasionally, he'd use a screwdriver to shove the strands of hemp into place.Thank God someone aboard knew something about repairing leaks!

The others had manned the long oars—four men to a side.

With help from the northerly wind, the oarsmen soon had us far enough out to sea to be out of gunshot range from shore. No one wanted to turn back. We, and our leaky Yacht, were committed. The sea was black and choppy, with two to three foot waves pushing against the hull. I heard several anguished groans as the boat alternately rose, then dropped with a sickening lurch, yielding to the motion of the waves. Giorgio worked nonstop, and finally made some headway against the leaks, reducing them to a mere trickle.

Feeling safer, we laid off bailing and relaxed a bit, while Vaughn, Todhunter, and Ranfurly hoisted the loose-footed lugger sail. They seemed well-schooled in sailing, jumping to with alacrity as Vaughn called out crisp commands. This was certainly not like blueblood sailing on the Thames--out on a breezy Sunday afternoon, in impeccable whites, the Union Jack snapping merrily at the top of the mast, everything shipshape and spotless. But they turned to with a will, and we let out a cheer as the north wind filled our patched and weathered sail, and began bowling us down the Adriatic at a good clip.

By midnight, we were scudding swiftly southward. The sea, only moderately choppy at first, became more agitated as the offshore wind became stronger. By then, most of the group were heaving and retching with seasickness—several so violently they couldn't even lift their heads. For Giorgio and me and several others, though, there was no respite. The leaks were once more gaining on the patching, and bailing was not only necessary, it was a matter of life or death for us all. My stomach felt queasy, too, but the constant need to shift my weight as I bailed, in order to keep my balance and not go overboard, kept my mind off it.

After several hours of Giorgio's persistent caulking with pitch and hemp, the leaks were once again under control. I stopped bailing, and flopped down, exhausted, taking it easy, enjoying the ride. For the first time, I allowed myself to think it might work--to believe that I might, this time, make it down the coast to Allied-held territory, if we encountered no enemy patrol boats along the way. Just then, there was a loud crack, closely followed by shouts of "Damn!" "Grab it!" "What the hell?" and the mast, sail and all, whizzed past my ear, crashing into the water. I jumped up. "NOW what?"

"The mast brace snapped," said Ranfurly. "This is a fine piece of work!" At almost the same moment, I felt the chill of cold water swirling around my ankles. There was a new leak—a big one! I began bailing. "Rieter! Man the other bucket!" I yelled. Jack sprang to help me bail, while Giorgio and two of the others, leaning precariously over the side, grabbed for the waterlogged sail. Bit by bit, with Herculean effort, they pulled it and the broken mast back aboard. "For God's sake Giorgio, leave that and fix this new leak, or the damn sail won't matter," I yelled.

Giorgio abandoned the sail to Vaughn and Ranfurly and attacked the new leak. I helped as much as I could, and with great effort, he finally brought it under control. I stopped bailing and peered around me. What a pathetic cargo of almost drowned rats we were! Soaking wet, streaked with pitch, sick, and half-frozen from the cold north wind which, even without a sail, continued to move us southward. Before long my teeth were chattering, so I grabbed the bucket and began bailing vigorously, just to warm myself. Giorgio returned to working on the mast, using what little rope we had left. I marveled at his energy and know-how. He was amazing!

Following his instructions, Vaughn, the tallest and strongest of the Brits, pushed, and several others held, and somehow they managed to re-secure the broken mast. We held our breath as Ranfurly carefully hoisted the sail again. We gave him a rousing cheer as the sail gulped a bellyful of air, and the mast held. We were once more running before the wind. A faint smattering of applause came from the seven or eight men whose spasms of seasickness had them almost beyond caring whether or not they drowned.

Bailing, checking sail and mast, keeping watch, and tending to the sick men kept us busy, although we stayed wet, freezing, and utterly miserable for the rest of that long night. I knew we were moving fast, but had no idea how far down the coast we might have traveled. I was fearful for what daylight would bring. We were probably far enough out to sea not to be visible from shore, but we didn't know with any certainty where the battle lines were drawn. Daylight might find us still deep in enemy territory, and then we'd have patrol planes and German boats to worry about.

Like a bugler signaling retreat, the night wind blew one final blast at the onrushing dawn, then slackened and died as daylight chased it. Glancing toward shore, we could see, silhouetted in the distance, the peaks of a high mountain range. "The Abruzzi?" I asked Giorgio.

"Sí, Signore, I think so," he replied. "It has to be them— we've come a good distance in the night." That gave us the will to resume rowing. We decided to put only two to each oar, in half-hour shifts, to conserve strength. Even those who had been immobilized with seasickness for most of the night manfully took their turn at the oars. No one looked to Giorgio or me to row, since we had spent the night bailing and repairing, and were completely exhausted. Soon, the rowers would be, too. We prayed for the wind to resume.

Around nine in the morning, a tiny gust nipped at us, ushering a moderate breeze along behind it, and the rowers gratefully shipped their oars. We continued to bail. "Water and food are getting low," Rieter murmured.

We hadn't figured realistically what it would require to supply fourteen men for more than twelve hours on the water, doing hard physical work all the way. We had to give the seasick men extra water, so they didn't become dehydrated. Our supply of fresh water was fast being depleted. "We'll have to ration water," I informed Vaughn. He nodded, "I hope we're behind the line of battle," he said wearily. "We're sitting ducks out here in broad daylight. I'd hate to get this far and be picked up by the bloody Jerries!"

"God, don't even think about it!" I said. "We have to make it now. We will."

"Men!" he called. "We're conserving our supplies. Limit water to two sips an hour, each. A mouthful each after a rowing stint. An extra mouthful every hour for the sick men." A murmur of alarm went through the group. "Ssh! Quiet, then!" Vaughn called suddenly. Everyone fell silent. "Hear that? That's artillery fire!"

I turned to Ranfurly. "We must be parallel with the battle lines! Another hour or so at most, and we'll be in Allied territory for sure!"

"Another hour or two, d'you think?" groaned Kerine, who was desperately seasick. "God, I don't know if I can make it!"

"Sure you can, old man," said Rieter. You'll make it. Before you know it, you'll be home having tea and toddies, and being nagged by your wife." We had to chuckle at Rieter's parody of the English.

Shortly after eleven a.m., our fickle breeze deserted us again, and we went back to the oars. The grunts of the rowers as they heaved and pulled at the heavy oars, the slosh of the bailing buckets, and an occasional weary groan or empty-stomached retch were the only sounds we heard until almost two o'clock that afternoon. We had been at sea for seventeen hours.

Then, two Allied aircraft buzzed over us. We nearly capsized The Yacht, all rushing to one side to wave at them. Two men whipped off their shirts and frantically waved them, too. But the planes flew onward and disappeared, without dipping their wings or giving us any signal that they had seen us. Dejectedly, we turned back to the oars. Breeze and sail finally finished flirting and decided to mate, so with full sail we were once again zipping along in a southerly direction. After about an hour, Ruggles-Brise spotted several boats to the west of us, also under sail. "Sail-ho!" he called out, pointing, and I felt my heart leap. I understood exactly how early explorers must have felt.

We altered direction, and attempted to steer our clumsy, leaky craft toward the sails that billowed enticingly in the distance. A cheer went up as we saw the men on one of the boats pull in the nets it was dragging, then turn and head toward us. They closed the distance rapidly, but we weren't afraid. We knew that all non-military boats were banned by the Germans in areas they controlled. The vessel approaching was a civilian fishing boat, which meant we had to be in Allied-held territory! "It's a friendly! It's a friendly!" shouted Rieter, pounding me excitedly on the back. "We made it, Orebaugh! We made it!" When they were close enough, they hove to and tossed a line to Giorgio, which he looped firmly around the wooden cleat at the prow of The Yacht.

I cupped my hands to my mouth and called in Italian, "Where are we? What port are you from?"

"Ortona, Signore," they replied. Ortona! We knew it had been liberated by the Allies only a few weeks ago. We shouted, hugged and pummeled each other. We had definitely made it to the Allied lines--by the skin of our teeth, to be sure, but who cared? The Yacht had gotten us there! We looked at our scow with new affection, and wished we could have sailed her majestically into port on her own.

Artillery fire roared deafeningly all around us as we were towed into the devastated port of Ortona, where we were greeted by British Marines. "Hullo! And who is this?" they inquired. On hearing the high rank of the British officers aboard, they snapped to attention and saluted, then rushed to help us debark. "Welcome back, sir !" they greeted Vaughn, as senior in command. "We'll see to your needs, and your people's needs, immediately, sir!"

"Thank you corporal," said Vaughn. Despite his filthy, unshaven, ragged appearance, he was every inch the Brigadier. "Carry on."

The corporal hustled us over to the beach hotel that served as headquarters. They immediately showed us to facilities where we could bathe and shave. While we were enjoying that welcome luxury, clothing and personal items were procured and brought to us. My clothes were little more than shreds, and they, and my body, were coated with black pitch. I barely recognized my companions, once they had shaved and cleaned up! In fact, everyone had shaved except me. I was determined to keep my "beard of many colors," as Amy had dubbed it, at least until after Marguerite saw it. I did trim it a bit, though. One of the British officers looked in on us. "Well, that's a lot better, eh? But now, I imagine you gentlemen must have a bit of a hunger and thirst. How about some dinner?"

"Captain, you've got yourself a deal!" I said, jumping up with alacrity. The others, laughing heartily, followed suit. We were ravenous! I had just finished my meal of field rations when a messenger appeared to inform several of us we were to come with him immediately. Bidding a hasty farewell to the others, I climbed into the waiting car with Vaughn and the other two brigadiers.

I had survived my capture and detainment in Italy, my raids with the San Faustino Band, my trek across the mountains, and the boat trip to Ortona, but I wasn't at all sure I'd survive the ride across Ortona to my next destination. German shelling was constant, and our British driver floored the accelerator and charged ahead at breakneck speed, bouncing through piles of rubble and deep shell craters. Several times I was certain we'd be thrown from the car. "Slow down!" I roared, but he paid no attention. As we sped along, bounding in and out of deep potholes with tooth-jarring regularity, the Allied artillery pieces aligned along the south side of the road were laying down a continuous barrage of fire. The shells whistled over us, clearing the roof of our vehicle by a margin of only inches! It was May 10, 1944, the first day of the major Allied offensive that culminated in the liberation of Rome.

Sometime after midnight, we arrived at Torino del Sangro, an advance Allied army base. We slept on army cots, and in the morning enjoyed our first hot showers. I felt like I was beginning to live again, despite my still purple, blood-congested feet, my aching shoulder, and the hundreds of sores from bedbug bites on my neck and body, which were to plague me with intermittent infection for years to come. While at Sangro, we were interrogated by Nile McNally of British Intelligence. He, like many after him, was astounded to hear the details of our escape odyssey. It was there that Jack Rieter and I said a fond farewell to our British friends. They had all been supplied with uniforms, and to see them spiffed up, in their khakis, bathed and shaved, brought a rush of warmth to me. We had all made it back safely. We shook hands all around, determinedly keeping a "stiff upper lip," although there was a trace of mist in every eye. We went through the ritual of parting wherein everyone vows eternal friendship and constant communication--vows sincerely spoken, rarely kept.

"Good luck," said Vaughn, "take care of your friends in Umbria." He shook my hand warmly, as did Ranfurly. "Call when you're in London, and we'll have a dram together."

"You'd bloody well better write," growled Ruggles-Brise, pressing a missive with everyone's home address in England into my hand. That done, we climbed into the car, they all saluted us, and we drove away in a cloud of dust.

The British driver delivered us to the American forces at 12th Air Corps Headquarters in Foggia. I dispatched telegrams to the Department of State and to Marguerite, informing them of my escape and of my intention to proceed to Algiers, which is where I thought the nearest American Embassy was situated, and then home.

Rieter and I parted, both to begin a whirlwind of interviews, interrogations, and debriefings. I asked everyone with whom I spoke to help me get an air drop arranged. I was told that I would have to handle that at Allied Headquarters in Caserta, and was reminded constantly not to discuss any of the details of my escape with anyone outside of military intelligence. The following day I was flown to Naples, where an American Consulate had been opened, and there I conferred with Ambassador Kirk and Consul General George Brandt about my San Faustini friends. The next day, I was in a jeep bound for Caserta, where I was to report to, and be the guest of, General Harold Alexander, the ranking Allied Commander.

A kindly man, with graying hair, a clipped mustache, and erect, military bearing, the general greeted me cordially. He had heard some sketchy details of my ordeal, and immediately offered me his personal trailer for my accommodations. When I politely refused, he insisted on giving me sleeping quarters in the headquarters building. Never had I dreamed I would one day sleep in a royal bedchamber. But that night, chuckling at the thought of my leap from cow and sheep stalls to this, I slept in one of the luxurious bedrooms of the Royal Palace of the House of Savoy, which was serving as headquarters for the Allied Command. There, tucked in a massive, gilded, canopied bed, under a satin goose down comforter, cosseted by sheets of the finest, softest linen, I curled up alone, in a room bigger than the whole Bruschi farmhouse, and slept like a baby.

"Good to see you Orebaugh," General Alexander greeted me warmly the next morning at breakfast. "Did you sleep well?"

"Well? I would say I slept exceedingly well, in absolute royal luxury, sir," I answered, smiling.

"I imagine you must have quite a tale to tell us," he said, leaning back in his chair, an interested gleam lighting his blue eyes.

"That I do, sir, I most certainly do! I think you'll find it an interesting one." He listened with rapt attention as I briefly described my activities since being captured in Monaco.

That afternoon, as I rested in my room and prepared reports, an aide knocked on the door to present the General's compliments. "He'd like you to join him at dinner tonight, sir."

"Tell the General that I am honored, and will of course be there."

That evening, at dinner, I felt incongruously out of place in the glittering assemblage of be-ribboned, high-ranking officers General Alexander had invited. My shaggy beard and nondescript clothing stood out like a sore thumb in those regal surroundings.

The dining room of the Savoy Palace was the most enormous room I had ever seen, outside the Palace of Versailles in France. Ornately carved and gilded borders outlined large portions of the room, and light from the hundreds of thousands of prisms in the twelve huge crystal chandeliers, each roughly the size of a jeep, danced off the mirrors and the gleaming table, laid with fine china and crystal, that ran the length of the center of the room. It could seat fifty with ease, and that night every seat was taken. I was placed to the right of the General, in the position of honor.

A memorable five course dinner was served. First a light chicken broth with spinach, then a simple pasta course of ravioli—but what ravioli they were! With the first mouthful, I knew my fate had been sealed—I would love Italian pasta for the rest of my days. This was followed by enormous platters of sliced roast veal in a delicious wine sauce, accompanied by an assortment of vegetable dishes—peas, artichokes, eggplant with tomatoes, tiny potatoes. It was all topped off by a magnificent "Zuppa Inglese," the liqueur-laced Italian version of English Trifle. With each course, an appropriate wine was offered. The military always knew how to "liberate" the best supplies for their tables! It was such a far cry from supper at the Bruschi's as to be almost unimaginable.

After dessert was cleared, as the servants poured real espresso into delicate china demitasse cups, and cordials into tiny crystal flutes, the general rose. I had my cup up to my nose, inhaling the aroma of the coffee. I didn't know if I'd be able to bring myself to actually consume such a rare treat. "Gentlemen," he began, "today I have heard a most amazing and interesting story. A very touching story. I think you'll find it fascinating too, and that is why I am now going to ask Mr. Walter Orebaugh, an American Foreign Service officer, who has just escaped after sixteen months behind enemy lines, to tell you some of it."

Startled, I almost dropped my cup. All eyes turned to me. I stood, feeling unkempt and insignificant, and skipped through the highlights of my story in as few words as possible. When I finished, there was stunned silence. Then the group of officers rose, to a man, and gave me a resounding ovation. I flushed with pride. The joy of actually being back struck me, and I felt a lump rise in my throat as tears flooded my eyes.

The next day, I was asked to meet with a Mr. Proctor and several OSS (Office of Strategic Services) officials. "Orebaugh, I'm almost sorry to see you here," said Proctor, without preamble.

"What?" I stared at him, shocked. "What do you mean?" "Well, we had counted on using you to our advantage in that district around Perugia. On May 2nd, we broadcast your code signal, advising that you were authorized to draw consular drafts for $2000 a month for your partisan activities. Unfortunately, you had already left the area, so you never got the message."Hearing that, my heart fell. If only I had delayed my departure from Morena a few more days!

"But sir," I protested, "does that mean I can't get help— ammunition and money and supplies—to the Band at San Faustino?"

"No, no, Orebaugh," Proctor hastened to reassure me, "don't you worry about that! We're getting ready to make an airdrop to them within the week. You just tell us what's needed."

I jumped up. "I have the list in my knapsack," I said . "I'll go get it now."

Proctor smiled again, puffing on his pipe, and held up his hand. "Tomorrow morning will be time enough. We have a pretty good idea of what's probably on the list."

I was elated. An air drop to Morena within the week! Bonfigli's smiling face flashed before me, and Pierangeli's. Giovanni's, and Ruggero's and Ramsay's. "What about a radio transmitter, and someone to operate it? Can we get someone up there? Maybe someone from A Force?"

"As a matter of fact, we'll soon be dropping two operatives behind German lines. One of them is intended for San Faustino."

"Thank you, sir, any Allied effort on behalf of these people will not be wasted, I can assure you." Then, briefly, I described the battle between the united Bands of San Faustino and Cantiano, and the Waffen SS troops. He whistled softly in admiration, making notes.

The next day, I talked at length to the two operatives who were scheduled to be dropped behind the lines, and set up the air drop for Morena. Then I left for Algeria.

As I was winging my way across the Mediterranean, my friend and companion Giovanni Marioli, monitoring the BBC at home in Pietralunga, heard the magic code words, "abbia fede" (have faith) and "puoi gioire," (You can rejoice) crackle from the radio. He raced to notify Pierangeli and Bonfigli. Darkness was falling as a squad of partisans arrived at the church in Morena and informed Don Marino Cecarelli, the bandit priest, that Il Console had succeeded in reaching Allied lines and that an air drop for the partisans was on its way! After saying a quick prayer of thanksgiving, Don Marino hurried out to round up his parishioners, who gathered materials for the six huge bonfires that were to be built in the field across from the church, then lighted to identify and outline the drop zone. Don Marino, the partisans, and the villagers worked feverishly against the ten–thirty deadline for the drop. By ten-fifteen the bonfires, and the torches to light them, were ready.

At ten twenty, one of the peasants gathered in the field called, "Attenzione! Ascoltate!" (Attention! Listen!) Everyone quieted. In the distance, the faint drone of an airplane motor sounded. "Light the fires!" commanded Pierangeli. A dozen torches were lit and touched to the six tall piles of dried brush and branches that lined the field. With a whoosh and a crackle, the bonfires blazed up in the night. A plane roared in low, and as they strained their eyes to see, twenty-three dark objects tumbled from it, down to the center of the flame-edged field, followed by a parachutist.

"God be praised!" murmured Don Marino Cecarelli, as he, the partisans, the peasants, and the townspeople of Morena rushed in to gather up the vital store of ammunition and supplies dropped on them from the heavens, courtesy of Il Console and the Allies. Within ten minutes, the bonfires had been extinguished and the debris cleared away. The supplies were hidden, and the field across from the church at Morena was nothing more than a field again. As Don Marino and some of his flock knelt in the tiny church, reciting prayers, silence settled on the Umbrian hills once again. But not for long--no, not for long.

Chapter 11

Welcome Freedom

From the moment I was arrested by the Italians in Monaco on November 20, 1942, I had lived in a round-the-clock culture of fear. From that day, until I reached U.S. 12th Air Force Headquarters at Foggia on May 12, 1944, and saw the Stars and Stripes waving at its entrance, I was never able to let down my guard or enjoy a completely carefree moment. Even when I was in the company of members of the Band of San Faustino, the physical sense of fear and danger was always present. Fortunately, very few people in our free society have ever known what it is like to live like a hunted animal, or a fugitive, over a long period of time.

Even in the relative luxury of the Brufani Hotel in Perugia, the fear that the Germans would arrive and deport us to prison camps was always with us. At the Bonucci flat, we couldn't set foot outdoors, and the prospect of random house searches by the enemy kept us on the alert day and night. In the hills of San Faustino, the lurking shadow of danger dogged my every move. During the trek to the Le Marche region with Giovanni, we repeatedly ran the gauntlet of terror and impending disaster. The time I spent trekking to the seaside at night, waiting to escape by sea, and the harrowing journey by boat to reach Allied lines, was hardly an exercise in relaxation. I had borrowed heavily against my physical reserves and my nerve centers for over a year and a half.

Reaching the front lines at Ortona, in the midst of a raging battle, afforded no immediate relief either, despite our elation at having at last reached the security of Allied-held territory. For me, one kind of stress was merely exchanged for another. Beginning at Foggia, and continuing at Naples and Caserta, I was subjected to an endless round of debriefings, and meetings, interspersed with hours of report writing. Readjusting to living by day and sleeping by night was no small feat, after months of doing just the opposite. Added to all that were the long, drawn-out luncheons and dinners at which, inevitably, I was called upon to "say a few words about your experiences."

My world had been one of stealth, silence, terse whispers. Now, ceaseless noise of vehicles, machinery and artillery fire, which went on 24 hours a day, kept my nerves on edge. I slept little. When I finally boarded the military plane for Algiers, knowing that the air drop to my friends was set and I could at last let my guard down, I was almost a basket case of nerves and fatigue. I was greeted personally on arrival by Ambassador Robert Murphy.

It was at the Ambassador's serene, luxurious residence in Algiers that I finally began to relax, and make the first tentative moves toward becoming a human being again. Bob Murphy, the antithesis of a stuffed-shirt, was a genial, charming and very considerate host. Almost as an order, he charged me to sleep late, and to order breakfast to be brought to my room at any hour that suited me. He introduced me to a number of high-ranking Allied officers, both British and American, who were based in Algiers. I had a long session with the head OSS man in Algiers, who took copious notes. To him, and to others, the story of the Italian partisans was fascinating.

"I have some news you'll be glad to hear, Orebaugh," he said, smiling. "The airdrop to your friends at Morena went off without a hitch! They have their supplies. The radio operator we sent made it, too, and he has been in touch." He would never know how welcome those words were to me! I thought of my "buddy" Mario Bonfigli, of Captain Pierangeli, Giovanni, the Bruschis, Don Marino,—and Bonuccio Bonucci.

Would I ever see any of them again? They had become so much a part of my life. I wondered what had happened after the air drop, and what raids the Band would make, now that they had ammunition and supplies. I missed them all, and wanted to be in on those raids. It was as if I were still two people—Walter Orebaugh, U.S. diplomat, Consul, married to Marguerite, father of young Howard, anxious to get back to them, and resume my former life. And I was also Michele Franciosi, peasant, fugitive, the guerrilla fighter known as 'Il Console'. Would I ever be able to reconcile the two personalities and become one person—my real self—again?

I gave the OSS the name of Signor Meletti, the banker in Gubbio. "I have a personal score to settle with that man," I said, and related the story of the loan, and Meletti's diatribe against Americans, Jews, and Roosevelt. "Okay, Walter," he said, "leave it to us. It will be a pleasure for us to settle this one for you."

I was finally able to shed some of my weariness and tenseness. The Ambassador's other house guest was Douglas Fairbanks Jr. Every bit as suave, urbane and witty as I had imagined him to be, he was fascinating company. After a couple of days of this relative indolence, however, I was ready to get moving, to return home, to be with my family again. That was quickly arranged.

My flight to New York left at night, and I slept most of the way, arriving at sunrise on May 21, 1944. Looking out with my forehead pressed to the window next to my seat, I wept unashamedly as the pilot swept past the Statue of Liberty, still holding aloft her torch of freedom, then made a banking turn that revealed the skyline of New York, bathed in the soft light of dawn.

I had been away a little over two years. It seemed more like ten. I sent Marguerite a telegram. "Arrived New York today, stop. Meet me Trailways stop, Centerville, tomorrow, May 22, 4 p.m. stop. All my love, Walter." Little did I know that telegram would be Marguerite's first word that I had escaped, left Italy, and was back in the United States! The next afternoon, with pink and white helmeted dogwoods standing guard of honor as we rolled along country roads, I finally reached Centerville, Virginia, not far from Washington, D.C.

As I stepped down from the bus, the lone passenger to alight, the expression on the face of the lovely, dark-haired young woman waiting there shifted, with kaleidoscopic speed, from stunned surprise, to shock, to dismay. I can only imagine how Marguerite must have felt—the man who stepped off that bus bore scant resemblance to the man she had kissed goodbye over two years ago! I was considerably thinner, and the rugged Italian winters had left their mark on my face—what face there was above the long, scraggly, multi-colored beard that camouflaged the Walter of old. The cane in my hand was also a surprise. Her first thought was that I had been wounded. She didn't yet know the story of the "man with the cane," or about the treasure in rolled-up bills concealed in its hollowed-out stem.

After those initial, very brief reactions passed, Marguerite smiled the radiant smile that had attracted me to her when we were still in high school, and lifted her arms in welcome. On cue from his mother, little Howard, now a sturdy young boy, cried "Daddy!" and followed her into my arms. I gathered them to me and held them close, tears streaming down my face. I was home again, at last.

I immediately sent word by diplomatic pouch to Nancy in Rome, letting her and Amy know that I had escaped and was safe in Washington. I asked her to send a postcard to "my friend in Trieste, telling him that Felice is visiting Marguerite." I fervently hoped that somehow Manfred would receive it and know I was safe, and had managed to escape.

In late June, I learned I was being assigned back to Italy— to Florence as Consul General—and that this time, even though the war was far from being over, my family would go with me—and a car! I was delighted. With Marguerite's loving care and tender ministrations, and after a month of respite from walking and carrying heavy gear everywhere I went, my feet were vastly improved, and my shoulder had begun to heal, too. I had shaved off my beard, and looked more like my old self, much to my wife's relief.

Finally, I finished my meetings and debriefings at the State Department, and we were ready to take some leave, to become a family again. Howard, initially extremely reserved with me, was beginning to accept the idea of having a Daddy around, but I needed to spend more time with him before the reunion would be complete. I was given 90 days home leave by the State Department, in recognition of the ordeal I had been through.

On our return to Virginia in late August, there was a letter from Ramsay. It had been forwarded, through the OSS and the State Department, from the Presidio at Morena. In it, Ramsay described the aftermath of the airdrop on May 19th:

> "For various reasons I cannot give you any details of what happened after you left, but there was absolute hell to pay! Morena was burnt and blown up by the Germans, and one or two people shot, but fortunately we all got away after the air drop, and after the Allied offensive started in earnest, we returned to Morena with 500 well-armed partisans, and got a bit of our own back.... The British officers living at Acqua Viva farm are back home in England. I have elected to stay here in Italy, and have been given command of the 273rd Armoured Delivery Squadron—also a promotion to major! I received your message by parachute along with the arms—thank you."

The euphoria created in San Faustino by the arrival of the air-dropped supplies was beyond description. Rebounding from a death-rattle state, the Band of San Faustino increased the tempo of its activities, and was able to carry out a number of daring raids during May and June. The Allies liberated Perugia and the surrounding areas of Umbria in the final weeks of June, 1944.

When stories of my adventures behind the lines, and my clandestine escape by boat, were released in the fall of 1944, I was hailed as a national hero. Unaccustomed to such publicity, I found it all rather embarrassing, and at times somewhat of a nuisance. I was featured as a hero in True Comics, and on an NBC radio program. I received letters and accolades from many high-ranking government officials, and a good deal of attention from the media. After my secretive, Spartan existence in the Umbrian hills, it was disconcerting.

In October, 1944, with the war in Europe still raging, Marguerite, Howard and I arrived in Rome. I couldn't wait to see Nancy and Amy again. I phoned Nancy at the Vatican. "Walter!" she screamed happily. "How wonderful to hear your voice! Where are you? When can we see you?" We agreed to meet for dinner that same evening at a small restaurant on the Via Veneto. As soon as she saw me, Nancy threw herself into my arms, and much to my surprise, the normally cool, reserved Amy burst into tears, and hugged me warmly. I felt tears in my own throat.

"Here, let me look at you," I said huskily, holding them both at arm's length. They looked wonderful—far better than when I had seen them last. Amy was less gaunt, though still rangy, and her blue eyes were clear and bright. Nancy was prettier than ever. She had regained her normal weight, lost the dark circles under her eyes, and looked positively radiant. She had cut her hair, and still wore her girlish grin, but she had acquired an air of sophisticated maturity, which only added to her attractiveness. As I looked them over, I couldn't help but chuckle, remembering the "make do" outfits both had worn in Gubbio and Perugia—where fashion took last place after warmth and availability. Now, they were attired in the latest designs— both walking proof that the Italian fashion industry had managed to survive both the German occupation and the Allied invasion.

Nancy turned to me. "You first, 'Felice,'" she teased, "We want to hear everything that happened to you after you left us!" We barely touched our food, so absorbed were we in catching up. Hours later, we were still lingering over coffee. After I finished with my tale, it was a contest between them as to which could do the most talking. It was like old times again, and there were a few tears, and many laughs. It was well past one o'clock in the morning when we finally said good night. As I gave them a farewell hug, I remarked, "You know, you're both looking great—years younger than when I last saw you in Perugia!" They smiled delightedly. Nothing I could have said would have pleased them more. Before we left Rome for Florence, we all had dinner again, and this time Marguerite and Howard were with us.

Our car finally arrived, creating a sensation in Rome. There had been no production of cars for the civilian market in Europe since 1939. The brand new, shiny gray DeSoto had the additional distinction of being the only civilian car permitted to circulate in Italy, and it drew swarms of curious people wherever it appeared. It even rated mention on the front page of the New York Times.

We were getting ready to leave Rome for Florence when I remembered the bags I had given to Alex Manz, the Swiss Vice Consul, when we were taken from Monaco to Gubbio. I decided to drop by the Swiss Legation in Rome and inquire. "May I help you sir?" said the young Swiss clerk politely. "Would you check and see if by chance a diplomatic pouch for Walter Orebaugh might have been left here for safekeeping? It would have been sometime late in 1942."

"Just a moment, sir, and I'll check," he said. In less than five minutes he was back, with the pouches. "Thank you--I never expected to see this again," I remarked. It was his turn to look surprised. How could one even think such a thing? The Swiss rarely lost anything--and NEVER money!

I was in for an even bigger surprise. While it had remained quietly in the custody of the Swiss, the money's value had grown considerably. General Charles De Gaulle, in his determination to restore France as a world power, had insisted

291

on revaluing the French franc. My hoard, large to begin with, had more than doubled in buying power against the lira!

I proceeded to Florence with my pockets bulging. If only the money-changer in Lisbon could have known what finally happened with those hundreds of thousands of "worthless" French francs he had stuffed into my diplomatic bags that day! I could just picture the look on his face.

A few days later, I visited the jewelry mecca of Florence—the Ponte Vecchio. Dating from before the time of Michelangelo and the Medicis, the narrow covered bridge over the Arno was home to scores of goldsmiths and jewelers, crowded together in tiny shops that lined both sides of the bridge. With part of my windfall of lire, I commissioned a very extravagant brooch, as a special gift for Marguerite. A week later, it was ready. When she opened the box, the beauty of it took her breath away. Nestled on black velvet was a finely wrought brooch, a jeweled rose. Icy diamonds sparkled from the center of petals made of dazzling red rubies. The graceful stem and leaves of the flower were set with emeralds. It was an artist's masterpiece in red, white and green—the colors of Italy.

We settled in, and I reopened the United States Consulate in Florence. It was November, 1944, almost two years from the day I had opened the ill-starred U.S. Consulate in the principality of Monaco, which was never reopened. At last I had time to begin checking up on old friends.

Through the Consulate in Nice, I received word that my staff there had made it through the war, somewhat the worse for the wear, but okay. Madame Goff Lowenstein, being a Jew, had been forced to hide out for months, but was grateful to be alive. The advancing Allied forces were just beginning to uncover the horrible results of Hitler's relentless persecution of the Jews of Europe.

In Gubbio, the banker Meletti had been arrested and imprisoned. The city officials came to me in Florence to plead for him. I told them that I would request his release only if he donated 12,000 lire, the amount he had cheated me out of, to the civilian hospital in Perugia. He promptly donated the money and was freed.

Bonuccio Bonucci somehow survived the brutalities of his imprisonment by the Fascists. He was freed by the Allies in June of 1944, in terrible physical condition as a result of all the torture. His back was scarred from the lash, and his eyes were sunken and dark-rimmed. He was, in truth, but a haggard shadow of his former robust and laughing self. After he was freed, he returned to his pre-war occupation as an agriculturist. Gigi, who had looked after his interests during his imprisonment, was still in his service.

Widely acclaimed as a partisan hero, Bonucci became president of the Agrarian Union of the Province of Perugia, a post he held for many years. For all his life he bore the agony, in the scars, and in the black and congested condition of his legs, of the terrible beatings he had endured at the hands of Rocchi and his neo-Fascists. Bonnucio Bonucci lived to age 73, dying in 1977. His name and deeds are forever enshrined in the memories of those of us who helped him lay the foundations of the partisan movement of San Faustino. His villa has been restored, and a memorial plaque of dedication to Bonucci and the Band of San Faustino is affixed to an outside wall.

For about a year following the end of the fighting in Italy, Nancy Charrier remained in Rome as an administrative assistant to President Roosevelt's personal representative to the Vatican. We kept in close touch. Later, she returned home to New Jersey, and eventually married attorney Sherman Burling. They now live in Savannah, Georgia, and have three grown children. Nancy pursued higher learning, doing graduate studies both at home and abroad. We are still in close touch. Between Nancy and me there remains an affectionate bond that neither time, age, nor distance will ever extinguish.

Amy Houlden remained single all her life. She stayed on at the Vatican until 1947, as a member of the same staff as Nancy. She left Rome to return to the French Riviera, her favorite playground, where she lived until her sudden death in1956.

Lester Maynard, arrested in Perugia by the Germans shortly after the girls and I went into hiding, was sent to a prison camp in Spoleto, where he was strenuously interrogated about me, and my whereabouts. It was a good thing I had told him nothing, so he was unable to give them any useful information about us. He managed to escape from the German military hospital in Spoleto, where he had been confined to await deportation to a concentration camp in Germany. He reached Perugia again, and went into hiding. Lester was the first person to meet the British advance patrol that arrived to liberate Perugia at dawn on the 20th of June, 1944. After the war, he and his wife and daughters lived in Perugia for several years, before returning to their home in Monaco. He died there in the early 1950's.

Mr. Scheck, the helpful manager of the Metropole Hotel in Monte Carlo, wrote to me in Florence in December, 1945:

> "It will interest our American visitors, when they return again to the Riviera, to hear about our brave American Consul. But we then had a hard time, and I was on the black list, and slept for several months with my bag, containing the most essential things, ready to go when forced to. Fortunately, it did not happen. We have just reopened the Metropole...."

To this day, the Hotel Metropole, now owned, I believe, by Hilton Hotels, remains a landmark luxury hotel in Monte Carlo. In Gubbio, too, the Albergo San Marco still endures, much renovated and improved. Signorina Vera has gone on to her reward; and the Piazza Italia, where Nancy and I often walked, was renamed Piazza di Quaranta Martiri, in honor of the forty innocent citizens of Gubbio,— heads of household, — who were chosen at random, lined up against a wall and machine-gunned to death by the Germans, in reprisal for partisan activities in the area.

The Hotel Brufani in Perugia has been renovated, enlarged, and restored to its former glory, and today, under the same name, it is ranked as one of the finest hotels in Italy.

Soon after we arrived in Florence in 1944, I invited Vittoria Vechiet to move to Florence to join our household staff. She was delighted. We enjoyed having her with us, and she was the same loyal, closemouthed Vittoria, worthy of implicit trust, that I had known in the Brufani Hotel, and at Margherita's apartment in Perugia. She remained with the Consulate for many years, and upon her retirement returned to her birthplace Gorizia, near Trieste.

Our beloved friend Margherita Bonucci carried on with her children in Perugia. Always a very proud and independent woman, she steadfastly refused any money or assistance from me. She was eventually reunited with her husband, Gregorio, who had miraculously survived his imprisonment in Germany. We visited them as often as we could during our stay in Florence.

Little Lucia, thin and frail, greeted me with joy. "I am so happy to see you again, Zio Gualtiero (uncle Walter)". She loved coming to Florence to visit us, and she often took little Howard for walks. In 1945, at fourteen, Lucia contracted typhoid fever. Despite all the effort I could expend, despite the best medical care available, the years of undernourishment and deprivation took their toll. She died, and I felt as if I had lost my own beloved daughter. Lucia Bonucci is buried in the Campo Santo in Perugia. Her sister Valentina grew up to be an outstanding beauty, and in her twenties she married a British non-commissioned officer, and moved to England. We lost touch with her after that, and have never regained it. Young Franco married a neighborhood Perugina, and still lives in Perugia with his family, in the same apartment where we sheltered with his mother and sisters.

Nancy visited Margherita in the late 1970's, and wrote me:

"Walter, my shock at seeing her cannot be

described. My last memory was of a sturdy, fast-moving woman. Instead, a bent, white-haired old woman came hobbling toward us! Her smile was warm, her eyes still bright, but old, as the contadine do become. My dear Walter, when I saw those rooms again, I could not believe it was possible we were ever able to stay there. The dank cold was terrible, and it was April. Nothing had changed. The kitchen table was still there. The smell from the sanitary arrangement permeated the rooms. How did we all stand it? I was profoundly moved.... Margherita and I talked about Lucia, and shed a few tears together. I looked at the spot where we kept the can of condensed milk. I can still remember how good that one teaspoon a day tasted! She insisted on walking with me to the bus stop—'only a short walk', she said, but you above everyone know how the 'short walks' are here, it seemed like miles!— I hugged her goodbye, and left with tears, and sad, mixed emotions."

Our beloved Margherita died only a few years later, in 1976.

As soon as we settled in Florence in 1944, I sent word to Ruggero Bruschi, asking him to pack up his family, close Fontanella, and come to Florence to join my staff. They were overjoyed! "Oh, Signore, Signore," Adalgisa said to me again and again, "Molto grazie! Never in my dreams did I imagine such beauty, such luck!" They loved the picturesque old city. We were living at that time in a 25 room apartment, in a wing of the Palazzo San Clemente. We installed the Bruschis in a couple of the large rooms downstairs, and they remained there, with us, until an apartment was ready for them in the annex to the Palazzo Canevaro—the new home of the Consulate. Adalgisa and Ruggero were loyal, devoted members of my staff, and, along with Vittoria, they managed to spoil the three of us outrageously, especially little Howard, whom they all loved on sight.

Ruggero remained with the Consulate in Florence until his retirement at age sixty-five. The family prospered and, with the marriages of Concetta and Pepe, grew in size. They were able to buy an apartment building in Sesto Fiorentino, a suburb of Florence, where they live to this day—one family to each floor. To our great sorrow, Adalgisa died of a heart attack at Christmas time in 1986. Ruggero still lives in the top floor apartment that he and Adalgisa once shared. Concetta and her husband Marino are on the second floor, and Pepe and his family occupy the ground floor.

At Adalgisa's request, Assunta, the young girl who lived down the hill from the Bruschis, and who always ran up to warn me of approaching Fascists or Germans, came to Florence and joined our household staff. She eventually married a young Italian Army veteran, Giuseppe Natali. He, too, became a member of our staff. I felt fortunate to have so many good friends around me. Their honesty and their fierce and unwavering loyalty were, in those trying times, beyond price. The Natalis, long since retired, now live on a farm on the outskirts of Pietralunga. I visit them whenever I'm in Italy, and we remain in touch by letter. They have been faithful friends for almost fifty years.

One day in January, 1945, Leonard Mills turned up, unannounced, at my office in the Consulate on the Via Tornabuoni in Florence. "Hello, Walter," he greeted me as though nothing interesting had transpired in the interim, and finding me ensconced as Consul, instead of running around the hills bearded, and in rags, was the most ordinary of occurrences! He asked me for a job. Given his high academic credentials, and his knowledge of several languages, I knew he would make a useful addition to my staff. Leonard did his job well, and some months later played a role in my acquisition, for the United States Government, of the massive Canevaro Palace in Florence. The acquisition of that valuable Palace, situated on the Arno river, in the very heart of the city, ranks as one of the best deals ever consummated for the benefit of the United States. To this day, it houses not only the various offices of the Consulate, but also provides living quarters for the entire American staff. Leonard left Italy in 1949 to embark on a teaching career with the University of Long Island, where he remained until his retirement.

Jack and Florence Kutsukian, ravaged by illness, died within a few years after the war ended.

I remained in touch with my former San Faustino comrades.My buddy Lieutenant Mario Bonfigli remained in the Italian Army following the cessation of hostilities. Later, he achieved recognition as the Director of the Provincial Postwar Assistance Program. Cultured and well-educated, he eventually attained a degree of doctor of economics. I was overjoyed to be reunited with him, and with Don Marino Cecarelli, "il prete bandito," in 1986, when I returned to Pietralunga for the 43rd anniversary of the organization of the Band of San Faustino. Although white-haired like the rest of us, and somewhat heavier, Mario was still the same bright and jovial person I knew from those perilous days of 1944. Don Marino was, incredibly, still serving the parish of Morena, as he had done for decades. Captain Stelio Pierangeli received widespread recognition for his bravery in the Northern Italian campaign, but declined public service following the war in favor of returning to his private practice as an attorney.

My erstwhile traveling companion Giovanni Marioli and I shared many a happy hour during my years in Florence, and I enjoyed watching his two young sons grow. I did not forget my deep debt to him, and his family, and did everything possible to make life pleasant for them. Of all my gifts to Giovanni, the most popular by far was a light motorcycle I gave him for his birthday. I can still see him, as he sat happily astride it. "Signor Console!" he exclaimed, "this is not 'just a gift'—it's a regalone!" (a very big gift!)

In March of 1969, Giovanni's delightful, mischievous sense of humor and his unabashed zest for life were snuffed out when a car, traveling too fast to stop, hit and killed him as he walked behind his cart on a narrow country road. To this day, I remain in close touch with his family.

Although valiant old Francesco Rossi and his wife died long ago, I have never forgotten them. In 1990, I searched out a grandson, Nello Rossi, in Fermo. At his home, we were joyously welcomed by Nello and his wife, his brother Leonardo, and their parents. The farm at Grottazzolina had been abandoned many years ago, they informed me. I had a memorable visit with them, and was once more extended the famous Rossi affection and generous hospitality. I knew then that Francesco Rossi's admirable values had been successfully bequeathed to succeeding Rossi generations.

"Cag", Lieutenant Cagnazzi of A-Force in Bari, survived the war and returned to his home in Durban, South Africa. Quinto Silenzi was killed in an accident in the late 1940s. Despite our entreaties to remain in touch, except for the note from Ramsay I never heard further from any of the Allied officers who escaped with me.

This postscript would not be complete, of course, without mention of Manfred Metzger. Dear Manfred! No one could ever hope for a more loyal or conscientious friend. After we returned to Washington from visiting family that spring of 1944, not only was there the letter from Ramsay, there was also one from Manfred, postmarked Switzerland, sent to me via the State Department. Anxiously, I tore it open. "Dear Felice," he wrote, "you will no doubt be surprised to learn we are now residing in Switzerland. When I was notified I was being conscripted into the German army, I escaped with my family to Switzerland, and we are now residing in Geneva." He was running the family tank car business from there. I was overjoyed to learn that he was safe, and well. I dashed off a reply, informing him about my posting back to Florence, but I didn't hear further from him, and that puzzled me. Then, one evening in June of 1945, Vittoria came in to announce we had "a distinguished visitor."

"Who is it?" I asked.

"I suggest you go see for yourself, Signore," she said, with a mysterious smile. I followed her to the front door, and there stood Manfred. We embraced joyously, and after much handshaking and backslapping, we sat down over a brandy to catch up on our lives. I noticed that Manfred was not himself, in fact he was uncharacteristically nervous.

"What's wrong?" I asked, concerned.

"Well," he said, "I may need your help, if you can do anything. My company and I have been blacklisted by the Allies. It's dangerous for me to even be here visiting you."

I immediately prepared and signed a declaration attesting to Manfred Metzger's assistance to me, and to the Allied cause. "It's little enough, considering all you've risked on our behalf." He and his company were removed from the blacklist, and he was able to resume his business. From that day on, rarely did more than a month or two pass without some contact between us.

During the years that followed, no matter where I was in the world, Manfred managed to come and see me at least once a year. We often relived our youthful adventures in Italy, and although he protested modestly, he was always pleased when the high point of his long and eventful life,— his heroic role in helping the partigiani, and in arranging the escape of Nancy and Amy—came up.

In May of 1985, it was my pleasure to be in Switzerland when his wife Nerina and daughters Hèliane and Adrìenne hosted a glittering celebration of Manfred's eightieth birthday. From the time we met in 1937, until his death while visiting in Fort Lauderdale, Florida, in January of 1986, Manfred was my closest friend.

Together, we established the Metzger-Orebaugh Friendship Fund for Youth in the Naples, Florida area to provide day care and other worthwhile youth activities for children. All proceeds from the telling of this story are donated to that fund. The affinity that existed between us for more than fifty years knew no limits, and was sealed with life's most precious gifts—mutual respect, and love. To this day I miss him, very much. Hèliane Metzger Kebaili recently honored me by representing me and her father's memory, at the ceremonies introducing the Italian language version of this book held in Umbria in the spring of 1994, for the 50th anniversary of the liberation of Italy.

In January 1947, I was summoned to Rome, and in the presence of my wife Marguerite, and my mother Imogene Orebaugh, I was awarded the Medal of Freedom, our nation's highest civilian award. U.S. Chargé d'Affaires David McKey made the presentation, on behalf of President Harry S. Truman, who had conceived the award, and Secretary of State Dean Acheson. I was among the first Americans to be so honored. Although I have received many medals and other honors in the years since, nothing has ever given me the intense feeling of awe, or the pride in myself and in my country, that receiving the Medal of Freedom did.

In 1948, Marguerite and I adopted a little sister for Howard. The addition of four year old Edith to our family made it complete, and has kept our cup overflowing ever since.

Now, in my eighty-fifth year, as I look back over those turbulent times of my youth, and the events of World War II, I can still recall the one brief encounter that was pivotal in restoring my life to its pre-war balance. It was mid-1946, a year after the end of the war. I had stepped out of the Consulate in Florence, bent on some errand not far away, (on foot, even though I had vowed never to walk anywhere again), and was making my way down one of the narrow, cobbled, pedestrian-only streets that branch off the Via Tornabuoni. As I threaded my way through the lunchtime crowds in the street, I saw coming toward me a dark-haired man, rather ordinary looking, pushing a bicycle. He was staring hard at me, with his brow wrinkled as though trying to recall something. As we drew abreast, his eyes suddenly lit with recognition. "Signor Console! Signor Console!" he exclaimed, startling me. I stopped, and he grabbed my hand and shook it, smiling warmly at me. "How are you, Signore? What in the world are you doing here? How is your beautiful secretary?" I stared hard at the man. A faint tinge of recognition stirred in the back of my brain. Then suddenly it dawned on me. The man facing me was one of the four OVRA guards,

Mussolini's former secret police, who had taken us to Gubbio from Monaco! He was the armed guard who had been callously indifferent to our comfort, or our basic human needs, during that long, cold and miserable trip. He was the guard who had kept all of us, including "my beautiful secretary," freezing on the station platform for hours. He, like the banker Meletti, was one against whom I had vowed to square accounts, if ever I had the chance.

And here he was--standing before me, smiling happily. He was obviously genuine in his pleasure at seeing me, when he could easily have passed me by. For an instant, I stood frozen,—then all rancor drained from me. I found I was able to smile back, and engage in polite conversation with him. No longer was I talking to a Blackshirt Fascist, but to a newborn Democrat. He, like so many of his countrymen, had "cambiato la camicia" (changed his shirt), to use a familiar Italian expression. As a member of Italy's postwar democratic society, he had changed the color of his shirt, and dismissed the dismal past. I too, had changed the color of my shirt. I had become a diplomat again, not a guerilla fighter. All desire for vengeance finally left me. It was in that moment that World War II ended for me. There was no longer any trace of Michele Franciosi, partisan guerrilla fighter, in me—there was only Walter Orebaugh, diplomat— "Il Console".

During the half century that has passed since, no matter where I have gone in the world, or what I have experienced in life, the words uttered by a seventeen year old girl, sitting at a poor kitchen table in Perugia, have echoed in my heart and remained my watchword as I served my country and raised my family:

> *"It is better to be in danger, and hope to live*
> *Than to be safe, and pray to die."*
> Valentina Bonucci
> December, 1943

Acknowledgements

Words cannot express my appreciation to my collaborator, writer Carol Jose. Her deep understanding of the people and the adventure, and her magical way with words, along with generous helpings of patience, dedication, and most of all, friendship, were instrumental in bringing this book to fruition, and helping me realize a lifelong dream.

I gratefully acknowledge the following assistance: use of the annals of the band of San Faustino sent to me by Don Marino Cecarelli, the Report of Colonel Guerrizzi, and the memoirs of other comrades of those times; the friendship and assistance of Nancy Charrier Burling (Mrs. Sherman Burling) of Savannah, Georgia, who shared the early part of the adventure; the photographs and mementos provided by Heliane Metzger Kebaili, and the Metzger family of Geneva, Switzerland; and Francesco "Franco" Bonucci of Perugia.

I am indebted to Signor Furio Benigni, Mayor of Pietralunga, Italy; to Signor Raffaele Mancini of Umbertide, Italy; Dr. Fabio Luca Cavazza of Milan, Italy; Giuseppe and Assunta Natale of Pietralunga; and Leo Teplow of Tempe, Arizona; for their unswerving faith, support, and friendship.

I gratefully acknowledge the encouragement of author Herman Wouk, who urged me to tell this story. Paul Maluccio of Blue Note added his vote of confidence by publishing this paperback reprint. Graphic artist Scott Patrick of Atlanta provided our fine cover design, Debra Nesbit provided computer support and Jan Harrison provided proofing.

Above all, I am deeply grateful for the never-ending love, encouragement and understanding of my wife and life companion of more than sixty years, Marguerite.

U.S. Chargé d'Affaires David McK. Key presents the Medal of Freedom to Walter W. Orebaugh, as his mother Imogene I. Orebaugh, his wife Marguerite, Italian Chief of Staff General Raffele Cordona, and Lt. General C. H. Lee, Commander of U.S. forces in the Mediterranean Theater, look on. Rome, January 17, 1946.

Citation to Accompany the Award of
The Medal of Freedom
to
Water W. Orebaugh

Walter W. Orebaugh, Consul of the United States, for exceptionally meritorious and courageous service in gathering military and political information behind the German lines during the Italian campaign of 1943. Mr. Orebaugh, Consul at Monte Carlo in November 1942, was captured after successfully destroying the codes and other confidential material entrusted to him. After a period of internment at Gubbio and Perugia, Italy, he joined a band of guerrilla troops, and, rejecting the opportunity to appeal to the protecting power for exchange, remained with the guerrilla band and became its leader. After harassing German communications in January, February, and March, 1944, at frequent risk to his life, he crossed territory constantly patrolled by German forces and made his way by foot and small boat to Ortona, within the Allied lines. There he gave the first accurate and detailed report on the guerrilla movement as well as other valuable military and political intelligence. Mr. Orebaugh voluntarily performed services beyond his normal duty as a Foreign Service Officer, and displayed courage, resourcefulness and coolness under fire, worthy of the best traditions of the Foreign Service.

> (signed) Dean Acheson
> Acting Secretary of State
> Washington, December 11, 1946

The Medal of Freedom

Now called The Presidential Medal of Freedom, this prestigious award, the highest civilian award of the United States Government, was established by order of President Harry S. Truman on July 6, 1945. It was amended by Executive Order 11085 in 1963, and again by Executive Order 11515 in 1970. Only about three hundred people have been awarded the Medal of Freedom since its inception in 1945.

The San Faustino Partisan Guerrilla Band
Brigata D'Urto Di San Faustino

The partisan guerrilla Band of San Faustino was established in late 1943 at a secret meeting at San Faustino, Pietralunga, in the province of Umbria. There, tasks were assigned to various parties and officers. It was the desire of Lt. Col. Guerrizzi and Bonuccio Bonucci and those establishing the Band to keep the movement free of political party attachment or ideological coloration. They adopted the following program of action:

"To fight without quarter against the German invader, to fight against Fascism, to obstruct recruitment to them for the so-called Republican Army, to impede collection of foodstuffs by them, and to educate the masses about the principles of a free society, devoid of partisan bias."

In December of 1943, eighteen officers took the oath, and each was assigned a nucleus of local patriots to aid them. In January 1944, through the Florence Committee of National Liberation (CLN) and the help of the newly recruited American Consul Walter Orebaugh, contact was made with the Allies, and code words were agreed upon as signals for air drops of arms. Several British officers also joined the Band.

Unfortunately, the Band's cause was severly damaged by betrayals. Colonel Guerrizzi and Captain Pierangeli reported:

"One Paciotti, caught carrying arms, fearful of being shot, to save his life spilled all he knew about our organization, naming me as its leader and also naming others of my command. Warned that an arrest warrant had been issued for me and Bonuccio Bonucci, our civilian advisor, we both went into hiding. Bonucci went to his villa at San Faustino, where he was arrested by a Fascist patrol."[1]

In reprisal for failing to apprehend Guerrizzi, Armand Rocchi, the notorious Fascist Prefect of Perugia, arrested Guerrizzi's wife and eighteen year old son, whom he held prisoner for two months. He issued an order that if found, Guerrizzi was to be "skinned on sight."

The Band of San Faustino kept an area of four hundred square kilometers out of the control of the Germans and Fascists for six months during the Italian campaign, thereby forestalling the conscription of thousands of young men into enemy service and avoiding the conscription of large quantities of foodstuffs and other supplies to the benefit of the German and Fascist cause. They successfully fought off the attempts of the Germans to capture them, and disband them, and were intact and active when the Allies liberated Umbria in July, 1944.

Initial promoters of the Band of San Faustino were:

Lt. Colonel Mario Guerrizzi	Bonuccio Bonucci
Lieutenant Mario Bonfigli	Captain Stelio Pierangeli
Lieutenant Vittorio Biagotti	Don Marino Ceccarelli
Lieutenant Livio Dalla Regione	Attorney Salcerini Gaetano
. . . . . . and many others	

Statistics of the Band of San Faustino:

Total Strength: Four battalions
Officers: 11   Men: 300
Killed: Officers: 2   Men: 35
Wounded: 27

---

[1]This quotation, and the details of this brief history of the Band of San Faustino, are taken from a translation of the official report of Lieutenant Colonel Mario Guerrizzi and Captain Pierangeli to the Allied Command, July, 1944.

ABOUT THE AUTHORS

Walter W. Orebaugh

Born in Kansas, WALTER W. OREBAUGH began his career with the United States Foreign Service in 1932. He was promoted to Consul in 1941, and transferred from Trieste, Italy, to Nice, in Vichy—controlled France. In November 1942, he opened the first U.S. Consulate in the Principality of Monaco. It was there that he and two members of his female staff were taken prisoner by the Italian Sixth Army and sent to Italy.

Hailed as a hero in the United States following his escape and repatriation in 1944, he was awarded, in 1945, the Medal of Freedom, the nation's highest civilian award, by Secretary of State Dean Acheson and President Harry S. Truman. He also received several medals for bravery from the Italian Government.

In 1945, Orebaugh returned to Italy as U.S. Consul in Florence, and continued his distinguished career in the

Foreign Service. From 1950-1955 he served as Chief of a branch of the CIA. Returning to the Foreign Service in 1956, Orebaugh served as U.S. Consul in Norway, Trinidad and Mexico, before retiring from his post as Senior Counselor for Career Development of the Foreign Service. He then accepted a position as Vice-Director of the Bologna Center of the School of Advanced International Studies for Johns Hopkins University, in Bologna, Italy.

After two full careers marked by national and international recognition, Walter Orebaugh retired permanently in 1975. Now 84, he lives in Naples, Florida with his wife Marguerite.

Carol Jose

CAROL JOSE is a freelance writer and journalist based in Satellite Beach, Florida. She has a degree in French Literature, speaks several languages fluently, and holds a Masters degree in Business Administration from the University of Central Florida. Widely traveled, she has written and collaborated on several books, and writes a weekly newspaper column and features on food, education, travel and current issues. She is a recipient of the National Education Association's Human Relations in Education Award for the State of Florida.

Additional paperback copies of THE CONSUL (English language edition) are available from your local bookstore, or from the publisher, Blue Note Books, 110 Polk Avenue, Suite 3, Cape Canaveral, FL 32920. Phone: 1-800-624-0401. (MC and VISA accepted.)

THE CONSUL has been translated into Italian and published in Italy by Edizioni Nuova Prhomos, Via R. De Cesare, 28, Città di Castello, 06012 (Perugia), FAX 00139758521167. The Italian language edition, entitled IL CONSOLE, can be ordered from Blue Note Books, Inc., 110 Polk Avenue, Suite 3, Cape Canaveral, FL 32920. Phone: 1-800-624-0401. (Price: approximately $25 plus shipping and handling.)

The original hardcover edition, which includes dustjacket, index, and bibliography, entitled GUERRILLA IN STRIPED PANTS: A U.S. Diplomat Joins the Italian Resistance, by Walter W. Orebaugh with Carol Jose, published in 1992 by Praeger, Greenwood Publishing Group, 90 Post Road West, Westport, CT 06881, is still in print. Hardcover edition ($45) can be ordered by calling Greenwood at 1-800-225-5800, Ext. 700.